Anthropologists and Anthropology

ADAM KUPER

Anthropologists and Anthropology

The British School 1922–1972

PICA PRESS
NEW YORK

Published in the United States of America in 1973 by
PICA PRESS
Distributed by Universe Books
381 Park Avenue South, New York, N.Y. 10016

First Printing: February, 1974
Second Printing: October, 1975

Library of Congress Catalog Card Number: 73-83487

Cloth Edition: ISBN 0-87663-711-X
Paperback Edition: ISBN 0-87663-930-9

Printed in the United States of America

FOR JESSICA

Contents

Preface

In 1908 Frazer delivered his inaugural lecture on taking up (very briefly) the first chair in social anthropology in Britain, at Liverpool University. He remarked on the paradox that the subject was granted recognition just as its object of study – 'savages' – was disappearing. In fact modern social anthropology was not yet properly born. It emerged only after the First World War and, as if to contradict Frazer, immediately produced a series of remarkable monographic studies of isolated, pre-industrial communities; and, soon, began to break down the categories of 'primitive' and 'civilized'. The baseline of this book is 1922, the *annus mirabilis* of functionalism. In that year Malinowski and Radcliffe-Brown both published their first major field-studies; and in that year too died Rivers, the greatest figure in the pre-functionalist generation. More than Frazer or any of his contemporaries, Rivers provided an intellectual measure. Malinowski once boasted that Rivers would be the Rider Haggard of anthropology, but he would be its Conrad; while Radcliffe-Brown – Rivers's first student in anthropology – was casting his arguments in the form of a critique of Rivers even twenty years after his death.

Frazer served as a rather baffled godfather to the new movement, but Malinowski and Radcliffe-Brown were its founders. They established the competing theoretical models and schools which were to give 'British social anthropology' its distinctive character for at least a generation. The past half-century has seen their students and students' students producing field-studies of the various exotic societies over which Britain used to rule, and evolving a distinctive mode of analysis.

The 'British social anthropologists' came from the most diverse backgrounds, and differed in every imaginable way but one: they were united in an exceptionally tightly-knit professional group, with a revolutionary methodology, shared standards of training and evaluation, and a fairly coherent theoretical framework. The Belgian scholar, Luc de Heusch, remarked perceptively, 'L'anthropologie sociale britannique diffère profondément de l'ethnologie française par un trait remarquable: elle a l'esprit de famille.' An American called them, less politely, a mutual admiration society of limited intelligence. The reader will judge for himself, but in any case they established a distinctive intellectual tradition, which has since been diffused to various parts of the world.

'British social anthropology' in its modern sense has already been led by three sharply defined generations. Malinowski and Radcliffe-Brown set it going, and they had all the lonely certainty of prophets and seers. Their students, trained in the late twenties and the thirties, took over the leadership of the profession after the Second World War. They were appointed to the chairs in the various old and new departments in Britain and the Commonwealth, and ruled for two decades. Between 1968 and 1972 they reached retiring age *en bloc*. This jubilee year of functionalist anthropology sees the final transfer of power to the third generation, which entered the profession in the late forties and early fifties, and now faces the problem of its reconstruction in a post-imperial world.

Not that social anthropology was ever just an exercise in the sophistication of colonialism. The British social anthropologists drew upon a foreign tradition of sociological understanding which gave their work a special character, although, of course, they shared many ideas current in Britain in the sciences and in the arts – and even on the P. & O. line. And although only a few of their works ever won a popular readership, their ideas have always seeped through into other disciplines and even into politics and the general intellectual life of the country. The interest of the common reader has perhaps never been so great, and I hope that this book will help to provide a perspective on the discipline and its subject-matter. Social anthropology has always been conscious of its broader implications, and I believe that a historical account is the best way of setting out its still unfolding message.

Professor Isaac Schapera invited me to write this book, and he has given me constant support – even selecting the appropriate title. (It was he who reminded everyone that social anthropology is concerned 'not with stones and bones, but rather Marx and Spencer'.) My dear aunt, Hilda Kuper, first took me into the field as an undergraduate, and I owe to her an early sense of the inner history of the subject, without which it all makes much less sense. Mr James Urry, a mine of information himself, compiled the index. My wife, Jessica Kuper has been my support throughout, and this book is dedicated to her.

Writing such nearly contemporary history one necessarily relies upon the willingness of good witnesses to talk, and on access to unpublished material, as well as upon published sources. Despite various efforts I have not been able to tap much unpublished material, but a number of my senior colleagues agreed to reminisce in a seminar I organized at University College London or to submit to interviews. I am very grateful to all of them, and hope they find my account reasonable and amusing. But my main source has been the published material, for this is not a story of private quarrels or loves – it is not an exposé of the secrets of the family. I have tried to write the intellectual history of a living and perhaps important tradition within the social sciences.

Adam Kuper

ONE

Malinowski

The magnificent title of the Functional School of Anthropology has been bestowed by myself, in a way on myself, and
to a large extent out of my own sense of irresponsibility.
                                                        – Malinowski[1]

. . . a unique and paradoxical phenomenon – a fanatical
theoretical empiricist.
                                                        – Leach[2]

I

Malinowski has a strong claim to being the founder of the
profession of social anthropology in Britain, for he established
its distinctive apprenticeship – intensive fieldwork in an
exotic community. For the fifteen years which he spent at
the London School of Economics after his return from the
Trobriand islands he was the only master ethnographer in
the country, and virtually everyone who wished to do fieldwork in the modern fashion went to work with him.

Yet Malinowski, and many of his students, felt that he was
much more than a pioneer in method. As one of his most
distinguished students has remarked, 'he claimed to be the
creator of an entirely new academic discipline. A whole
generation of his followers were brought up to believe that
social anthropology began in the Trobriand islands in
1914.'[3] This grander reputation persists, despite the poverty
of Malinowski's explicit theoretical formulations. His ethnographic triumph was based upon a novel perspective which
is still an integral feature of British social anthropology,
however much it may have been obscured by his attempts at
formalization and his incessant polemics. There *was* a
functionalist revolution, and Malinowski was its leader. But
it did not establish functionalist theory as Malinowski propounded it.

II

The subject-matter of anthropology was fairly clearly defined in the early twentieth century, although it was called by various names – social anthropology, cultural anthropology, or ethnology, ethnography and sociology. Its core was the study of 'primitive' or 'savage' or 'early' man, and by the last third of the nineteenth century the study of 'culture' – in Tylor's sense, embracing social organization – was clearly distinguished from the biological study of man. There was, then, a specific study concerned with 'primitive culture'. This field was conventionally considered under various heads – material culture, folklore, religion, magic, and 'sociology'; perhaps also language, law, even environment.

There was also by the early twentieth century an accepted distinction between a broadly geographical approach, which was concerned with migration, cultural diffusion and the classification of peoples and objects, and what was generally called the sociological approach, which dealt with the development of social institutions. Exponents of the former approach tended to be more descriptive and particularistic; while the sociologists were more comparative and theoretical. The distinction between them had been formalized at least as early as 1909, when, according to Radcliffe-Brown,

A meeting of teachers from Oxford, Cambridge and London was held to discuss the terminology of our subject. We agreed to use 'ethnography' as the term for descriptive accounts of non-literate peoples. The hypothetical reconstruction of 'history' of such peoples was accepted as the task of ethnology and pre-historic archaeology. The comparative study of the institutions of primitive societies was accepted as the task of social anthropology, and this name was already preferred to 'sociology'. Frazer, in 1906 had already defined social anthropology as a branch of sociology that deals with primitive peoples. Westermarck had the position of Professor of Sociology, though his work was really in the field of social anthropology.[4]

A similar distinction was made in the syllabus adopted for the newly-established diploma in anthropology at Oxford in 1906. 'Cultural anthropology' was distinguished from physical anthropology, and it was considered under four heads – archaeology, technology, ethnology and sociology. The distinction between ethnology and sociology was clear. Ethnology included

The comparative study and classification of peoples, based upon conditions of material culture, language, and religious and social institutions and ideas, as distinguished from physical characters. The influence of environment upon culture.

Sociology was concerned with

The comparative study of social phenomena, with special reference to the earlier history of –
  (a) Social organization (including marriage customs), government and law;
  (b) moral ideas and codes;
  (c) magical and religious practices and beliefs (including treatment of the dead);
  (d) modes of communicating ideas by signs, articulate language, pictographs, and writing.[5]

Each of these approaches to 'primitive culture' was associated also with a particular theoretical tendency. The ethnologists inclined towards diffusionism. Cultures were patchworks of traits, borrowed from others, the superior traits moving outwards from a centre like the ripples made by a stone thrown into a pond – to echo a favourite analogy of diffusionist writers. These cultural traits could be classified, on stylistic or other criteria, and their movement, or the movements of their bearers, reconstructed. Diffusionism was given a great impetus in Britain by the dramatic discoveries of Egyptian archaeology, and the development of the theory that the 'fertile crescent' was the cradle of most of the artifices of civilization – a theory propagated in the twenties by Elliot Smith and Perry at University College London. The sociologists, on the other hand, were by and large evolutionists, though their views diverged from each other, and none any longer favoured the unilinear evolutionary schemes so fashionable in Victorian England. Speaking very generally, they tended to see cultures as systems with an interior dynamic, rather than as the products of haphazard borrowings; but they varied as to whether the dynamic element was intellectual, economic, ecological, or whatever.

This is a simplified version of the situation, but it permits the immediate identification of the impact of functionalism. The functionalists took over 'sociology', but dropped the 'special reference to the earlier history of . . .' which had been the hallmark of the evolutionists. They also rejected not only diffusionism but the whole ethnological enterprise, so that for a generation the preoccupations of the ethnologists, including specific histories, were disregarded by British social anthropologists.

In the concluding pages of his first Trobriand monograph, *Argonauts of the Western Pacific* (1922), Malinowski set out his own point of view with reference to the preoccupations of these major schools. He wrote:

. . . it seems to me that there is room for a new type of theory. The succession in time, and the influence of the previous stage upon the subsequent, is the main subject of evolutional studies, such as are practised by the classical school of British Anthropology (Tylor, Frazer, Westermarck, Hartland, Crawley). The ethnological school (Ratzel, Foy, Gräbner, W. Schmidt, Rivers, and Eliott-Smith [sic]) studies the influence of cultures by contact, infiltration and transmission. The influence of environment on cultural institutions and race is studied by anthropogeography (Ratzel and others). The influence on one another of the various aspects of an institution, the study of the social and psychological mechanism on which the institution is based, are a type of theoretical studies which has been practised up till now in a tentative way only, but I venture to foretell will come into their own sooner or later. This type of research will pave the way and provide the material for the others.[6]

A few years later Radcliffe-Brown wrote, more directly:

I believe that at this time the really important conflict in anthropological studies is not that between the 'evolutionists' and the 'diffusionists', nor between the various schools of the 'diffusionists', but between conjectural history on the one side and the functional study of society on the other.[7]

Nevertheless it is misleading to see functionalism triumphing over the orthodoxies of evolutionism or diffusionism. The

16

hallmark of British anthropology in the first two decades of this century was a cautious and sceptical attitude to any grand theoretical formulation, evolutionist or diffusionist. Frazer's work was being treated with a certain derision, even at the turn of the century, in the anthropological journals; and in the hands of men like Westermarck or Marett evolutionism was only an ultimate point of reference, not a central organizing concept. It is true that the extreme Egypto-centric diffusionism of Elliot Smith and Perry was a force in the twenties, and that even Rivers was a convert, but the theory did not gain much credence in professional circles. Indeed, Myers, as president of the Royal Anthropological Institute, had a difficult time preventing Elliot Smith's resignation in 1922 as a protest against alleged censorship of his ideas; and he wearily complained about the absurdities of the great man's evangelical fervour. Malinowski spent a good deal of time in the twenties in debate with Elliot Smith and Perry, but this was for popular rather than professional audiences. It was as though a modern social anthropologist were to spend a lot of time in very public debate with Robert Ardrey and Desmond Morris. The functionalist oral tradition has greatly exaggerated the significance of these confrontations.

There was also the counter-influence of Durkheim and his school in Paris, which had attracted the attention of Radcliffe-Brown and Marett before the First World War, and which continued to influence the British 'social anthropologists'. Durkheim's theories were particularly influential in the study of religion, and they led away from the concerns of the diffusionists, and also of the intellectualist evolutionists, like Tylor and Frazer.

But if one were to characterize the mood of British anthropology in the first decades of this century one would have to stress the overriding concern with the accumulation of data. The ultimate goal might still be the reconstruction of culture history, or evolutionist generalization, but these interests were overlaid by a strong resurgence of British empiricism. There was a feeling that the facts which were increasingly becoming available made facile evolutionist and diffusionist schemes look rather silly. Further, these 'facts' might soon disappear, with all 'primitives'. Their collection was an urgent matter. 'In many parts of the world,' Rivers wrote in 1913, 'the death of every old man brings with it the loss of knowledge never to be replaced.'[8] One might detect incipient moves away from evolutionism or diffusionism towards some sort of functionalism; but more obviously there was a change of emphasis, away from theoretical preoccupations and towards field-research. The rivalries of 'sociologists' and 'ethnologists' seemed in general less urgent than the calls of 'ethnography'.

The demand for professional fieldwork was the motive force behind the Cambridge expedition to the Torres Straits in 1898-9, organized by Haddon and including Rivers, Seligman and Myers. Despite this business-like start, and the general eagerness for more, the follow-up was not particularly impressive. Seligman worked in Melanesia in 1904, among the Veddas in 1907-8 and later in the Sudan, and Rivers worked among the Todas and in the Pacific. A. R. Brown (Radcliffe-Brown) was sent by Haddon and Rivers, from Cambridge, to study the Andaman islanders in 1906-8. There was, of course, a grave shortage of funds and of trained workers, but still very little professional work involved more than a few days in any exotic area. Despite the obvious dangers, the workers had to rely upon interpreters, or evolué informants.

Nonetheless, this represented a departure from the traditional system, whereby – as Marett described it – 'The man in the study busily propounded questions which only the man in the field could answer, and in the light of the answers that poured in from the field the study as busily revised its questions.'[9] It was now realized that the man in the field should be expert in the discipline, and that the European resident in the tropics was not generally a reliable informant. Some of these, particularly among the missionaries, had produced masterly ethnographies, but they were very much the exception; and even the best of them relied too heavily upon selected informants. Even Junod says that his information came almost entirely from three men. Two were Christians; the third 'a Bantu so deeply steeped in the obscure conceptions of a Bantu mind that he never could get rid of them and remained a heathen till his death in 1908'.[10]

It is a measure of the hunger for information that Hartland, reporting to the readers of *Man* on the meeting of the British Association for the Advancement of Science in South Africa in 1905, could write with some enthusiasm:

. . . specimens of several Bantu tribes were kindly brought together at the Victoria Falls by the Government of Rhodesia for anthropological study. Time was short, and only admitted of a few measurements and photographs.

And further,

I had the pleasure of travelling a few days later with Dr. Kannemeyer of Smithfield, a gentleman who was born in Cape Colony, by descent, on the father's side German, on the mother's side French, both families having been colonists for some generations. He is in practice as a medical man. Some of the notes I made from his conversation follow. He has learned from more than one person intimately acquainted with Bushmen . . .[11]

Even the faith in the ethnographic expertise of professional anthropologists may have been rather excessive. As late as 1915, in a glowing review of Rivers's *History of Melanesian Society*, Hocart wrote:

The idea still persists that no trustworthy material can be collected in a few hours, and that it requires a long sojourn among savages before we can understand them. This idea being based on no proof will persist in spite of all proof.[12]

Although he had spent three years in Fiji to Rivers's three days, Hocart said, he could testify to the accuracy of Rivers's material, He did not add that he was Rivers's main source on Fiji.

Rivers himself took a more perceptive line. He distinguished between what he called 'survey work' and 'intensive work'. Survey work involved visits to tribes over a wide area, in order to map distributions and identify problems requiring investigation. Rivers's own work in Melanesia was a good example of this; another, of more enduring value, was Seligman's survey of the Sudan. Intensive work was a different matter. Rivers wrote, in 1913,

> The essence of intensive work . . . is limitation in extent combined with intensity and thoroughness. A typical piece of intensive work is one in which the worker lives for a year or more among a community of perhaps four or five hundred people and studies every detail of their life and culture; in which he comes to know every member of the community personally; in which he is not content with generalized information, but studies every feature of life and custom in concrete detail and by means of the vernacular language. It is only by such work that one can realize the immense extent of the knowledge which is now awaiting the inquirer, even in places where the culture has already suffered much change. It is only by such work that it is possible to discover the incomplete and even misleading character of much of the vast mass of survey work which forms the existing material of anthropology.[13]

Since Malinowski was the first British social anthropologist, professionally trained, to carry out intensive research of this kind, it is perhaps impossible to answer the question which must suggest itself – does fieldwork of this kind inevitably demand a synchronic, functionalist perspective? Rivers might have had good grounds for doubting this, since Boas in America had done fieldwork which approached the intensive ideal and had still remained an ethnologist. Yet despite his own ethnological and diffusionist bent, Rivers pointed out that a lone ethnographer engaged in intensive work in a small community would be bound to demonstrate how the different domains of culture are interconnected – 'Thus, for instance, among peoples of rude culture a useful art is at the same time a series of religious rites, an aesthetic occupation, and an important element in the social organization.'[14] Even Marett, one of the last of the armchair anthropologists, came to stress synchronic analysis. Ironically in a lecture in which he was concerned to salvage the reputation of Frazer from the attacks of Elliot Smith, he said:

Some of us, indeed – and I can at least speak for myself – are so greatly preoccupied with the study of the mind of the savage as it works here and now under social conditions complicated by all the contaminating influences of modern civilization that, while fully allowing that anthropology is purely historical in its scope, we are more immediately interested in analysing existing tendencies than in using such analysis as a key to the past.[15]

The influence of Durkheim was at work here; and, of course, the most important of the evolutionists, Spencer, had recognized the place of synchronic study. Nevertheless it does seem that the intensive study of small communities was recognized to imply a commitment to synchronic analysis of a type which later came to be called functionalist. This was not seen as something which would displace evolutionist and diffusionist concerns, but rather as something to be added to them.

This was Malinowski's own view. He remained an evolutionist throughout his career, and like his orthodox colleagues he believed that the collection of living cultural facts would ultimately yield evolutionary laws. In the special foreword to the third edition of *The Sexual Life of Savages* Malinowski published a 'recantation from evolutionism'. He admitted that he had been concerned with origins as late as 1927, and even now he was not prepared to abandon evolutionism. Simply, he had 'grown more and more indifferent to the problems of origins'. But even this was a tempered indifference:

My indifference to the past and to its reconstruction is therefore not a matter of tense, so to speak; the past will always be attractive to the antiquarian, and every anthropologist is an antiquarian, myself certainly so. My indifference to certain types of evolutionism is a matter of method.

Anthropologists should concentrate upon the processes 'which can still be observed in present-day stone-age communities' in order to provide a firm base for reconstruction. Once he understood how culture meets man's needs the anthropologist would be in a position to say something about the gradual evolution of institutions in response to the growing complexity of derived needs. Therefore, he wrote,

21

I still believe in evolution, I am still interested in origins, in the process of development, only I see more and more clearly that answers to any evolutionary questions must lead directly to the empirical study of the facts and institutions, the past development of which we wish to reconstruct.

And after completing his cycle of Trobriand monographs, with the publication of *Coral Gardens and their Magic* in 1935, he turned back to the classical problems of cultural evolutionism.

This brief review of the situation may serve as an initial perspective on the 'functionalist revolution' in British anthropology. When *Argonauts of the Western Pacific* was published in 1922 it was welcomed as a useful addition to the literature rather than as a call to revolution. This was by no means a crass response, and Malinowski's initial caution supported the reaction. The book was dedicated to Seligman and even carried a generous preface by Frazer, who remained sufficiently favourably disposed several years later to introduce Malinowski's inaugural lecture as professor at the London School of Economics. As a percipient reviewer might have remarked, the book answered a felt need. Yet at the same time the type of material Malinowski had collected, and the manner in which he presented it, did amount to a radically new view of a 'primitive culture'. Malinowski was fully conscious of this, as few others were at first; and he soon showed that the material for revolution was there.

III

A new mode of action requires a mythical charter, and Malinowski in his prime developed a personal myth which his followers passed on to later generations. It runs something like this. Malinowski, a brilliant young Polish student, becomes ill when on the point of entering a professional career in science. (His *Who's Who* entry always stressed two elements in his background – 'parentage on both sides Polish *szlachta* [landed gentry and nobility]'; and 'Ph.D. 1908 with the highest honours in the Austrian Empire

[*Sub auspiciis Imperatoris*].') He is told he is too ill to continue his scientific research. In despair he decides to divert himself with an English classic, chooses *The Golden Bough*, and is at once bound in the service of Frazerian anthropology. In due course he sets off for England (after a detour in Germany) and becomes a student at the L.S.E. After precociously solving the problems of Australian aboriginal family organization he finds himself in Australia with an anthropological mission when the First World War erupts. He is an Austrian citizen, an enemy alien, and may be interned. Fortunately he is permitted to spend his internment in the Trobriand islands. There he passes the war inventing intensive fieldwork by participant observation, working through the vernacular, and living as one of the people, in total isolation from European contacts. After the war he returns to England, and in the face of pig-headed opposition from reactionary evolutionists and mad diffusionists he builds up a group of dedicated disciples who go forth, etc., etc. . . .

In whatever version, the myth presents the classic story of a prophet. The false start, then the illness and conversion, followed by migration; the earth-shattering calamity – no less than a world war – leading to isolation in the wilderness; the return with a message; the battle of the disciples. I have presented the outline of his career first in this form, since it brings out more profoundly than any contemporary account the messianic self-image of the man. A version of the myth is embedded in any oral account of Malinowski's 'functionalist revolution'. The myth is important to the understanding of the man and his career; but a more conventional biographical review brings out other significant, if less apocalyptic, features.

Bronislaw Malinowski was born in Cracow in 1884, the son of a distinguished linguist, professor of Slavic philology at the Jagellonian University. His childhood was passed among the intellectuals of Cracow and Zakopane, the resort which was known as the 'summer capital of Poland'.[16] His father pioneered the study of the Polish language and its folk dialects, and was something of a folklorist and ethnographer, publishing some studies of Polish folklore in Silesia. He died in 1942.

There was then an anthropological element in his family background. However, when he went up to the Jagellonian University, Malinowski read the exact sciences. At the time when he was taking his Ph.D. examinations he first read *The Golden Bough*, and this, he claimed several times, made him an anthropologist. He had to take an English examination in connection with his degree, and probably chose to read Frazer for his style, much admired at the time. But at the same stage he fell ill and was advised to abandon his scientific researches briefly, and evidently he consoled himself over his convalescence with Frazer. In any case, however great an impression Frazer might have made on him he did not become an anthropologist straight away. His next move was to the University of Leipzig (where his father had also studied) and there at first he continued to work in physics and chemistry.[17]

At Leipzig he later branched out, and studied experimental psychology under Wundt and economic history under Bücher. The importance of these two years at Leipzig should not be underestimated. In particular Wundt was a major influence – he had already trained both Durkheim and Boas, and he was very interested in anthropology. Wundt's 'folk-psychology' was concerned with culture, with 'those mental products which are created by a community of human life and are, therefore, inexplicable in terms merely of individual consciousness, since they presuppose the reciprocal action of many', a conception related to Durkheim's notion of the 'collective consciousness'.[18] Wundt objected to the tracing of the development of one cultural phenomenon in isolation, whether language, or myth, or religion, for 'the various mental expressions, particularly in their early stages, are so intertwined that they are scarcely separable from one another. Language is influenced by myth, art is a factor in myth development, and customs and usages are everywhere sustained by mythological conceptions.' He preferred to take another option, which consisted 'in taking transverse instead of longitudinal sections, that is, in regarding the main stages of the development with which folk-psychology is concerned in their sequence, and each in total interconnection of its phenomena'. This was possible, since at each evolutionary level 'there are certain ideas, emotions, and springs of action about which the various phenomena group themselves'.

If the major elements of functionalism can be discerned in Wundt (and many of his students), it is perhaps even more interesting to note that Malinowski's first anthropological study, on Australian family organization, was already well begun before he left Leipzig for the London School of Economics in 1910.[19] At the L.S.E. he worked under Westermarck, the man who had so definitively criticized earlier theories of 'primitive promiscuity', 'group marriage', etc. and argued for the primacy in evolutionary terms of the monogamous family. But this was also a theme of Wundt's, and Wundt and his circle were also very concerned with the Australian material – as were many of the social scientists of the day, of course. During 1912 and 1913 major publications on the Australian aborigines appeared not only from Malinowski and Radcliffe-Brown, but also from Durkheim and Freud; all, apparently, working in ignorance of each other. That Malinowski should have been stimulated in Leipzig to begin a monograph on the family in Australia, and should have chosen to complete it under Westermarck, makes good sense.

At the L.S.E. Malinowski encountered the British desire to support more ethnographic work. In 1912 Seligman, who became his patron, asked the director of the L.S.E. for a small grant to allow Malinowski to do four months' research among Arab tribes in the Sudan. This was refused, but Malinowski continued to write, publishing *The Family among the Australian Aborigines* in 1913 (for which the university awarded him a D.Sc.), and a book in Polish on *Primitive Religion and Forms of Social Structure*. The Australian book was commended in *Man* by Radcliffe-Brown as 'by far the best example in English of scientific method in dealing with descriptions of the customs and institutions of a savage people'.[20] He delivered lectures on 'Primitive Religion and Social Differentiation', which, like his Polish monographs, reflected a Durkheimian orientation, and in particular a close interest in Durkheim's work on Australian totemism.

Then came the break, through the intervention of Marett, who later described it in this way:

> As Recorder of Section H. of the British Association, about to visit Australia in 1914, I needed a Secretary, whose travelling expenses would be found for him. Thereupon that brilliant pupil of mine Miss M. A. Czaplicka (for whom, I hope, a special niche is reserved in the Polish Temple of Fame) besought me to assist her compatriot that he might see with his own eyes those peoples of the Antipodes about whom he had hitherto known from books alone; and thus began a friendship which if on my part wholly delightful, soon proved for him disastrous, at least at first sight. For as our ship was on its way from West to South Australia, the War descended upon us, and Malinowski as an Austrian subject, became technically an enemy, and who as such must be interned. Nothing, however, could have been more generous than the treatment by the Australian authorities of the young scholar, for they not only granted him a *libera custodia* so that he could explore where he chose within their vast territories, but actually supplied him with the funds to do so.[21]

In fact all enemy scientists who chose to do so were allowed to return to Europe. Malinowski was making the most of an opportunity. He might have been planning to remain in any case, for he came with two scholarships from London University and the L.S.E. which Seligman had negotiated for him, and upon which he depended entirely for a year until the Australian funds became available.

IV

Malinowski was thirty when he began his career as an ethnographer, with six months' fieldwork in southern New Guinea. The shortcomings of his work there persuaded him of the advantages of working in the vernacular and in more immediate contact with the tribesmen. He also found he had a convenient facility for picking up the local languages. (After six months in the Trobriands he was proficient enough in the vernacular to dispense with an interpreter.) The Mailu study was no more than an apprentice's trial run, conventional enough in method and results. After a break in Australia Malinowski returned to the field, in May 1915, and partly by accident fixed on the Trobriand islands off New Guinea for his next study. Seligman had wanted him to investigate Rossel island, but his contacts there failed him. This Trobriand study provided the basis for his later reputation, and its pioneering quality is highlighted by a comparison with the earlier Mailu work. He really did invent modern fieldwork methods in the two years he spent on the Trobriand islands, from 1915–16 and from 1917–18.

Malinowski wrote with great candour about his fieldwork methods, but the posthumous publication of some of his field diaries provide a much more intimate view of his experiences in the Trobriands than his dissertations on method. Yet while the diaries bring out the personal stresses of the fieldwork, they also make his achievement at once more comprehensible and more admirable. As Malinowski told his students, he saw the personal diary of the field-worker as a safety-valve, a means of channelling the personal cares and emotions of the ethnographer away from his scientific notes. The diaries deal with the private life of the fieldworker, and show Malinowski struggling with boredom, anxieties about his health, sexual deprivation, loneliness, and what Georges Mikes once called the Slav Soul. They also contain outbursts of irritation directed against the Trobrianders. They reveal that he did not achieve that separation from European contacts which he advocated. But above all they illustrate how hard he worked, and how creatively. Here is part of an entry for a good day – the 20 December 1917:

I got up at 6 (awoke at 5.30). I didn't feel very buoyant. Made the rounds of the village. Tomakapu gave me explanations concerning the sacred grove near his house. It had been raining all night; mud. Everybody was in the village. The policeman joined me at 9, I set to work with him. At 10.30 they decided to go for a *poulo* (fishing expedition) and I set out with them. *Megwa* (magical rite) in the house of Yosala Gawa. I felt again the joy of being with real *Naturmenschen*. Rode in a boat. Many observations. I learn a great deal. General *Stimmung*, style, in which I observe tabu. Technology of the hunt, which would have required weeks of research. Opened-up horizons filled me with joy. We made a cruise around this part of the lagoon – as far as Kiribi, and then to Boymapo'u. Extraordinary sight of fishes darting through the air, jumping into nets. I rowed with them. I removed my shirt and had a kind of sun bath. The water attracted me, I wanted to bathe, but somehow I did not – why? Because of my lack of energy and initiative, which has done me so much harm. Then, this began to weary me; hunger. The charm of open expanses gave way to feeling of absolute emptiness. We returned (by way of) Kaytuvi and Kwabulo . . .

His servant comes by boat with his shoes and billycans, and he returns for a late lunch.

Then, around 5, I went to Tudaga where I took a census. I came back; the sunset was a blazing brick colour. Some natives observed a Tumadawa fish and 12 or 13 boats set off in pursuit of it. I tried to catch up with them, but I felt a bit tired.

He puts down his oars and sinks into a reverie about a romance in Australia. The entry ends on a domestic note:

I felt poorly when I returned. Drank tea only. I chatted a bit, but without any specific aim. Enema . . . Slept well.[22]

Then there were the periods of depression and inactivity. In one entry he wrote:

As for ethnology: I see the life of the natives as utterly devoid of interest or importance, something as remote from me as the life of a dog. During the walk, I made it a point of honour to think about what I am here to do. About the need to collect many documents (i.e. texts dictated by informants, and charts of activities, maps, etc.). I have a general idea about their life and some acquaintance with their language, and if I can only somehow 'document' all this, I'll have valuable material. – Must concentrate on my ambitions and work to some purpose. Must organize the linguistic material and collect documents, find better ways of studying the life of women, *gugu'a* (implements), and system of 'social representations' . . .[23]

The emphasis on 'documentation' here is significant. Malinowski was very concerned with the way in which his observations could be translated into systematic bodies of evidence. Rivers had developed a useful technique for the collection and recording of genealogies, but Malinowski had to develop a whole series of techniques to cope with other kinds of data.

In his research Malinowski came to the view that there were three broad kinds of data, each of which demanded specific techniques of collection and recording. First there was the outline of institutions, of customs, which he studied by what he called 'the method of statistic documentation by concrete evidence'. The aim was to build up a series of synoptic charts, in which one entered the range of customs associated with particular activities. The chart at once summarized the elements of the activity, and indicated the connection between its aspects. The data one included came from opinions and descriptions which were elicited from the people, and from the observation of actual cases. This systematic charting of activities was crucial – 'Indeed,' he wrote, 'the object of scientific training is to provide the empirical investigator with a *mental chart*, in accordance with which he can take his bearings and lay his course.'[24]

However, these charts reflected only one level of reality. The fieldworker must also observe the actualities of social action, what Malinowski called the imponderabilia of everyday life, minutely recording his observations in a special ethnographic diary. His gloss on this is of the greatest interest:

In working out the rules and regularities of native custom, and in obtaining a precise formula for them from the collection of data and native statements, we find that this very precision is foreign to real life, which never adheres rigidly to any rules. It must be supplemented by the observation of the manner in which a given custom is carried out, of the behaviour of the natives in obeying the rules so exactly formulated by the ethnographer, of the very exceptions which in sociological phenomena almost always occur.

A third kind of data must also be collected:

A collection of ethnographic statements, characteristic narratives, typical utterances, items of folk-lore and magical formulae has to be given as a *corpus inscriptionum*, as documents of native mentality.

These prescriptions reflect a perception of the systematic divergence between what people say about what they do, what they actually do, and what they think. It is this perception, almost certainly born partly of his field experience, which is the hallmark of Malinowski's work. Customs cohere around activities; but individuals manipulate the rules to their advantage when they can. And finally the understanding of the rule and the action must be put in the context of the way of thinking characteristic of the culture, for the ultimate goal 'of which an Ethnographer should never lose sight' is 'to grasp the native's point of view, his relation to life, to realize *his* vision of *his* world'.

This awareness of the different layers of ethnographic reality pervades Malinowski's first essay on the Trobriands, his minor masterpiece 'Baloma', published in 1916 and written during a break between his two field expeditions. He vividly describes the divergence between informants' descriptions of the solemn farewell to dead spirits and the observed reality:

When the *saka'u* was heard, everybody went quietly away – the young people in pairs, and there remained to farewell the *baloma* only five or six urchins with the drums, myself and my informant . . . A more undignified performance I cannot imagine, bearing in mind that ancestral spirits were addressed! I kept at a distance so as not to influence the *ioba* – but there was little to be influenced or marred by an ethnographer's presence! The boys from six to twelve years of age sounded the beat, and then the smaller ones began to address the spirits in the words I had been previously given by my informants. They spoke with the same characteristic mixture of arrogance and shyness, with which they used to approach me, begging for tobacco, or making some facetious remark, in fact, with the typical demeanor of boys in the street, who perform some nuisance sanctioned by custom, like the proceedings on Guy Fawkes' day or similar occasions.

This essay was not simply a splendid demonstration of the

dangers which anthropologists ran in trying to deduce psychological attitudes to religious events from formal descriptions. It was a vivid realization of the multi-layered character of ethnographic reality. Behind Malinowski's concern with field methods, then, there was a grasp of the complexity of social reality which amounted, almost, to a theory.

To what extent was this realization of the nature of ethnographic phenomena the product of field experience; to what extent did it derive from theoretical predisposition? I have indicated the kind of proto-functionalist awareness which Malinowski must have found even in the work of Rivers and Wundt, let alone Durkheim, who had influenced his ideas so markedly before his departure for Australia. One does not have to sift a great deal of material in order to find even more striking anticipations of his approach, in even less likely places. Marett, the office-bound don, was writing in 1912:

I deem it, then, most important at the present juncture that some anthropologist should undertake the supplementary work of showing how, even where the regime of custom is most absolute, the individual constantly adapts himself to its injunctions, or rather adapts these to his own purposes, with more or less conscious and intelligent discrimination. The immobility of custom, I believe, is largely the effect of distance. Look more closely and you will see perpetual modification in process; and, if the underlying dynamic be partly due to physical and quasi-physical causes, such as changes in climate, movements of people following the consequent variations in the food-supply, and so forth, yet, most fundamental condition of all, there is likewise at work throughout the will to live, manifesting itself through individuals as they partly compete and partly cooperate one with the other.[25]

This could stand as the motto to any of Malinowski's Trobriand monographs. Yet the fact that Malinowski followed these prescriptions through in the field gave him a special grasp of their implications. It also provided him with material of unprecedented richness and complexity, with the result that Marett had foreseen:

We portray the wood after a fashion. It suits our sketchy methods well enough to represent it as a dead mass of colour. But we have not sought, so far, to render the subtle values of the individual trees. Yet only by so doing can we hope to do justice to the spirit of the wood, which is a spirit of life and growth.

It was not a wood in which one would expect to find Frazer's sacred grove.

V

Despite the completion of his fieldwork, and the end of the war, Malinowski's return to the London School of Economics was delayed, first by his marriage to the daughter of an Australian professor, and then by ill-health. In 1920 and again in 1922 he lectured at the School during the summer term, and in 1923 he was recognized as a teacher of social anthropology by the University of London. In 1924 he took up an appointment as Reader at the School. University College London had just made a similar appointment, in 'Cultural Anthropology', and in response to questions about a suitable title for his own appointment Malinowski wrote to Beveridge, Director of the L.S.E.:

> I suggest the title Social Anthropology, so that we are distinct from the U[niversity] C[ollege] people, who no doubt will insist on being *Cultural* since Cultural is their *mot d'ordre*. Social will also indicate that our interest is mainly sociological, the School being the centre for sociology and all that pertains to it. Social Anthropology has also its good English tradition by now – I think this was the title under which Edward Tylor lectured in Oxford, Frazer in Liverpool and this is the way in which the science of primitive culture is usually distinguished from Physical Anthropology. Cultural is really borrowed from German, where Kultur means civilisation with its fine shade of meaning not implied in the English Culture. The School needs Anthropology or Ethnology to fit into the general teaching of Social Science and broaden it perhaps, to supply the modest comparative basis for the Modern Humanism, for which the School in its theoretical role stands, if I understand it rightly.[26]

In 1927 he was appointed to the first Chair in Anthropology

at the University of London (Seligman held a Chair in Ethnology). He remained at the L.S.E. until 1938 when he went to the United States on sabbatical leave, only to be stranded there by the outbreak of the Second World War. He taught at Yale, and did some vacation fieldwork on peasant markets in Mexico. He died in New Haven in 1942, at the age of fifty-eight.

Malinowski's seven monographs on the Trobriand islands appeared between 1922 and 1935. They constitute the overwhelming bulk of his publications during the years he spent as a teacher in London, and his Trobriand material also provided the core of his lectures and courses. It was now that he built up his following, introducing students to the fascinating Trobriand Man, compelling belief in his own role as prophet of a new science, and despatching them around the world to do field studies of their own. One cannot easily separate his Trobriand writings from his success as a teacher in this period, but I shall first attempt a brief assessment of his role as professor, before examining the message of the Trobriand monographs.

Within the L.S.E. Malinowski stood between Seligman, the ethnologist, and the sociologists, Westermarck, Hobhouse and Ginsberg. From 1925 Seligman lectured on 'General Ethnology', dealing with prehistory and the distribution of human races. Malinowski taught 'Social Anthropology', covering a variety of topics, but always with primary reference to his Trobriand material. The sociologists were concerned with the evolution of institutions. There was a good deal of interdisciplinary teaching, and Malinowski held joint seminars with the others, but he was given in effect a clear field for his own interests. He soon made use of it, building up his seminar and in time breaking his friendly personal contacts with his colleagues.

Several of his students have described these seminars. M. F. Ashley Montagu has a certain priority, however, for, as he wrote:

In point of time I believe that I was actually the first of Malinowski's students. Evans-Pritchard arrived from Oxford a few weeks later, and Raymond Firth from New Zealand several months later. I had come to the London School of Economics from University College [London] where I had enjoyed the doubtful distinction of being the first of W. J. Perry's two students. As a gestating Child of the Sun it was late in October 1923 that I presented myself at Malinowski's office at the London School of Economics, a handsome room which at that time Malinowski shared with Professor C. G. Seligman. Malinowski received me most cordially, and I was at once enchanted. There was nothing of the stuffed shirt about him; he put you at your ease at once, and made you feel that you and he were going to have a fascinating time exploring human nature together . . .

Following some preliminary enquiries Malinowski suggested that I read Lévy-Bruhl and work up a critical paper on 'Primitive Mentality' for the first seminar of the session. I did this, and when I had presented my paper, Malinowski, in a manner so eminently characteristic of him, thanked me, and added 'I could hardly have done as well myself' . . .

In the classroom I have never experienced a more interesting or stimulating teacher. Malinowski would enter the room with a sheaf of papers in his hand, and without much formality would begin reading his typescript. After a few minutes of this, some passage which particularly interested him would cause him to stop, and looking round the class he would suddenly fire the question, 'Well, what do you think of that?' If no one answered he would call upon some student by name, or a colleague, and thus often a discussion would begin which would last for the rest of the period . . . At almost all of Malinowski's classes there were generally present several members of the faculty, and often enough there were visitors from other colleges both at home and abroad.[27]

Malinowski would recruit people from all over to attend these seminars, and, perhaps, to be converted; and those students who did attach themselves to him soon became an integral part of his world. A Chinese student once remarked, 'Malinowski is like an Oriental teacher – he is a father to his pupils. He has us to his home; he gets us to run messages for him; sometimes we even cook for him. And we like to do these things for him.'[28] When he moved to his Tyrolean retreat in the summer some students would go with him, and spend the vacation working at the inn, walking with him, and taking part in informal seminars in the evening.

But if he drew his favourite students into his family, he demanded their complete loyalty. He came increasingly to see himself as engaged in a battle for truth against the forces of darkness, and as his influence waxed he could not tolerate the mature differences of even his closest colleagues, Seligman and Westermarck.

The mood he created has been strikingly evoked by Leach:

The fervour that Functionalism aroused among a limited intellectual circle was not based in reasoned analysis. Malinowski had many of the qualities of a prophet, he was a 'charismatic' leader and such men always express their creed in slogans . . . Prophets are conscious of their powers. Malinowski had no doubts about his own greatness; he regarded himself as a missionary, a revolutionary innovator in the field of anthropological method and ideas. Like all such revolutionaries he tended to belittle the significance of his more conservative contemporaries and their immediate predecessors. His published comments on fellow anthropologists are seldom flattering and in verbal discourse he was even more explicit; he claimed to be the creator of an entirely new academic discipline.[29]

In fact his published criticisms tended to bypass the real establishment of British anthropology – Marett, Frazer, Haddon, Myers, Seligman, They were aimed rather at Rivers, who had died in 1922, at Elliot Smith, a professor of anatomy, and at Freud or Durkheim. In discussion he was equally scathing about his powerful contemporaries, however, and virtually every idea he put forward was presented – as Fortes has noted – 'in the form of an assault on the *ancien régime*'.[30] These attacks were often outrageously irresponsible. In the first pages of *Argonauts* he wrote, for example,

It is a very far cry from the famous answer given long ago by a representative authority who, asked, what are the manners and customs of the natives, answered, 'Customs none, manners beastly', to the position of the modern ethnographer.

Who on earth was this 'representative authority'? The footnote to the paragraph reads, 'The legendary "early authority" who found the natives only beastly and without customs is left behind by a modern writer . . .' and he proceeds to satirize one Rev. C. W. Abel of the London Missionary Society in New Guinea.[31]

Still, this was obviously heady stuff for the students. As one of them put it, 'The secret of Malinowski's charisma was that you thought you were being given an entirely new revelation that was known only to the favoured few and that solved all problems – could put right the experts in every other field.'[32] The message had its political dimension too, for if cultures were delicately attuned mechanisms for the satisfaction of men's needs, then each had its value, and one tampered with it only at great risk. This had to be taught to colonial administrators and missionaries. And more generally, the theory implied a relativistic approach, a suspension of those ethnocentric judgments on other peoples' cultures which were such a feature of smug, bourgeois Philistines. Malinowski had the truth, and it was a truth which must urgently be propagated.

While many found him bewitching, there were others who could not bear his rudeness and intolerance, and found the overpowering personality oppressive. It is difficult to find a single objective portrait of him. Perhaps to round out this sketchy portrait it is best to listen to his own voice, in a joking exchange with Bertrand Russell. In 1930, when Russell was running an experimental school, Malinowski wrote to him:

Dear Russell,

On the occasion of my visit to your School I left my only presentable brown hat in your anteroom. I wonder whether since then it has had the privilege of enclosing the only brains in England which I ungrudgingly regard as better than mine; or whether it has been utilized in some of the juvenile experimentations in physics, technology, dramatic art, or prehistoric symbolism; or whether it naturally lapsed out of the anteroom.

If none of these events, or shall we rather call them hypotheses, holds good or took place, could you be so good as to bring it in a brown paper parcel or by some other concealed mode of transport to London and advise me on a post card where I could reclaim it? I am very sorry that my absentmindedness, which is a characteristic of high intelligence, has exposed you to all the inconvenience incidental to the event.

I do hope to see you some time soon.

Yours sincerely,
B. Malinowski.

Russell's reply makes a nice contrast:

My secretary has found a presentable brown hat in my lobby which I presume is yours, indeed the mere sight of it reminds me of you.

I am going to the School of Economics to give a lecture . . . , and unless my memory is as bad and my intelligence as good as yours, I will leave your hat with the porter at the School of Economics, telling him to give it to you on demand.[33]

It is not surprising that a man like this should have his enemies. Those outside his circle particularly resented his presumption. The American scholar, Kluckhohn, dismissed him as 'a pretentious Messiah of the credulous',[34] and his colleague Lowie remarked, 'Malinowski is forever engaged in two favourite pastimes. Either he is battering down wide open doors; or he is petulantly deriding work that does not personally attract him.' But, he added:

His intolerance of other approaches, his adolescent eagerness to shock the ethnological bourgeois – that figment of his fancy, the mere technologist or oddity-monger – must not blind us to his soundness on problems of social organization, his vital ideas on primitive law and economics.[35]

VI

Each of Malinowski's Trobriand monographs was concerned primarily with a single institutional focus – trading, family life and procreation, myth, the enforcement of norms, gardening. Although in each case he moved outwards from this centre, following various threads to show the ramifications of each activity, he never produced a single coherent statement of Trobriand 'culture' as a whole. Perhaps he could not, for despite his insistence upon interconnections he lacked the notion of a system. His monographs recall the spiritual, 'The toe bone is connected to the foot bone, The foot bone is connected to the ankle bone,' etc. – very just, but not a theory of anatomy. His own explanation for this failure is nonetheless reasonable enough. In a letter to his student Firth, shortly after the latter had returned from the field in 1929, Malinowski wrote:

> You have, no doubt by now, already a general plan of your future work. I wonder whether you will proceed at once to a full straightforward account of the Tikopean [sic] culture or whether you will do what I did – that is write it up piecemeal. I hope you will do the former, as I would do now, if I could go back ten years. I had, of course, my good reasons for proceeding as I did. One of them was, as you know, the poor health with which I had to fight at that time, and which prevented me from really taking in hand the difficult task of handling my full material. The other reason was that, at the time when I started my work, it was rather urgent to present the theoretical point of view which we now label 'functional', and which I could only do by presenting some fragments of my stuff, well placed in an extensive theoretical setting.[36]

To put it slightly differently, he was always concerned to deploy his ethnography to make critical points against what he considered to be general, or perhaps merely popular, but at any rate dangerous misconceptions about the 'primitive'. Trobriand Man was often set in a complex institutional context, but more often he was summoned on parade to controvert, by his flesh-and-blood reality, some scholarly theory.

There are three central themes in all his monographs. First, aspects of culture cannot be studied in isolation; they must be understood in the context of their use. Secondly, one can never rely on the rules, or on an informant's description, for the social reality; people always say one thing and do another. Finally, if one understands what is really being done, and puts it in its proper context, one will be forced to recognize that while the 'savage' may be no more rational than ourselves, he is at least as reasonable. Moreover he is, as a reasonable man, manipulating the possibilities to

My object in publishing this monograph was to demonstrate the main principle of the functional method: I wanted to show that only a synthesis of facts concerning sex can give a correct idea of what sexual life means to a people.

This was not merely tautologous, because as Malinowski showed again and again in his monographs, the connections between different aspects of culture are not necessarily obvious. It might be illuminating to consider, say, boat-building in relation to magic as well as economics; and, so far as he was concerned, you could not claim to understand boat-building unless you examined all the activities associated with it.

This sense of culture as comprising a set of tools led on to his other axioms. Beliefs, however magical, had to contain a utilitarian core; for the rest they served psychological functions. Rules and some magical and religious rites served to ensure the minimum of necessary cooperation, and to provide a plan for the realization of a task. But cooperation was not an end in itself. Man was self-seeking, and he cooperated only as a form of enlightened self-interest. Malinowski wrote that 'whenever the native can evade his obligations without the loss of prestige, or without the prospective loss of gain, he does so, exactly as a civilized business man would do'.[37] Only the enlightened self-interest implied by the principle of reciprocity ensured some sort of mutual accommodation. Where rules inhibited the realization of satisfactions they would be broken where possible, or convenient. One might sum up by saying that Malinowski's perspective depended (like all sociological theories) upon a view of man – in his work, represented by the archetype, Trobriand Man – and, in Malinowski's view, man was down-to-earth, reasonable, rather unimaginative, perhaps, but able to discern his true long-term interests. In short, he was very different from the figments of armchair anthropologists. It is this insistence upon the living, acting, calculating individual which gave Malinowski's monographs their vitality, and made them such a startling, refreshing contrast to the work of other anthropologists.

The contrast emerges clearly in his treatment of two major

contemporary themes, the Frazer/Tylor problem of magic, science and religion; and the Westermarck/Freud problem of the central importance of the family. Tylor and Frazer did not dispute that the beliefs of savages made some kind of sense; but they were concerned with what kind of sense they made. Did the savage make a radically logical kind of sense, as Tylor believed, leading Andrew Lang ironically to remark that 'We must ever make allowance for the savage habit of pushing ideas to their logical conclusions, a habit which our English characteristics make us find it difficult to understand'?[38] Or did he make sense in terms of what was later called a logic of the concrete, associating different things on the basis of external resemblances? This was basically the view of Frazer and of Lévy-Bruhl. Malinowski's answer was simply that apparently irrational beliefs and rites made sense when their *use* was appreciated. 'Thus,' he wrote,

in his relation to nature and destiny, whether he tries to exploit the first or to dodge the second, primitive man recognises both the natural and the supernatural forces and agencies, and he tries to use them both for his benefit.[39]

Magic worked, for it relieved anxiety about the uncontrollable elements of the future. With religion, it arose and functioned in situations of emotional stress, and the function of magic was 'to ritualize man's optimism, to enhance his faith in the victory of hope over fear'. This left room for a Frazerian analysis of the components of magical activity, and equally for a Tylorian view of utilitarian knowledge. These were problems which Malinowski thought rather marginal. He once wrote:

From my own study of living myths among savages, I should say that primitive man has to a very limited extent the purely artistic or scientific interest in nature; there is little room for symbolism in his ideas and tales.[40]

The family was, to Malinowski, also basically a means – it domesticated sex and coped with the care and training of children. It was also the mould of personality, the locus of

41

man's primary emotional attachments, and the nexus within which his primary social emotions were formed. Thus he tended to argue in phylogenetic terms, deriving kinship institutions from the experiences of growing up within a family. He also tended to identify the family and the interests of the individual, so that familial emotions and loyalties were the mainspring of self-interest, while the demands of the broader society were often in conflict with these more natural claims. This is not very far from Freud, despite his divergences from the psychoanalysts.

> To put it clearly, though crudely [he wrote], I should say that the family is always the domestic institution *par excellence*. It dominates the early life of the individual; it controls domestic co-operation; it is the stage of earliest parental cares and education. The clan, on the other hand, is never a domestic institution. Bonds of clanship develop much later in life, and though they develop out of the primary kinship of the family, this development is submitted to the one-sided distortion of matrilineal or patrilineal legal emphasis, and it functions in an entirely different sphere of interests; legal, economic, above all, ceremonial.[41]

The Trobriand islanders were matrilineal. A man inherited from his mother's brother, and exerted jural control over his sister's son. Although fathers and sons were not involved in these crucial relationships of authority and transmission of property, they nevertheless developed strong bonds of affection and mutual concern. This provided Malinowski with a major theme – the conflict between the interests of the father and the legal claims of the mother's brother. He could even demonstrate the limitations of Freud's theory of the Oedipus complex, for in the Trobriand islands boys resented not their father for his sexual enjoyment of their mother, but their mother's brother for his authority. Yet typically this insight was never embedded in a systematic consideration of Trobriand kinship; it was always simply an example of how emotions might pull against the rules, and how people manoeuvred in order to bend the rules. It was left to his students, Audrey Richards and Meyer Fortes, to show how these differing interests in

42

matrilineal societies formed two poles of a single system, and found concrete expression in forms of household which varied in time and space according to the strength of family or matrilineage.[42]

Both in his writings on magic, science and religion, and in his writings on the family, Malinowski's emphasis was all on the individual and his goals. The advantages of this emphasis were great, but the price was a failure to treat beliefs, or kinship, as systems in themselves. As others have shown, systems of beliefs and ritual action do form integrated wholes, and (turning Malinowski's rhetoric against himself) they could not be understood simply by tearing out elements and showing that these had a function. In kinship Malinowski focused on the 'initial situation', the child growing up in the supposedly universal nuclear family, and gradually generalizing the sentiments for his parents on to their kin until he had created afresh a whole system of kin and clan. There was no allowance for the system as a pre-existing structure which the child learnt rather than created.

Fortes has pointed out that Malinowski was always promising a book on Trobriand kinship, and he suggests that the book was never written precisely because Malinowski could not conceive of a 'kinship system'.[43] But so far as Malinowski was concerned, *The Sexual Life of Savages* was a book on Trobriand kinship. In that book he showed that love and sex must be considered together with courtship, that this led to marriage, which produced the family, and that in the family sentiments were generated which provided the basis for relationships of kinship and clanship – 'and all these subjects, so intimately bound up with one another, constitute really one big system of kinship'. To Malinowski any set of connections constituted a system. He recognized, of course, that he had not touched the sorts of problems with which Rivers had been concerned in much of his writings. This was his perception of the issues involved:

. . . starting with the problem of sex, I was led to give a full account of the kinship system, and of its functions within the Trobriand culture. I have left out, or rather I have only briefly indicated, the linguistic aspect of the question – the ill-omened kinship nomenclatures – a subject so wildly over-discussed, so often exaggerated in records of field-work, that one is sometimes led to suspect that it is nothing but an avenue to anthropological insanity. This aspect of kinship I have reserved for publication in a separate volume, hoping that by an overdose of terminological documentation and linguistic detail I can administer a cathartic cure to social anthropology.[44]

It may have been true that the sociological study of kinship was still, in the twenties, too much tied to a concern with kinship terminologies. Nevertheless Malinowski was not merely ignoring problems of terminology. Reviewing his early study of the Australian family, Radcliffe-Brown had tempered his praise with the criticism that 'the Australian notions relating to kinship cannot be studied without reference to what the author calls "group relationships"; in other words, the relationship systems, classes and clans.'[45] Malinowski never took the point. He was never able to study social systems, or group relationships.

VII

In the Trobriand monographs things 'hang together' because in accomplishing any task the Trobriander mobilizes practical knowledge and techniques, magical aids and rituals, social relationships and the mechanism of reciprocity. In his more theoretical work, published during and after his great London period, he stressed a different kind of integration, which was expressed in his theory of needs and institutions. If his Trobriand work describes the horizontal integration of beliefs and activities, this theory concentrated upon a sort of vertical integration. Culture existed to satisfy needs, either biological needs or the secondary, derived needs, which arose from the acquisition of culture itself. Each need gave rise to an institution, and the institution was made up of various layers. To carry out the necessary need-satisfying activity there must be a material apparatus; this is deployed by a social unit, with its appropriate rules of organization and procedure; and the whole complex is finally legitimized by a mythical charter. This is Malinowski's own formulation, with special reference to the Frazerian problem of magic, science and religion:

> . . . human culture is primarily founded on the biological needs of man. Following this cue, we can add that in satisfying his primary biological needs through the instrumentalities of culture, man imposes new determinants on his behaviour, that is, develops new needs. In the first place he must organize his tools, his artifacts, and his food-producing activities through the guidance of knowledge. Hence the need for primitive science . . . Human action must be guided by the conviction of success . . . Hence, magic . . . Finally, once man develops the need of building up systems of knowledge and anticipation, he is bound to inquire into the origins of humanity, into its destinies, and into the problems of life, death, and the universe. Hence, as a direct result of man's need to build systems and to organize knowledge, there emerges also the need for religion.[46]

The reasoning is straightforward: show me a complex of customs and I will intuitively decide which need, basic or derived (by which he means, for the most part, biological or putatively psychological) it subserves. The underlying psychological theory was an ill-considered mix of Mc-Dougall's 'instincts' and Shand's 'sentiments', each searching out an appropriate expression. It reads like a tinny echo of Marx, with its materialistic base, social structure, and ideological justification, and indeed it is not unreasonable to see the theory as an attempt to counter Marxism. The crudity of his theory could hardly be better demonstrated than in his comments on Marxist theory:

> It is one of the remarkable paradoxes of social science that while a whole school of economic metaphysics has erected the importance of material interests – which in the last instance are always food interests – into the dogma of materialistic determination of all historical process, neither anthropology nor any other serious branch of social science has devoted any serious attention to food. The anthropological foundations of Marxism or anti-Marxism are still to be laid down.[47]

Of all the triumphs of Malinowski's reductionist impulse, this must surely be the greatest, the reduction of Marxism to a sort of dietetics.

Malinowski, like all functionalists, has been accused of being indifferent on the one hand to the historical development of societies, and on the other to the radical changes which have affected all tribal cultures in this century. At a theoretical level, it is true, he was not concerned with problems of history, except in the guise of diffusionism or evolutionism. However, his later London years saw him becoming more and more engaged with the political issues of colonial countries, and much of his writing in the late twenties and early thirties was concerned with what he called 'culture change'. This was due in part to his missionary zeal, and his determination to take the functionalist gospel to colonial officials, some of whom were drawn into his seminars while on leave. In part, his new interest came with the foundation in the late twenties of the International Institute of African Languages and Cultures, which was committed to applied studies and which supported the research of his students in the African colonies. But, as perhaps was inevitable in his case, these new interests were crystallized by direct observation. In 1934 he attended a conference in South Africa. He then spent several months visiting students in the field in South and East Africa, including Hilda Beemer (Kuper) in Swaziland and Audrey Richards among the Bemba. In 1938 he wrote:

As soon as the 'plane crosses the border between Nilotic and Bantu peoples, it becomes obvious that it is a transformed Africa over which we are moving. Among the Baganda the houses are new, square, built on the European pattern; even from above, the dress and equipment of the natives spell Manchester and Birmingham. Roads and churches, motor-cars and lorries, proclaim that we are in a world of change in which two factors are working together and producing a new type of culture, related both to Europe and Africa, yet not a mere copy of either.[48]

And in the slums of Johannesburg he found what he took to be a symbol of the new situation, the illicit brew *skokiaan*, blended from all sorts of noxious ingredients, including methylated spirits and calcium carbide, a potent, quickly maturing, easily-hidden spirit. As he wrote, 'in the general puritanic drive against native beer – itself an entirely innocuous drink – and the police control by which it was enforced, the native was driven to invent *skokiaan* and its peers'.[49]

Malinowski argued that the ethnographer in Africa should consider three distinct cultural realities: the living 'traditional culture', a shrinking area; the intrusive European culture; and, above all, the expanding band in-between, the *tertium quid*, in which a new syncretic culture was emerging, the culture of the mining camp and the urban slumyard, symbolized by the illicit brew *skokiaan*. This was not quite a diffusionist view, for the elements taken from the traditional and colonial cultures were transformed by their blending in a new, heady brew. But like diffusionism, it was essentially an unsociological point of view. In the collection of essays on the problem to which Malinowski contributed the introductory review, from which I have been quoting, Meyer Fortes and Isaac Schapera both argued that the social field should be considered as a unity, and that the focus should be upon the system of social relations encompassing tribesmen, migrant labourers, colonial administrators and missionaries. As Radcliffe-Brown observed, in 1940:

> The study of composite societies, the description and analysis of the processes of change in them, is a complex and difficult task. The attempt to simplify it by considering the process as being one in which two or more 'cultures' interact, which is the method suggested by Malinowski . . . , is simply a way of avoiding the reality. For what is happening in South Africa, for example, is not the interaction of British culture, Afrikander (or Boer) culture, Hottentot culture, various Bantu cultures and Indian culture, but the interaction of individuals and groups within an established social structure which is itself in process of change. What is happening in a Transkeian tribe, for example, can only be described by recognising that the tribe has been incorporated into a wide political and economic structural system.[50]

Whatever his contemporaries may have felt about the adequacy of Malinowski's 'cultural' approach to colonial societies, his characteristic determination to embrace the realities as he observed them, and to accept the consequences, is remarkable. The implications were certainly radical:

The anthropologist [Malinowski wrote] is now faced with the tragic situation which has often been bewailed in lecture-rooms and in print, even by the present writer. Just as we have reached a certain academic status and developed our methods and theories, our subject-matter threatens to disappear. In some parts of the world it has been wiped out – as in Tasmania, the eastern states of America, and certain islands of the Pacific. Instead, however, of lamenting the inevitable, we must face the new, more complex and difficult task which history has set before us, the task that is of building new methods and new principles of research in order to reclaim the 'anthropological no-man's-land' and take up 'the new branch of anthropology . . . the anthropology of the changing native'.[51]

He even came to castigate himself for having falsely obscured the realities of change in the Trobriand islands. In an appendix to his final monograph on the Trobrianders, *Coral Gardens and their Magic*, which appeared in 1935, he wrote: 'The empirical facts which the ethnographer has before him in the Trobriands nowadays are not natives unaffected by European influences but natives to a considerable extent transformed by these influences.' He now believed that this recognition should guide the fieldworker, but he admitted that he had failed to take it into account while he was in the Trobriand islands, concluding, 'This perhaps is the most serious shortcoming of my whole anthropological research in Melanesia.'[52]

This was a remarkable admission. Malinowski came to *see* ethnographic reality as not 'savage cultures' but rather colonial cultures in process of rapid change. His ethnographic masterpieces did not embody this insight, and they served as a potent example of how tribal cultures might be described as if they were 'untouched'. Further, his theory of culture change was so unsatisfactory that the impetus he gave to the study of colonial realities was gravely impaired. Malinowski might have revolutionized the British social anthropologist's conception of his proper subject-matter, but this radical change of paradigm was not accomplished.

IX

In 1957 one of Malinowski's most devoted pupils, Raymond Firth, collected a series of essays by his contemporaries on aspects of Malinowski's work, in order to provide a fresh estimate of his contribution, and perhaps revive his reputation.[53] It is significant that few of his ex-students had a good word to say about the functionalist theories. For many of Malinowski's contemporaries his theoretical naïveté was apparent from the first, and his crude utilitarianism could arouse derision. As Raglan asked in 1930, 'Does Professor Malinowski really believe that subincision was invented to detach boys from their mother's apron strings?'[54] The period of Radcliffe-Brown's great influence on British anthropology had intervened too, and Malinowski's blindness to the notion of a social system was fully appreciated.

But, as one can now see perhaps more clearly than ever, Malinowski's greatness lay in his ability to penetrate the web of theories to the real man, boasting, hypocritical, earthy, reasonable; and he passed on to his students an invaluable awareness of the tension which is always there between what people say and what they do, between individual interests and the social order. It was Malinowski too who was the first to show the way in which the principle of reciprocity might serve to bind the individual, in his own interests, to the community. *Argonauts of the Western Pacific* explored the dynamics of a system of ceremonial exchange, and stimulated the analysis of Mauss in *The Gift*, which in turn provided the central inspiration of Lévi-Strauss. *Crime and Custom in Savage Society* showed that the principle of reciprocity was a crucial element in the operation of social control, providing the means to maintain social relationships of all kinds. This was to be the central theme of 'transactional' analysis, which provided the main challenge to the French structuralist position in the late sixties.

But perhaps it is not vital to demonstrate Malinowski's

49

place in the history of anthropological ideas. His real greatness was his recognition of Trobriand Man in his full humanity. 'What is the deepest essence of my investigations?' he wrote in his diary in 1917, in the Trobriand islands. 'To discover what are his main passions, the motives for his conduct, his aims . . . His essential, deepest way of thinking. At this point we are confronted with our own problems: What is essential in ourselves?'[55]

TWO

Radcliffe-Brown

I have been described on more than one occasion as belonging to something called the 'Functional School of Social Anthropology' and even as being its leader, or one of its leaders. This Functional School does not really exist; it is a myth invented by Professor Malinowski . . . There is no place in natural science for 'schools' in this sense, and I regard social anthropology as a branch of natural science . . . I conceive of social anthropology as the theoretical natural science of human society, that is, the investigation of social phenomena by methods essentially similar to those used in the physical and biological sciences. I am quite willing to call the subject 'comparative sociology', if anyone so wishes.

– Radcliffe-Brown[1]

I

Malinowski brought a new realism to social anthropology, with his lively awareness of the flesh-and-blood interests behind custom, and his radically new techniques of observation. Radcliffe-Brown introduced the theoretical discipline of French sociology, and brought a more rigorous battery of concepts to the aid of the new fieldworkers. He also established several new centres for the science. Three years Malinowski's senior, he survived him by eleven years and took over the leadership of British social anthropology from him in the late thirties.

Some saw Radcliffe-Brown as the classic to Malinowski's romantic. In fact he too was a man of extremes, obsessed by his message; like Malinowski, an egomaniac and a dogmatist. Both men had pretensions to aristocratic, even superman status, and I think it is symptomatic of their essential similarity and oddity that both were valetudinarians. In short, both men saw themselves as prophets. But where Malinowski gushed, Radcliffe-Brown disciplined his flow, guided by his unswerving if somewhat naïve adherence to the canons of the natural sciences at the turn of the century.

Radcliffe-Brown came under the influence of Durkheim's

sociological theories before the First World War, and the productive years of his career were dedicated to the application of this theory to the discoveries of the ethnographers; an enterprise he shared for much of his life with Durkheim's nephew Mauss. He established social anthropology in Cape Town and Sydney, and recreated it in his own image at Chicago and Oxford. His tenure of the Oxford Chair permitted him to establish an ascendancy over British social anthropology which lasted almost until his death in 1955.

II

Alfred Reginald Brown was born at Sparkbrook, Birmingham, in 1881. When he was five his father died, leaving his mother penniless. She worked as a 'companion', while her mother looked after the children. 'Rex' was a scholar at King Edward's School in Birmingham, but he left school before he was eighteen for a job in the Birmingham library. His elder brother, Herbert, encouraged him to study further, and supported him while he did a year of pre-medical science at Birmingham University. He then won an Exhibition at Trinity College, Cambridge, and in 1902 he began to read for the Moral Sciences tripos. His brother, now established in South Africa, continued to give him financial support, in part from the proceeds of a wound gratuity, deriving from the Anglo-Boer war.[2]

Brown had wished to take the Natural Sciences tripos at Cambridge, but his tutor insisted that he was better advised to read Mental and Moral Sciences. Here his teachers included Myers and Rivers, both medical psychologists and veterans of the Torres Straits expedition, Cambridge's pioneering venture in anthropological field research. The course covered psychology and philosophy, including the philosophy of science, which was taught in part by A. N. Whitehead. In 1904 he took a first, and became Rivers's first pupil in anthropology.

Cambridge was enjoying its greatest modern period at the turn of the century. Brown was in the university of Moore,

52

Russell, Whitehead, Sedgwick and Keynes. Great advances were being consolidated in the natural sciences, and at the same time there were the first stirrings of a novel, still intensely private culture, francophile, personal, élitist but not without a social conscience, the culture which was later to emerge from its charming adolescence into the neurotic maturity of 'Bloomsbury'. Bertrand Russell, who also read Moral Sciences, and was a fellow of Trinity, spanned the Victorian Cambridge of Moore and the Edwardian Cambridge of Keynes and Lytton Strachey. He has identified the essential spirit of the place at that time as one of intellectual honesty – 'This virtue certainly existed not only among my friends, but among my teachers. I cannot remember any instance of a teacher resenting it when one of his pupils showed him to be in error, though I can remember quite a number of occasions on which pupils succeeded in performing this feat.'[3] Rivers had the virtues of contemporary Cambridge, and Brown was fortunate in his teacher. As a Cambridge man of his day, he later concluded that Rivers was fundamentally in error.[4]

Guided by Rivers and Haddon, Brown made a study of the Andaman islands from 1906–8. His report won him a fellowship at Trinity, which he held from 1908 to 1914, though during this period he also held briefly a teaching appointment at the London School of Economics. His initial Andaman report was concerned with problems of ethnology, and it reflected the diffusionist proclivities of Rivers. However, he was soon converted to a Durkheimian view of sociology.

A preliminary essay by Durkheim, which foreshadowed the argument of *The Elementary Forms of the Religious Life*, made a considerable impact in England at this time. In Cambridge the classicist Jane Harrison immediately adopted the new point of view, and Marett at Oxford thought (erroneously) that he discerned a fundamental similarity to his own position.[5] In 1909–10 Brown gave a series of lectures at the L.S.E. and at Cambridge in which he advanced the essentially Durkheimian point of view which he was to maintain for the rest of his life.[6] In 1913 he delivered a similar series of lectures in his home town, Birmingham, which were reported in the local press. After reading the programme of these lectures, Durkheim wrote to him: 'It has brought me a new proof of the understanding which reigns between us on the general conception of our science.'[7]

Radcliffe-Brown never published a record of his conversion but he did remark that his switch from the ethnological interests of Rivers and Haddon was quite sudden. Conversion to a new paradigm is usually rapid and not, in detail, a matter of logical analysis, and in turning to Durkheim he was part of a fairly widespread movement in Britain at the time. The episode parallels the reception of Lévi-Strauss's structuralism in Britain in the fifties. At the same time one can appreciate what the conversion offered: scientific method, the conviction that social life was orderly and susceptible to rigorous analysis, a certain detachment from individual passions, and a fashionable French panache. Like Kropotkin's anarchism, to which Brown had been attracted as a student, Durkheim's sociology contained an essentially optimistic vision of the possibility of man's self-realization in a properly-ordered society; but at the same time Durkheim's socialism played down the 'class war', and this too may have attracted Brown. In short Brown's devotion to the natural sciences and his vague Utopian anarchism were both provided for in a new creed which was at once scientific, humanitarian, in a mass sort of way, and, very important, French. His fundamental fanaticism was now directed for good. Later passions, as for Chinese philosophy, and earlier passions, for French culture, were swallowed up in it. In the twenties British intellectuals turned pessimistic and mystical; in the thirties, optimistic and communist. Brown never wavered.

III

We are fortunate to possess a perceptive portrait of Brown in his Cambridge years. He made friends with a student slightly junior to him, E. L. Grant Watson, who read natural sciences but later became a novelist and something

of a mystic. Watson accompanied Brown on his first Australian field expedition, and described him in some detail in
his autobiography, *But to What Purpose*. He recalled:

Towards the end of the first term in my fourth year I met
A. R. Brown, who was recently returned from the Andaman
Islands, where he had been studying the social organization of
the islanders. He was now planning an expedition to North-West
Australia, and it was mooted that I might possibly go with him
as Zoologist to the expedition. Brown, Anarchy Brown, as he
was then called, for he had been a declared Anarchist, had a
peculiar reputation at Trinity. In spite of his having passed all
examinations with distinction and being a Scholar and Fellow of
the college, there were many of the erudite who looked on him
with suspicion. He was too dramatic a personality to fit easily
into the conservative life of a college. He often made wild statements, he was brilliantly informed on *all* subjects. That, of
course, told against him, and then he had lived as a primitive
autocrat, exercising a beneficent but completely authoritarian
sway over the simple Andamanese, who had not been in a
position to criticise his grand gestures. He was in fact a bit of a
superman, and one who strove, more consistently than any other
man I have met, to live consciously and according to a set plan
dictated by his reason and will. It is true that he sometimes
lapsed from his high standard, and was led by his inventive
genius to fabricate the stories he told, and often it was not
difficult to see this invention in process. This made the scholarly
and conscientious distrustful of him, but I have every reason to
believe that these extravagances, which he allowed himself
in talk, never once found their way into his published work.[8]

Watson seems to have been one of the few men whom
Brown took into his confidence:

He expounded to me some of his philosophy. One must culti-
vate style. He dressed like a Paris *savant*, faultlessly. He aspired
to be conscious of every gesture; had even thought out the best
position in which to sleep. Not on the back, not wholly on the
side, and not like a foetus. He pictured himself even in sleep.

Indeed Brown had developed a complete, and rather inhuman plan of living in which all irrelevancies were ex-
cluded. Watson describes how 'He made, in fact, no least

effort towards people who seemed to him superfluous. They might talk to him, expecting an answer, but his eye would be fixed on the distance, and no reply would be forthcoming.' And he comments, 'This, I think, was all part of his system of using his time to the best advantage.' In fact, Watson wrote, 'I have never known a man be more ruthless, and can well understand the exasperated women who found cause to hate him, and who so often declared that he was "no gentleman"' – despite his handsome appearance, and elegant dress.

But Watson's conclusion is surely ingenuous – 'he was as unaffected by traditions as any man might be, whose contention was that everything should be judged and acted on from a self-made rational foundation'. On the contrary, his style and his later conduct reveal a determination to adopt the manner of an English aristocrat, rather romantically conceived. In 1926 he changed his name by deed-poll to Radcliffe-Brown, incorporating his mother's name, and in his long exile in South Africa, Australia and the United States he played the rather archaic part of the eccentric English nobleman abroad, even affecting a cloak and opera-hat on inappropriate occasions in the egalitarian milieu of Sydney in the twenties.

It is tempting to trace the roots of his later manner in the deprivations of his childhood and, perhaps, his uncertainty as a young man in the rather awesome Cambridge of his day, but such speculation can have no firm basis. Nevertheless one may discern a connection between the way in which he presented himself, and saw himself, and the theoretical position he adopted in his writing. His work has a glacial clarity, and his concern was always with the formal situation, the rules and the rituals. He lacked completely Malinowski's sympathy with the subjects of his study, and so not only failed to make that transference of the sympathies which is the precondition of good fieldwork, but failed also to cope with the flesh-and-blood individual whom Malinowski thrust under the noses of his students. His detachment was a source of strength too, for it gave a controlled power to his analyses of social systems, which Malinowski never achieved.

IV

Radcliffe-Brown's first field-study, in the Andaman islands, was in his view characterized by an unusual methodological rigour, but it belongs firmly in the pre-Malinowski era of fieldwork. The same is true of his work among the Australian aborigines, in 1910–12, which was survey work of the kind practised by Rivers or Seligman. But the results of his work, which formed his earliest publications, demonstrated his analytical powers, and constitute an important contribution to the subject.

Most of Radcliffe-Brown's work in the Andaman islands was done on the Grand Andaman, this for reasons of linguistic difficulty. He camped for three months in the Little Andaman and made a great effort to learn the language, finally giving up in despair. In the Great Andaman he worked at first in Hindustani, which was generally, if imperfectly, understood by the younger adults, and after a time to some extent in the local dialects. However, he found that he only made substantial progress in the latter part of his stay, when he discovered an intelligent, English-speaking informant. The contrast with Malinowski's work in the Trobriands is striking. Even his methods of data collection were inadequate. His teacher Rivers had developed the genealogical method, but Radcliffe-Brown confessed: 'I collected a number of genealogies from the natives, but unfortunately my own experience in the use of the genealogical method, and my consequent inability to surmount the difficulties with which I met, made this branch of my investigations a failure.'[9]

The Andamans had a population of under 1,300, and by the time of Radcliffe-Brown's study they had already been sadly affected by epidemics of measles and syphilis, following the establishment of a penal colony and European settlement. In Radcliffe-Brown's view, 'What is really of interest to the ethnologist is the social organization of these tribes as it existed before the European occupation of the islands.'[10] Therefore direct observation was of little use, and he had to depend on the memories of informants. He suggests that they could report 'What was the constitution of the islands in former times', but later, describing the kinship system, he confessed: 'It would not be safe, however, to base any arguments of importance to sociology on the above description of the Andamanese system of relationship alone.' As he explained:

> The difficulty of being really sure on these matters is due (1) to the fact that the breaking-up of the old local organisation has produced many changes in their customs, and (2) to the difficulty of questioning the natives on matters connected with relationships when they have no words in their language to denote any but the simplest relationships.[11]

By the time his monograph was published in 1922 its real importance to Radcliffe-Brown was as an example of analytic method; so far as the fieldwork went, he was content to describe it as an apprentice study, and he relied heavily on the ethnographic reports of a former resident on the islands, E. H. Man, while dissenting from his speculative interpretations. He went into the field an ethnologist, and his initial aim, reflected in his first report, was to reconstruct the history of the Andamans and of the Negritos in general. Later he was converted to the Durkheimian view that the meaning and purpose of customs should be understood in their contemporary context, and it was this that he set out to demonstrate in the book.

Radcliffe-Brown divided 'customs' into three types – techniques, rules of behaviour, and what he called ceremonial customs, on which he concentrated his attention. Ceremonial customs included those collective actions conventionally performed on occasions of changes in the course of social life. Their purpose, as he believed, was the expression of collective sentiments relating to such changes. In the first part of the book he described a series of such customs, mainly ceremonies and myths. The latter part of his study was concerned with their interpretation. This is the core of the book.

Interpretation should be concerned with meaning and purpose, for 'Every custom and belief of a primitive society plays some determinate part in the social life of the community, just as every organ of a living body plays some part in the general life of the organism.'[12] The purpose of ceremonials was the expression, and therefore the maintenance and transmission, of the sentiments by which the conduct of the individual is regulated in conformity with the needs of the society.[13] To appreciate how this works one must plumb the meaning of the custom. This is done by taking into account the explanations of the members of the society, and secondly, by comparing the different contexts in which a custom appears in a society, so abstracting its essential significance.[14]

A good example of the method is his analysis of the place of formal weeping in various Andamanese ceremonies. The Andamanese weep if friends or relatives meet after long separation; at peace-making ceremonies; when a man returns to his friends after a period of mourning; after a death; after the exhumation of a corpse; at a marriage; and at various stages of an initiation ceremony. The connection between these occurrences of ceremonial weeping lies, he argued, in the fact that they all mark situations 'in which social relations that have been interrupted are about to be renewed, and the rite serves as a ceremony of aggregation'.[15] This type of procedure, extended to the study of myths and legends in another chapter, recalls the methods of the diffusionists, searching out the pure form of an artifact by comparison; and it recurs as a feature of many of Radcliffe-Brown's analytic procedures. The theory of the function of these ceremonial customs is taken straight from Durkheim, and applied rather mechanically. There is no whiff of that reality which Malinowski had insisted upon in 'Baloma', and which future fieldworkers were regularly to find in the casual, apparently impious performance of sacred ceremonies.

v

When Radcliffe-Brown went out to Australia in 1910 he took Grant Watson with him, so that we have a vivid description of the expedition, which is very revealing of

Radcliffe-Brown's character and methods, and in general helpful in understanding the field conditions of the time. There were two other members of the expedition, Mrs Daisy Bates, an amateur ethnographer and philanthropist, whom Radcliffe-Brown took on in a show of sexual egalitarianism, but with whom he soon quarrelled; and a Swedish sailor, Olsen, who came as a servant. The party was put on a sound financial footing by a gift from a sheep-farmer, who heard Radcliffe-Brown lecture on the purposes of the expedition and decided that this was a good opportunity to repay some of the profits his Aboriginal labourers had earned for him.

The expedition's first destination was the site of a corroboree east of Sandstone, and the party was just settling down to 'the main business of our task, which was to tabulate facts pertaining to the four-class marriage system',[16] when they were interrupted by a police raid. Radcliffe-Brown kept cool, upbraiding the posse for their unbridled behaviour, and even, it transpired, sheltering the miscreants for whom the police were searching. However, after this incident the Aborigines were unwilling to continue their ceremonies. Radcliffe-Brown decided to leave, and after a row abandoned poor Mrs Bates on her own. He took the rest of his party to Bernier island, the site of a lock-up hospital for Aborigines infected with venereal disease. The occupants had mostly been kidnapped and forcibly removed there, but the party spent several months on the island pursuing with these unfortunate informants their researches into the traditional Aboriginal marriage systems. After a year in the field Watson left, and Radcliffe-Brown went on with Olsen to study other Aboriginal communities settled around mission stations along the Gascoyne river. His work in Western Australia was guided in part by his conclusion, from a study of the literature, that a certain variation of the typical structure might be expected to appear in the area, and this surmise was rewarded by his discovery of the Kariera system in the field in 1911.

Despite this triumph, it is clear once again that his work was 'survey and salvage' ethnography, and it was sterile as compared with the type of fieldwork Malinowski was to prosecute in the Trobriands. As one of his Australian students pointed out, there were still functioning tribes available for study in Australia, and because he did not go to them Radcliffe-Brown was reduced to the study of formal structures – 'he could not observe how this ideal and logical structure worked. It was form without content.'[17] On the other hand, in his reports, beginning in 1912 and culminating in the famous essay, 'The Social Organisation of Australian Tribes', published in 1930–31, he brought the complex Australian material into some kind of order.

Radcliffe-Brown's central concern in his Australian work was with the system of kinship and marriage, something he had not treated with great authority in his Andaman study. The orthodox view of the day was that the division of the Australian tribes into two, four, or eight 'classes' was the basis for the regulation of their extremely complicated marriage system. Radcliffe-Brown decided that this was not the case, and that marriages were regulated rather by the kinship system working independently of the division into 'classes'. He identified two main types of Australian system. In the Kariera-type systems marriage is with a woman who falls into the category 'mother's brother's daughter'. In the Aranda-type systems it is with a woman in the category 'mother's mother's brother's daughter's daughter'. Radcliffe-Brown argued that this reflected the existence of two 'descent lines' in Kariera systems, as opposed to four in the Aranda systems.

As a modern authority has pointed out, Radcliffe-Brown's assumption that the marriage systems and class systems varied independently 'is presumably false, for while he shows that neither uniquely determines the other, his own evidence suggests that incompatible marriage and class systems never co-exist within the same society'.[18] Despite this error, and despite his refusal to acknowledge all he took from the earlier work of R. H. Mathews, the Australian studies stand as a remarkable synthesis, and they mark a significant advance in our understanding of the intractable problems of Australian social organization.

VI

Radcliffe-Brown returned briefly to England (and his newly-married wife) in 1913, when he delivered the lectures in Birmingham which aroused Durkheim's enthusiasm. In 1914 he found himself once again in Australia, at that fateful meeting of Section H of the British Association for the Advancement of Science at which Malinowski served as secretary. When war broke out Malinowski took the opportunity to undertake fieldwork. Radcliffe-Brown, however, withdrew from anthropology for the duration of the war. He became a school-master in Sydney, and was later appointed Director of Education in the Kingdom of Tonga, a post in which he served, evidently without great pleasure or profit, between 1916 and 1919.

Immediately after the war the Great Flu reached Tonga. Radcliffe-Brown became ill, and on medical advice he left to join his brother in Johannesburg. Here he held some minor museum and academic appointments – including a lectureship in English at the new university. Then came a breakthrough. Haddon had been lobbying from Cambridge for the institution of anthropological studies in South Africa, and in 1920 General Smuts invited Radcliffe-Brown to establish the subject at the University of Cape Town. Smuts had been interested in the scientific study of South Africa's population for some time (and, indeed, his nephew and his wife, J. D. and E. J. Krige, were to become distinguished anthropologists). Nonetheless it is possible that Haddon's influence, and so perhaps Radcliffe-Brown's appointment, were due to the fact that both Haddon and Smuts were fellows of Christ's College in Cambridge.

Almost forty years old, Radcliffe-Brown now entered a new phase in his career. Fieldwork was behind him. From now on he was concerned with teaching, writing, and the development of theory. Practically all his important publications appeared after this first appointment to a professorship.

In Cape Town Radcliffe-Brown established a School of African Studies, organized around the new anthropology department. In addition to his teaching and administrative duties he had some impact on government thinking, mounting special 'applied anthropology' courses for administrators of the tribal areas, and giving many successful public lectures, which were often fully covered by the press. He did not, however, make specific recommendations for reform, and in general his message was hardly contentious:

The one great problem on which the future welfare of South Africa depends is that of finding some social and political system in which the natives and the whites may live together without conflict; and the successful solution of that problem would certainly seem to require a thorough knowledge of the native civilization between which and our own we need to establish some sort of harmonious relation.[19]

He argued, now and for the rest of his career, that the anthropologist's job was simply to provide a scientific appraisal of the situation which the administrator faced; he should not attempt to advocate any particular policy.

In 1926 he returned to Australia, to take up a new chair at Sydney. This was the first chair to be established in anthropology in Australia. It is interesting that this post was secured for him by that distinguished Sydney alumnus, the anatomist Elliot Smith, whose extreme diffusionist theories Radcliffe-Brown considered so ludicrous. Once again he built up an undergraduate programme, and mounted special offerings for colonial officers and missionaries (which, however, were generally thought to be much too theoretical, and which suffered also from his total lack of interest in Papua and New Guinea, territories he never even visited). With the help of substantial government grants he also established research projects on the Aborigines, and started a new journal, *Oceania*.

Despite all this activity, Radcliffe-Brown's tenure of the Sydney chair was in the end only just short of disastrous. He began under the most promising auspices, but his overbearing ways and political maladroitness alienated his supporters. In a period of growing financial stringency he turned the state governments against his schemes, and when he left Sydney in 1931 the department and all the subsidiary activities he had initiated were on the point of collapse. Firth took over to supervise the dissolution, but he and his successor, Elkin, managed to re-establish the department and most of its programmes. On the credit side, Radcliffe-Brown trained a few students, and organized a little – surprisingly little – research. Perhaps his most enduring contribution was the essay, 'The Social Organisation of the Australian Tribes', which provided a jumping-off point for the researches of the next generation.

After another brief visit to England, Radcliffe-Brown went on to Chicago in 1931. Here he was free of administrative duties, and was treated with exaggerated respect by his talented coterie of students. Outside this circle he aroused considerable antagonism, by his manner rather than his ideas, although there were many who found his generalizing 'natural science' approach unsympathetic. American anthropology, dominated by Lowie and Kroeber, was in a creative and transitional phase. The main trends were on the one hand a development of Boas's historical and historicist approach, and, on the other, a movement towards 'culture and personality' studies, influenced by developments in psychology, particularly psychoanalysis and gestalt theory. The work of those whom Radcliffe-Brown influenced showed the impact of his sociological perspective in a manner which was new within the American tradition. Eggan, Tax, and Warner came to represent a Radcliffe-Brownian theoretical school, centred in Chicago. It was always something of an anomaly within American anthropology, but the distinctive contribution of the school has been widely acknowledged.

In 1937 Radcliffe-Brown was appointed to the first established chair in social anthropology at Oxford, so that he returned to England shortly before Malinowski finally left. His inaugural lecture rehearsed his familiar views concerning the distinction between historical and sociological studies, and the superiority of the latter in anthropology. It had a tepid reception, and he never made an impact on the wider community of the university. Within the small world of British anthropology, however, his presence was of the utmost importance. He took Malinowski's place at the head of the profession, and at one time or another the members of his department included (as staff or as students) some of the leading figures of the next generation.

To those who worked with him at the time, Radcliffe-Brown was the leader of a long overdue challenge to Malinowski, representing sense, clarity and sociology. But some of Malinowski's more constant followers regarded Radcliffe-Brown as little more than a figure-head for the rebellious young men, E. E. Evans-Pritchard and Meyer Fortes. It is true that the new generation of fieldworkers were already turning to sociology in the thirties, before Radcliffe-Brown's return to Britain; but although this was in part a direct response to the complexity of their field-material, and the analytical weaknesses of Malinowski's theory, the influence of Radcliffe-Brown can be traced as well. He had trained a number of the students who later came to Malinowski for their fieldwork – Schapera, Hogbin and Stanner, for example. Moreover his brief visit to the country in 1931 had brought his work to the attention of some of the young anthropologists. Evans-Pritchard fêted him, and propagated his reputation. Of course, the commerce between Radcliffe-Brown and younger men of the calibre of Evans-Pritchard and Fortes was never a one-way business. Nevertheless one must recognize that Radcliffe-Brown had a very direct and personal impact upon British anthropology, particularly after 1937. This may be measured by the violence of Evans-Pritchard's later repudiation of his central dogmas, and by Fortes's no less impassioned defence.

During the war Radcliffe-Brown served as President of the Royal Anthropological Institute, and he spent two years on a British Council mission in São Paulo. Immediately after the war he had to retire from the Oxford chair, which he vacated reluctantly in 1946. He remained a man of influence in the profession after his formal retirement, and partly as a result of his poverty he even continued teaching for some years, holding positions in Cambridge, London, Manchester, Grahamstown and Alexandria. He died in London in 1955. Raymond Firth recalls visiting him in hospital a year before his death and asking whether he could bring him something to read. Radcliffe-Brown answered that he was interested only in reading about theoretical advances in social anthropology.[20]

VII

The sociology of Durkheim was the most important influence on Radcliffe-Brown's mature thinking, but he also remained an evolutionist in the tradition of Spencer. Cultures (later societies) were like organisms, and therefore they should be studied by the methods of the natural sciences. Like organisms, they evolved in the direction of increasing diversity and complexity. Evolution in this sense was sharply distinguished from progress, for evolution was a natural process, while progress implied an evaluation of a moral process. Many so-called evolutionists, including Morgan and Frazer, were really rather woolly-minded apostles of progress, from the smug viewpoint of Rochester N.Y. or some other pinnacle of modern man's achievement. The organic analogy should not, of course, be taken too literally. As Radcliffe-Brown once remarked, 'Societies are not organisms; they do not experience parturition nor death.'[21] The thrust of his argument was really to insist upon the use of methods parallel to those that, at the time, exemplified the 'natural sciences' at their most successful, the methods of biology and zoology.

Despite the initial talk of 'culture' and 'psychological' explanation his orientation from about 1910 was definitely sociological. Sociology to him meant the sort of work carried out by Durkheim, and, he sometimes added, Steinmetz and Westermarck, but certainly not the general run of social survey and reportage which passed for sociology in the U.S.A. He was apparently unaware of the work of Weber and Simmel, but their theories only became widely known in Britain in the forties.

Durkheim had begun with an insistence that social facts should be treated as objective phenomena. They could be explained in terms of other social facts. A social fact (exemplified by a grammatical usage, a taboo, a ceremony,

66

a courteous gesture) was characterized by its external and coercive nature. It was prior to any individual, and exercised a constraint upon his behaviour. One could not understand a mode of sacrifice, or a dietary custom, in terms of the psychological make-up of any individual. The custom existed before his birth and would endure after his death. Nor did he freely choose to adopt it, any more than he could freely choose to create a new language in which to communicate with his fellows. These 'social facts', in a sense external to individuals and exerting a force upon them, should also not be reduced to other kinds of reality, as Malinowski liked to do. The set of social facts with which the analyst was concerned must be treated as forming a system, and the meaning and purpose of a custom could be understood only by relating it to the total set of relevant social facts. Finally, the search for 'origins' must be abandoned. The 'contemporary origin', the function of an institution, must be found in its present use.

In Durkheim's view society was essentially a moral order. Increasingly in his later work he concentrated upon what he called the 'collective consciousness', the values and norms of a society. These were embedded in the individual's consciousness through the process of socialization. In 'primitive societies' this socially conditioned sphere of individual consciousness was predominant, while in societies with complex systems of division of labour the area of individuality was greater.

The persistence of the social order depended upon the maintenance of sentiments of solidarity. In 'primitive societies' one found a series of similar local groups, and these groups and their members were mutually replaceable. The group could segment without altering the form and function of the local units, and individuals could be born or die without changing the social order. In societies of this kind – segmental societies – social solidarity was based upon the recognition of mutual resemblance. In societies which enjoyed a complex division of labour, and, therefore, were of larger scale, and more highly centralized, the solidarity of the members derived from their sense of mutual dependence.

In all societies the forms of social grouping determined the social consciousness of their members, and the forms of consciousness were maintained and invigorated by being re-enacted in symbolic rituals. It is not only ritual in the usual sense which had this effect. Even crime was necessary to society, since by dramatizing deviance and retribution it strengthened the sentiments which supported the moral order.

Such a brief résumé is unavoidably distorted. One cannot easily convey the sweep of Durkheim's thought, which was developed in a series of exquisitely presented monographs dealing with particular topics. Moreover Durkheim was not working alone. The group he built up around the *Année Sociologique* included such great names as Mauss, Granet, Hubert, Halbwachs and Hertz, and in their journal they worked out their ideas in a cooperative fashion. Even some French scholars outside this group, including Lévy-Bruhl and the neglected master Van Gennep, contributed to the same broad enterprise.

The First World War destroyed this magnificent nursery of sociology. Some of Durkheim's most brilliant students, including his son, were killed in action; and Durkheim himself died in 1917. Only his nephew Mauss survived long to carry on the tradition. The war interrupted the plans for fieldwork which the *Année* group had been developing. It was many years before another cadre was built up, and when it emerged it dedicated itself to field-research. As Lévi-Strauss reported in 1947, 'The younger generation of French sociologists, which came to maturity around 1930, have over the last fifteen years almost completely renounced theoretical work – though doubtless only temporarily – in order to fill this gap.'[22]

And so after the First World War Mauss and Radcliffe-Brown were left to work parallel with each other to develop Durkheimian sociology. One may summarize the development from Durkheim to Mauss and Radcliffe-Brown by saying simply that Malinowski's studies of the Trobriand islands had intervened. Curiously, these influenced Mauss more than they did Radcliffe-Brown, and Malinowski himself soon turned away from Durkheim's preoccupations and ideas.

But I have exaggerated the unity of Durkheim's legacy. One may distinguish at least two divergent threads, one of which Mauss followed, while Radcliffe-Brown took up the other. First there was the study of social relationships, 'social morphology', as exemplified in the *Division of Labour in Society*; secondly the study of societies as moral systems, the view which dominates *Suicide* and *The Elementary Forms of the Religious Life*, and which led Durkheim and Mauss to anticipate many future developments in their essay *Primitive Classification*. Both approaches may be found in the work of Radcliffe-Brown and Mauss, and it is arguable that they are not divergent but rather complementary perspectives. However, Radcliffe-Brown turned more to the study of social relations, while Mauss continued to develop the study of cosmological notions.

Mauss lived to endure the Nazi occupation of Paris, which ended his active career. It is ironic that this was the period when Radcliffe-Brown finally succeeded in joining his theory to the Malinowskian tradition of holistic fieldwork. The two world wars had a calamitous impact on French sociology, but by a series of chances they did not greatly disturb the development of social anthropology in Britain. These accidents secured the predominance of British social anthropology for a generation.

VIII

The only extended statement of Radcliffe-Brown's theoretical position which has been published is the transcript of a seminar he gave at the University of Chicago in 1937. This circulated widely for many years in typescript, but was published only after Radcliffe-Brown's death, under the title *A Natural Science of Society*. The seminar was a response to a series of lectures by a leading psychologist, who claimed that all social sciences must begin and end with individual psychology. Radcliffe-Brown was moved to formulate in detail his own vision of comparative sociology as the master social science. The only substantial statements published in his lifetime were two essays, on the concept of function (1935) and on social structure (1940), and the introduction to his collected essays, *Structure and Function in Primitive Society* (1952). However, he repeatedly made declarations of faith, usually as preliminaries to particular analyses, and it is relatively easy to abstract the central features of the theoretical position he maintained at least from the twenties onwards, and probably earlier.

The object of study was the social system or social process. These were systems 'of real relations of connectedness between individuals', or more properly, between individuals occupying social roles, between 'persons'.[23] This constituted the 'social structure', which was not an abstraction. It 'consists of the sum total of all the social relationships of all individuals at a given moment in time. Although it cannot, naturally be seen in its entirety at any one moment, we can observe it; all of the phenomenal reality is there.'[24] But while this was what the fieldworker observed, he described something different, the 'structural form', that is the normal pattern of relationships which he abstracted from the flux of observed reality. Radcliffe-Brown is often criticized for his refusal to recognize that 'social structure' is an abstraction, and it is tempting to reply that his notion of 'structural form' corresponds to what is today generally termed the 'social structure'. This is true to a certain extent, but even the 'structural form' was a generalized description rather than a model. As he once wrote to Lévi-Strauss:

I use the term 'social structure' in a sense so different from yours as to make discussion so difficult as to be unlikely to be profitable. While for you, social structure has nothing to do with reality but with models that are built up, I regard the social structure as a reality. When I pick up a particular sea shell on the beach, I recognize it as having a particular structure. I may find other shells of the same species which have a similar structure, so that I can say there is a form of structure characteristic of the species. By examining a number of different species, I may be able to recognize a certain general structural form or principle, that of a helix, which could be expressed by means of logarithmic equation. I take it that the equation is what you mean by 'model'. I examine a local group of Australian aborigines and find an arrangement of persons in a certain number of families. This, I call the social structure of that particular group at that moment of time. Another local group has a structure that is in important ways similar to that of the first. By examining a representative sample of local groups in one region, I can describe a certain form of structure.

I am not sure whether by 'model' you mean the structural form itself or my description of it. The structural form itself may be discovered by observation, including statistical observation, but cannot be experimented on.[25]

The structural form is explicit in 'social usages', or norms, which are generally recognized as binding and which are widely observed. They therefore have the characteristics of Durkheim's 'social facts', but once again Radcliffe-Brown insisted that they were not deduced but observed. A social usage or norm 'is not established by the anthropologist . . . it is characterized by what people say about rules in a given society and what they do about them'.[26]

Having abstracted the social form of a number of societies one proceeds to comparison and classification, which is the basis of proper scientific procedure. One can then pose the fundamental questions of social morphology, 'How many different kinds of societies are there, and in what respects do they differ from one another? What is the range of variation, and, more important, what common characteristics are there discoverable by analysis which are characteristic of all human societies?'[27] Despite the significance he attached to comparison, there is, however, a certain ambiguity about the procedures he advocated. He often proceeded as though one should always in the first instance compare societies which are culturally or ethnically related – the various Andamanese groups, the Australian tribes, the Southern Bantu groups. The goal often seems to have been to uncover the general characteristics of the 'culture area', to strip away local variations from (say) the typical Andamanese form, and at times Radcliffe-Brown seems to retain elements of diffusionist method. At other times the goal was rather to understand peculiarities and variations by comparison with better-known or more readily understood examples. Finally, he was never clear as to the units of comparison. He sometimes wrote as though one could compare the structural forms of total social systems, but at other times he suggested that it was possible to compare only sub-systems, such as kinship or political systems.

In any case the ultimate goal was not in doubt. This was to formulate generalizations about the common features of all human societies. These generalizations would constitute social laws.

Radcliffe-Brown argued that although social structures were in flux, social forms were comparatively stable. New members of the society are born, the old chief dies and is replaced, people divorce and remarry; but the same social usages persist. The stability of the structural form depends upon the integration of its parts, and the performance by these parts of particular tasks which are necessary for the maintenance of the form. These are the 'functions' of the parts of the system. Laws of social statics would be statements about the needs which had to be met if social forms were to persist.

The basic need of all societies was what Radcliffe-Brown called 'coaptation', the mutual adjustment of the interests of the members of the society. This necessitates some standardization of behaviour, and it is here that 'culture' comes in, for culture is the realm of learnt ways of feeling, thinking and behaving. Ultimately coaptation requires the standardization of beliefs and sentiments, which are kept alive through rituals and symbols. But this area of social life – corresponding to Durkheim's 'collective consciousness' – could not be studied in isolation, as Malinowski and most American anthropologists believed. 'You cannot have a science of culture. You can study culture only as a characteristic of a social system . . . if you study culture, you are always studying the acts of behaviour of a specific set of persons who are linked together in a social structure.'[28]

Having established taxonomies and formulated the laws of social statics, that is the laws of persistence of social forms, there remained a third set of problems. These were concerned with the manner in which societies change their type – with what Spencer had called problems of social dynamics. Radcliffe-Brown believed that these problems were logically secondary to problems of continuity. The laws of social change would be deduced from the laws of social continuity. He never devoted serious attention to them.

The conclusions of these investigations are disappointing. The fundamental laws of social statics turn out to be statements of this sort:

There have to be as part of the social coaptation of any given society a certain common set of ways of feeling and a certain common set of ways of thinking.[29]

There must be a certain degree of functional consistency amongst the constituent parts of the social system. (Functional inconsistency 'exists whenever two aspects of the social system produce a conflict which can only be resolved by some change in the system itself'.)

To this law of the necessity of a certain degree of functional consistency we may add a second, which is a special instance of the first. Any human social life requires the establishment of a social structure consisting of a network of relations between individuals and groups of individuals. These relations all involve certain rights and duties which need to be defined in such a way that conflicts of rights can be resolved without destroying the structure. It is this need that is met by the establishment of systems of justice and legal institutions.[30]

Explanation consists in showing how a social usage fulfils one of these basic functions, upon which the maintenance of stable social forms depends. Thus a ritual sustains sentiments of social solidarity. These sentiments must be maintained in order to make people play their appointed parts – that is, they sustain the degree of coaptivity upon which the system depends. This sort of argument is often plausible enough, but it does not seem to lead anywhere. Ultimately it is tautologous. If you have to start off knowing what are the basic functions upon which society depends, you have settled the important questions before even beginning to sort out the details.

Fortunately Radcliffe-Brown's actual procedure was usually far superior to his prescription. Again and again his papers start with some banal statement about societies being like organisms, which should therefore be studied in pseudo-physiological terms, etc.; but he then proceeds to develop particular analyses as examples of what he means, and these analyses are generally original and illuminating. This is because he was not merely a functionalist, in the jargon of a later generation, he was also a structuralist. That is, he was concerned with the relationships between social relationships of different kinds, and in exploring these he allowed himself intuitive leaps which often yielded insights which have still to be superseded. His best work is concerned with 'totemism', and with kinship – that is, with special cases of cosmology and social organization. These were to be two of the central topics of the new structuralism which came into fashion after his death.

IX

'Totemism', broadly defined as an aspect of the way in which man conceives of the relationship between the social and the natural world, was a classical issue in British anthropology, and it was one of Radcliffe-Brown's preoccupations from the time of his Andaman study. In totemism a specific group within a society adopts a ritual attitude towards a particular natural species or object. Durkheim had argued that certain groups are the objects of sentiments of attachment. These sentiments must be collectively expressed in ritual and symbolism if they are to be maintained, and one obvious way of symbolizing the social group was with reference to natural species. Radcliffe-Brown accepted this argument as far as it went – 'it is a normal procedure that the sentiment of attachment to a group shall be expressed in some formalised collective behaviour having reference to an object that represents the group itself'.[31]

But Durkheim failed to examine the next question – why are natural species generally selected as totems? Characteristically Radcliffe-Brown insisted that this question must be placed in the context of a broader problem, the ritual relationships between men and natural species in all, including non-totemic societies. He recalled his study of the Andaman islanders, who lacked totems but expressed 'ritual attitudes' to a range of natural species. His initial conclusion was that species important to the livelihood of the group are given 'ritual value'.

This crude statement was elaborated. Totemism was 'a mechanism by which a system of social solidarities is established between men and nature'.[32] It is a way of bringing the natural world within the social or moral order. Totemism was therefore not only a mode of symbolizing social groups; it was also a way of domesticating nature. In this sense totemism was a prototype of religion, for the essence of religion is the conception of the universe as a social, that is, a moral order.

The method is characteristic. The particular problem is set in a broad context. One then states the fundamental laws which determine a kind of activity – e.g., groups must express sentiments of solidarity, through rituals, which employ symbols. Or, human beings must be able to see nature as somehow part of the same moral order as society . . . The particular phenomenon under consideration is then related to these broad generalizations. This constitutes explanation.

The other element of the method is comparison, and it was in a later essay on the comparative method that Radcliffe-Brown elaborated his argument. It had presumably become clear to him that totems are not generally selected because of their importance as food, and he now explored the problem of why particular species were selected to symbolize particular group relationships. He observed that in some tribes in New South Wales there was a division of the society into two exogamous moieties. The moieties were named respectively after the eaglehawk and crow, and eaglehawk men married crow women, and vice versa. He observed that parallels could be found elsewhere: the Haida of north-west America also have a division into two matrilineal moieties, and these are named after the eagle and the raven. In Australia there were many examples of exogamous moieties being named after pairs of birds, and these birds tended to be linked also in myths. Moreover one could find in Australia other kinds of dual divisions, including endogamous moeities, or even alternating generations, which were similarly named after pairs of birds – and not only birds, but sometimes after pairs of animals, such as two species of kangaroo, or the bat and the tree-creeper.

Further, where these divisions are found, the two birds or animals in question are usually represented in myths as being opponents in some sort of conflict. Radcliffe-Brown continued:

A comparative study therefore reveals to us the fact that the Australian ideas about the eaglehawk and the crow are only a particular instance of a widespread phenomenon. First, these tales interpret the resemblances and differences of animal species in terms of social relationships of friendship and antagonism as they are known in the social life of human beings. Secondly, natural species are placed in pairs of opposites. They can only be so regarded if there is some respect in which they resemble each other. Thus eaglehawk and crow resemble each other in being the two prominent meat-eating birds (. . . and the Australian aborigine thinks of himself as a meat-eater).

We can now answer the question 'Why eaglehawk and crow?' by saying that these are selected as representing a certain kind of relationship which we may call one of 'opposition'.

The Australian idea of what is here called 'opposition' is a particular application of that association by contrariety that is a universal feature of human thinking, so that we think by pairs of contraries, upwards and downwards, strong and weak, black and white. But the Australian conception of 'opposition' combines the idea of a pair of contraries with that of a pair of opponents. In the tales about eaglehawk and crow the two birds are opponents in the sense of being antagonists.[33]

A comparative study of moieties shows that they too are seen as locked in a sort of competitive alliance, at once paired and opposed. This is the sort of relationship which is often expressed in formalized 'joking'. It is therefore appropriate that they should be symbolized by two linked natural species, which are in turn represented as being in some sense contraries, and also competitors.

Lévi-Strauss has seized upon this last development of Radcliffe-Brown's theory of totemism, and suggested that it represented a departure for him and, incidentally, an approach to a structural linguistic mode of argument.[34] In fact Radcliffe-Brown's notion of opposition did include the linguistic level of binary pairing, but it applied more particularly to a social opposition between groups, which was expressed in some form of conflict. Nevertheless in this theory the structuralist dimension of Radcliffe-Brown's thought may be clearly discerned, side by side with the insistence upon function.

x

Radcliffe-Brown's particular specialism was kinship, and this was the field in which he was freest to develop his own insights, since Morgan and Rivers had relied upon historical explanations of kinship systems, and the *Année Sociologique* school had neglected the topic.

Radcliffe-Brown saw a system of kinship and marriage as a set of interrelated social usages which were based upon the recognition of certain biological relationships for social purposes. The systems included the kinship terminology; the actual networks of relationships between kin; the set of rights, duties and usages associated with particular kinship roles; and the beliefs and ritual practices associated with kinship, including, for example, beliefs about procreation, or the veneration of ancestors.

In investigating a kinship system he concentrated upon two of its aspects: (i) the usages governing the relationships between kin; and (ii) the terms used in addressing kin, and referring to them. The kinship terminology had a certain priority, both in logic and with respect to method. This was because 'The actual social relation between a person and his relative, as defined by rights and duties or socially approved attitudes and modes of behaviour is then to a greater or lesser extent fixed by the category to which the relative belongs.'[35] At the same time he would not admit any attempt to argue that one part of the kinship system had priority in causal terms. For example, Rivers had argued that the form of the marriage rules determined the terminology. This was unacceptable. The marriage regulations and the terminology were necessarily consistent, but there were no grounds for arguing that one or the other came first, or determined the other.

Societies such as the Andaman islanders and the Australian aborigines were organized by the principles of kinship and residence, and residential groups were themselves informed by the principles of the kinship system. Therefore in societies of this sort the study of social structure meant essentially the study of the kinship system. The hub of the kinship system was the family – this he took over from Westermarck. However, there were various possible ways of treating kin outside the circle of the family. Broadly the option was to classify them together with members of the family, as happened in the 'classificatory' kinship systems which Morgan had identified; or members of the family could be distinguished from other relatives, as was the practice among the Eskimo and in contemporary Europe. Radcliffe-Brown concentrated upon the logic of 'classificatory' systems of kinship terminology.

Every classificatory system operated with some combination of three basic principles. First of all, brothers and sisters shared a feeling of solidarity, and they were treated as a unit by outsiders. This generated the principle of 'the unity of the sibling group', which influenced the categorization of relatives. For example, in some South African tribes I call my mother *mma*, extend the same term to her sisters, and even call her brother *malome*, or literally 'mother male'.

Secondly, societies operating classificatory kinship terminologies commonly also had lineages – that is, there were solidary groups formed by the descendants in one line (traced through males only or females only) of a single ancestor. The members of the lineage, like siblings, shared a sense of unity; and outsiders treated the lineage as a unit.

This gave rise to 'the principle of the unity of the lineage group', which explained further peculiar features of classificatory kinship systems. For example, among the patrilineal Fox Indians I call all the men of my mother's lineage 'mother's brother' and all the women 'mother's sister', regardless of generation. This is because I belong to a different lineage (my father's), and so, to me, they are all alike members of another corporate group, to which I am linked through my mother.

Thirdly, Radcliffe-Brown described the generation principle. In all kinship systems members of consecutive generations are distanced from each other, for reasons which go back to the necessity for transmitting culture and socializing new members of the society, functions which demand discipline and control. But members of alternate generations (grandparents and grandchildren) tend to be 'merged'. Their relationships are easy and egalitarian, and in many societies there is a notion that the grandchild replaces the grandparent in the social system. These generational combinations and oppositions may also be reflected in the terms used for the classification of kin. Indeed some kinship systems, the 'Hawaiian' systems, classify relatives on the basis of generation alone.

These three principles, then, reflecting underlying social conditions of great generality, generate the various systems of kinship terminology. The approach developed by Radcliffe-Brown contrasted sharply with the classical method, whereby kinship terminologies were regarded as fossils, pertaining to a vanished system of kinship. For example, it might be suggested that in those societies where the term 'father' embraces a large number of men, this reflected an earlier period of promiscuity when one could not be sure who one's father really was. Radcliffe-Brown rejected all such speculative and reductionist explanations. The terminology made sense in terms of the contemporary kinship system.

But while the study of the terminology was the best approach to the understanding of kinship systems, the systems were essentially systems of social relationships, and these were patterned by the kinds of solidarity and opposition which governed all social relationships. Radcliffe-Brown's most interesting analysis of these principles came in his discussion of 'joking relationships', a problem to which he returned again and again in his work.

One of the classic examples of joking relationships was provided by Junod in his report on the Thonga of Mozambique, and this was an example which stimulated Radcliffe-Brown's first essay on the problem. Among the Thonga there is a relaxed and friendly relationship between a man and his mother's father –

However should a child take too much liberty with his kokwana, the old man will say to him: 'Go and play with your malume (mother's brother)'. The malume, indeed, for his uterine nephew, is quite different from any other relative. No respect at all is necessary towards him! 'You go to *bombela* in his village; you do what you please. You take all the food you want without asking permission. If you are ill, he will take special care of you and sacrifice for you . . . When the mupsyana goes to his maternal uncle, accompanied by his comrades who scent a good meal, the wives of the malume (mother's brother) call him: "Come along, husband! Look here, your malume has hidden some food in the back part of the hut . . . behind the large basket. Go and take it". The boy steals the food, runs away with it and eats it to the last bite with his friends. The malume comes back and is angry. But when he hears that the trick has been played by his mupsyana, he shrugs his shoulders . . . When another day the nephew comes again, the malume says: "You have killed us the other day by famine!" – "Is there any more food handy that I may do it again?" answers the boy.'
Sometimes the malume (mother's brother) himself points to one of his wives and says to the ntukulu: 'This is your wife. Let her treat you well!' This woman much enjoys the situation, which she finds quite entertaining. She makes a feast for the ntukulu and calls him *nkata*, husband. It goes so far that sometimes the nephew says to the uncle: 'Please make haste and die that I may have your wife'. – 'Do you intend killing me with a gun?' says the malume . . . But all this talking is mere joke.[36]

What is the explanation of this extraordinary behaviour – 'joking', as it came to be called in the literature, characterized by the breaking of even the fundamental conventions governing the use of food and sex, and by insults which would not be tolerated in any other situation? This sort of behaviour is to be found in a number of societies, between individuals and also, as Radcliffe-Brown recognized, between groups. Characteristically for his time, Junod explained the Thonga customs in terms of a conjecture about prehistoric Thonga society. He suggested that although they were now patrilineal, the Thonga had formerly been 'matriarchal'. The customs which subsisted in the relationship between mother's brother and sister's son were the relics of a former age, when both would have been members of the same corporate group, and a boy would have succeeded to the position of his mother's brother.

In his first essay on the problem, published in 1924, Radcliffe-Brown was concerned only with this relationship between mother's brother and sister's son. He disposed of Junod's unsupported historical conjectures, and insisted that the explanation must be found in the contemporary situation. Among the Thonga a man is disciplined and controlled by his father. His mother by contrast is a loving and tolerant figure. The sentiments he feels towards his mother are extended as he grows up to her siblings, including her brother who is regarded and treated as a 'male mother'. The mother's father is similarly regarded as a tolerant and permissive figure, and indeed all the men of the mother's lineage will be grouped together and treated in similar fashion. Even the ancestor spirits on the mother's side will be regarded as more kindly and forgiving than those on the father's side.

This sort of explanation was often invoked by Malinowski, and it has come to be known as an 'extensionist' hypothesis, since it argues from relationships within the family to relationships with more distant kin, and assumes that as a child grows up he actually extends the sentiments he has developed for his parents to their siblings. The weaknesses of the argument are numerous. It is sufficient for the moment to note that it assumes that every child builds up the customary relationship with his mother's brother from scratch; and it fails to account for the tolerance of the mother's brother to his demanding sister's son. (Evans-Pritchard was later to attempt to salvage Radcliffe-Brown's argument by means of an ingenious solution to that problem.[37])

Later Radcliffe-Brown took a different tack. Instead of arguing in terms of the extension of sentiments, he placed the problem – and more broadly the whole question of joking relationships – in the context of the range of possible forms of 'alliance'. Social relationships were divided into those between members of one corporate group, and those between members of different groups. The latter were further sub-divided. Some depended upon common membership of a political community. Others were contractual relationships. Finally there were relationships of 'alliance' or 'consociation' between individuals or groups which were otherwise socially separated. Such relationships of consociation were in turn classified into four types: (i) based on intermarriage; (ii) based on the exchange of goods or services; (iii) based on blood-brotherhood or a similar institution; and (iv) those which were in the form of joking relationships. A joking relationship was therefore identified as one of a limited range of possible relationships between members of socially separated groups. It might be found in isolation, or together with one of the other forms of consociation.

That might set the relationship in its proper context, but why was it expressed in *joking*? To understand this one must examine the whole range of etiquette regulating behaviour in kinship roles. The general types of behaviour associated with kinship may be classed in two sets of oppositions: respect *v.* familiarity, and joking *v.* avoidance. Respect typifies relationships with parents, familiarity relationships with siblings. Joking and avoidance are characteristic of relationships with certain kin and affines who do not belong to your lineage. They are extreme forms of familiarity and respect. Joking is most commonly found in the relationships between cross-cousins; avoidance is more typical of relationships between members of alternate generations, between men and women and their parents-in-law. But joking and avoidance serve a similar purpose: both protect the delicate relationship between people who are joined in one set of ties, but divided by others – for example, between members of different lineages who are allied in marriage. As Radcliffe-Brown recalled:

I once asked an Australian native why he had to avoid his mother-in-law, and his reply was, 'Because she is my best friend in the world; she has given me my wife'. The mutual respect between son-in-law and parents-in-law is a mode of friendship. It prevents conflict that might arise through divergence of interest.[38]

The analysis then concludes with a generalization. Both joking and avoidance are 'modes of organizing a definite and stable system of social behaviour in which conjunctive and disjunctive components . . . are maintained and combined'.[39]

Here again the analysis concludes with a statement of function, but its enduring value derives from the preceding statement of the structural forms in which 'alliance' appears. At this level the analysis joins up with his analysis of totemism, particularly the relationships of the eaglehawk/crow type, between moieties which exchange women and are united in their opposition. It has also been remarked that although he did not cite Freud, the theory of joking relationships is congruent with Freud's famous theory of the joke.

XI

Radcliffe-Brown's list of publications is not large, considering his reputation and the impact which his ideas had in social anthropology. Much of it consists of occasional essays, and a striking feature is the recurrent statements of policy, the manifestos of his comparative sociology. In these he set out the place of social anthropology among the social sciences, and prescribed its proper methods and goals. The first of these, published in 1923, marked his appointment to the chair of anthropology at Cape Town. The last to appear in his lifetime, a note in *Nature*, in 1944, rehearsed similar themes, and these were stressed once more in the uncompleted manuscript of a textbook on which he was working at the time of his death. One may discern minor shifts in his position, notably a new conceptual emphasis on 'social structure' rather than 'culture' after about 1930, but he maintained a remarkably consistent position for most of his professional life.

His primary concern was always to distinguish social anthropology – or comparative sociology, which he equated with the sociology of the *Année* school – from ethnology. Ethnology was a real force in Britain until the late twenties, and it continued for much longer to be the central interest of American anthropologists. Radcliffe-Brown's first objection was that the ethnologists argued from inadequate evidence. They were not strictly historians, since the societies with which they were concerned lacked a historical consciousness, and their history was undocumented. Like the eighteenth-century Scottish savants, the ethnologists were engaged in 'conjectural history', a completely unscientific enterprise.

Not, he stressed, that he had anything against history. Proper history might illuminate social studies. But – and this was his second, and perhaps more important argument – one could always understand societies from an ahistorical point of view. A study of the British Parliament would conventionally begin by tracing its development over a long period of time, perhaps for a millennium. But it would be quite possible to write an enlightening study of Parliament which dealt only with its contemporary structure and role. This apparently platitudinous statement was not without significance. Both common sense and scholarship in Europe and America were imbued with a historical point of view. The question normally posed was, how did this come to be . . . ? It took an act of imagination to grasp the new question which Durkheim was asking – what does this mean, and what are its concomitants? – and to recognize that it could be answered without first dealing with the historical question.

Although Radcliffe-Brown always identified the pseudo-historical point of view as the main threat, he was concerned to defend the integrity of social anthropology on other fronts as well. Like Durkheim he was ambivalent about psychology. Social facts could not be explained in terms of individual psychology, but it was possible that some forms of psychology might assist sociology. Like Malinowski, he was for some years an advocate of Shand's theory of sentiments, but while Malinowski later proclaimed himself a behaviourist, Radcliffe-Brown simply dropped his psychological assumptions – or left them implicit. He argued that the new sociology should maintain a guarded but neighbourly relationship with psychology. Their relationship should be rather like that between physics and chemistry, which also studied a single reality with different methods and in terms of different theories. Unlike Malinowski he never experimented with psychoanalytical theory.

The battle in the latter part of his life was extended to Malinowski and those American anthropologists who, like Malinowski, were urging the development of a 'science of culture'. These writers treated social relations as a part of the total configuration of behaviour with which they were concerned, but by no means as the primary part. Nor did they regard social relations as constituting a distinct system, which should not be reduced to other kinds of relations. This was the crux of the dispute. The differences between Malinowski and Radcliffe-Brown which developed particularly in the thirties were perhaps in part a matter of 'politics'; but there was also an important and growing divergence on matters of theory.

After his retirement Radcliffe-Brown – stung by being grouped with Malinowski as a 'functionalist' – charted the history of their differences. When Malinowski had first come to Britain, in 1910, he had shown Radcliffe-Brown a paper he had written on the Australian aborigines which contained a Durkheimian point of view on social function. In 1914, at the historic meeting of Section H of the British Association in Australia, 'We had many lengthy discussions on anthropology and the aims and methods of field research, and we reached fairly complete agreement.'[40] But then in the late twenties Malinowski began to propagate a theory of 'functional anthropology' which dealt with a whole range of non-social functions. In the thirties he was increasingly inclined to explain social facts with reference to biological or culturally derived needs. 'He had gradually come to think of the subject as concerned not with the social relations and interactions of human beings but with "culture".' In contrast Radcliffe-Brown always shared the view of Durkheim and Roscoe Pound, a view 'concerned not with biological functions but with social functions, not with the abstract biological "individual", but with the concrete "persons" of a particular society. It cannot be expressed in terms of culture.'[41] Indeed, he later wrote, 'As a consistent opponent of Malinowski's functionalism I may be called an anti-functionalist.'[42]

Radcliffe-Brown would sometimes concede that ethnology, or psychology, or cultural anthropology might be able to develop their own valid frameworks for the analysis of custom, but he was sceptical. However, his main concern was to establish the boundaries of the pursuit he considered to be the most promising, and to maintain it against all challenges.

The outstanding feature of Radcliffe-Brown's mature work is its single-mindedness. Again and again he set out his vision of sociology as a sort of natural science, and therefore as opposed to conjectural reconstructions. He kept returning to the same problems – totemism and ancestor worship; kinship terminologies, the avunculate and joking relationships; and law. And he remained faithful to the same set of examples, drawn from Australia, North America, and occasionally South Africa, the ancient Romans, Teutons, or Chinese. His strength lay in his clarity, his certitude, and his dedication. These enabled him to win disciples.

XII

So few people were involved in British social anthropology before the Second World War that one can be schematic about the history of the interwar period without serious distortion. The twenties saw the challenge to the classical historical approach, and the acceptance of intensive field-work by participant observation, as the basis of a career in anthropology. The thirties was the decade of Malinowski and the London School of Economics. At this time it seemed possible that anthropology in Britain and the United States might make a similar shift in concert, in the direction of a synchronic approach. In 1930 Boas, the leading American ethnologist, wrote:

If we knew the whole biological, geographical and cultural setting of a society completely, and if we understood in detail the ways of reacting of the members of the society as a whole to these conditions, we should not need historical knowledge of the origin of the society to understand its behaviour . . . An error of modern anthropology, as I see it, lies in the over-emphasis on historical reconstruction, the importance of which should not be minimized, as against a penetrating study of the individual under the stress of the culture in which he lives.

As Eggan remarked, 'some of Boas's students came to believe that "they had known it all the time" '.[43] But the American anthropologists went in a different direction, towards a psychological interpretation of culture, with gestalt psychology, learning theory and psychoanalysis coming together in the well-known studies of Margaret Mead and Ruth Benedict.

The real split between the American and British traditions came with the dominance of Radcliffe-Brown in British anthropology after his return to Oxford in 1937, and Malinowski's subsequent departure for the United States. The forties in Britain was the decade of Radcliffe-Brown, Oxford, and a sociological structuralism.

I cannot help speculating as to what would have happened if Malinowski had remained in London, and Radcliffe-Brown had stayed in Chicago; or, indeed, if both had been working in Britain in the thirties and forties. The question highlights the importance at this period of the chance movements of a couple of individuals between the small number of powerful posts which existed. Yet there are indications that even in the thirties the new generation of British anthropologists were moving towards sociology, in their search for analytical frameworks which would help them interpret the rich material they had brought back from the field. One sees this in the contributions of Fortes and Schapera to the symposium on culture change in Africa, which appeared in 1938, and in some of the monographs produced by Malinowski's students – sporadically in Firth's *We the Tikopia* (1936) and more consistently in Schapera's *Handbook of Tswana Law and Custom* (1938) and Hogbin's *Law and Order in Polynesia* (1934), to which Malinowski contributed a fiery introduction, restating his fundamental tenets in order to strengthen the reader against the heresies to follow.

But even this brief list includes several scholars who had been exposed to Radcliffe-Brown's teaching in Sydney or Cape Town. There can be little doubt that he did provide a more satisfactory framework for analysis than did Malinowski, although he and Malinowski both had to the full the weaknesses of their strengths.

THREE

The thirties and the forties – from function to structure

> My hunch is that at least some of the difference between
> the work of Malinowski and that of Radcliffe-Brown could
> be correlated with their personalities. Radcliffe-Brown, in
> sharp contrast to Malinowski, seemed to be more aloof from
> life, modern or tribal, and without close family ties . . .
> Again, compared to Malinowski, his relations with men
> seemed to be easier than those with women. Also, Radcliffe-
> Brown had disciples in the real sense of the word. Malinow-
> ski's students learned from him, but they also argued, talked
> back, and made jokes about him. He wanted loyalty (you
> had to be on his side) but not reverence . . . Radcliffe-
> Brown, on the other hand, gathered about him a group of
> worshiping young disciples. I never heard any of them snipe
> or ridicule him. Today, some of these British anthropolo-
> gists, now middle-aged, seem to belong to an ancestor
> cult.[1]
>
> – Hortense Powdermaker

I

Almost all the first generation of anthropology students in
the functionalist era passed through Malinowski's seminars.
Even those who were attached to other universities made a
point of attending. For the decade after 1924 this was the
only school which counted. The seminar included all
interested students, whatever their status, various members
of the faculty, academic visitors from other departments
and from abroad (including, for a while, C. K. Ogden and
Talcott Parsons), administrators and missionaries on home
leave from the colonies, and periodically, bewildered amateurs, some of whom might even be recruited into the profession and sent off to do fieldwork in some exotic spot.

There was no formal teaching. The participants in the
seminar came expecting to be stimulated by the discussion
rather than by formal contributions; and, particularly, by

Malinowski's interventions. As the first students went out into the field and returned, the range of material available increased, and the theoretical notions were stretched, questioned, vindicated and, occasionally, relinquished, though seldom by Malinowski himself. All the major monographs of the period show the imprint of these discussions. Perhaps as much as his ideas Malinowski's personality imposed itself – arrogant, enthusiastic, irreverent.

The new anthropology, established by a Pole at the academically unconventional London School of Economics, attracted an unusual collection of students. Foreigners predominated, and most were experts in other fields who had been brought in as fairly mature scholars. They came from diverse backgrounds, but they were a small group and formed a tightly-knit professional cadre. As late as 1939 there were only about twenty professional social anthropologists, in the modern sense, in the British Commonwealth, and most of them had spent some time with Malinowski. These features of the profession are significant, for they facilitated the interchange of ideas, and the concerted shifts to new points of view.

The American Hortense Powdermaker, a trade union organizer, arrived at the L.S.E. in 1925. She wrote:

During my first year at the L.S.E. only three graduate students were in anthropology. The first two were E. E. Evans-Pritchard and Raymond Firth. Isaac Schapera came the second year and we were soon joined by Audrey Richards, Edith Clarke, the late Jack Driberg, Camilla Wedgwood, and Gordon and Elizabeth Brown. Strong personal bonds developed between us and with Malinowski; it was a sort of family with the usual ambivalences. The atmosphere was in the European tradition: a master and his students, some in accord and others in opposition.[2]

Evans-Pritchard was the only British native of the three men. Firth was a New Zealander, and Schapera was the first of a long line of South African recruits, many of them Jewish. He had been a student of Radcliffe-Brown in Cape Town, and when he completed his masters degree, Radcliffe-Brown advised him to choose between studying further under Malinowski in London or Lowie in the United States. He considered them to be at that time the only two other men in the world who were competent to train social anthropologists.

The high proportion of women among the early students of Malinowski is noteworthy; like the foreigners, they were a marginal group being drawn into this fledgeling enterprise. Many of them became professional anthropologists, and Audrey Richards, a natural scientist from Cambridge, very soon became a leading figure.

The first organized group on a research grant were the initial set of Rockefeller research fellows of the new International African Institute. These were Fortes, Nadel and Hofstra, who joined Malinowski's seminar in the early thirties, and whom he termed collectively 'the Mandarins'. Fortes – another South African Jew – already had a doctorate in psychology, and had worked for some years in the East London child guidance clinic. Nadel, however, had the most romantic background. By the age of thirty he had taken a doctorate in psychology and philosophy at the University of Vienna, and was an accomplished musician. He had published studies on the philosophy of music, including a book on musical typology, and a biography of Busoni. He had also produced programmes of exotic music for Radio Vienna, and toured Czechoslovakia with his own opera company.[3]

There is a perceptible generation gap between these students, who attended the seminars during the initial Malinowskian decade, and those who went to the L.S.E. during the last few years of his régime. The first group of students were all specialists in other fields who had been converted to anthropology (with the exception of Schapera). The next group started younger, on the whole, and included a larger proportion who had been trained in anthropology at the undergraduate level. Some came from South Africa, where Schapera and Winifred Hoernlé preached the new gospel. In 1930 Schapera, after returning to South Africa, replaced Mrs Hoernlé for a year at the University of the Witwatersrand in Johannesburg. His first class included Max Gluckman, Ellen Hellman, Eileen (Jensen) Krige, and Hilda (Beemer) Kuper. All of them became professional anthropologists, and with the exception of Eileen Krige, all went on to study with Malinowski. There was a similar migration from Australia, after Radcliffe-Brown had established the department of anthropology at Sydney. Students began to come to Malinowski from Australia and New Zealand, including Hogbin, Hart, Piddington, Kaberry, and Stanner.

II

Malinowski's dominance lasted roughly from 1924 to 1938. It was superseded by a sociological movement, led by Radcliffe-Brown. The shift is evident in the monographs of the period. There is a period of 'functionalist' studies in the thirties; then a period of transition; and, after 1940, a wave of neo-Radcliffe-Brownian studies. There is a time-lag between the emergence of a new theoretical consensus and its public appearance in monographs. This is inevitable, given the length of time which elapses between the departure of the ethnographer for the field and the publication of his book. There is therefore some overlap, but the phases I have distinguished may nevertheless be identified with some precision.

A second shift at this time was not entirely the result of initiatives within the profession. This was the move from the Pacific to Africa. Anthropologists now began to study large-scale societies, which were often difficult to demarcate geographically, and which had complex political institutions. These new interests were to have a distinct influence upon theoretical developments, particularly after the publication of *African Political Systems* in 1940.

But beneath all this there remained the Malinowskian emphasis on fieldwork by participant observation. This became the hallmark of British social anthropology. The rules were clear: one had to spend at least a year, preferably two, in the field, working as soon as possible entirely in the vernacular, living apart from other Europeans and to some extent as a member of the community one was studying; and above all the anthropologist had to make a psychological transference – 'they' had to become 'we'. Of course, not everyone kept all the rules. Indeed it is now clear that Malinowski himself did not. However, as Hortense Powdermaker recently remarked, the guide-lines which he laid down for his students represented an ideal:

His students, like followers and new converts in general, may have lived up to the tenets of the myth more than did the medicine man who gave them to us. I, for one, have always been grateful. We were all, probably, more successful because of the myth than we would have been without it.[4]

III

The monographs of the thirties which are usually called 'functionalist' might more precisely be termed Malinowskian. They reflected his interests, even when the authors differed from him on particular points. They dealt with family life, with economic activities, and with magic. They were not particularly concerned with kinship systems, with politics, or with religion. Malinowski's example also permeated the presentation. The authors often included a typical biography – a development from the old-fashioned catch-all 'life history' presentation – and this helped them to integrate their descriptive material in a coherent but non-structural fashion. The monographs moved from the particular institution along the whole gamut of the culture, achieving a thematic integration, if not a more analytical coherence. Individual misbehaviour was generally stressed, and the reader was introduced to particular characters, and offered evocative descriptions to give life to the culture.

The best-known monographs in this genre are Firth's *We the Tikopia* (1936), Richards's *Land, Labour and Diet in Northern Rhodesia* (1939), and Schapera's *Married Life in an African Tribe* (1940). Fortune's *Sorcerers of Dobu*, published in 1932, dealt with the ethnographic region Malinowski had made his own, and although he cannot be considered in the usual sense a student of Malinowski, this book is a good example of the kind Malinowski's students were writing.

Studies of this sort continued to appear well into the forties, particularly in the outposts of the anthropological world.

Some British anthropologists were writing work of a different kind. For example, Schapera's *Handbook of Tswana Law and Custom* appeared in 1938, before his Malinowskian study of family life, and it was a constitutional study of the sort which became familiar in the following decade. Nevertheless these Malinowskian studies belong to the thirties, and they typified the work being done in Britain at the time.

Both *We the Tikopia* and *Married Life in an African Tribe* were primarily concerned with the family. Like Malinowski in the *Sexual Life of Savages*, their authors presented the family in terms of its 'functions', mainly procreation and socialization, and worked out from there to the implications of these processes for other aspects of the social situation. Audrey Richards's massive account of the Bemba treated the economy in terms of the simple, inescapable function of providing food. These are long, discursive books, and would soon seem old-fashioned and undisciplined in their manner. *We the Tikopia* runs to almost 600 pages, and because there is not a theoretical framework of any substance, one wonders almost why the author stopped when he did. The authors did not abstract. Principles of social organization were shown immanent in concrete activities, rather than as forming systems which could be comprehended. There is no notion of a kinship system in these early monographs of Firth and Schapera, and no notion of an economic system in Richards's book.

The weaknesses were recognized. Firth has written of the late thirties – 'The basic problem raised by the functional theory of anthropology in its less sophisticated form – if everything is related to everything else, where does the description stop? – was much before the writers of the period.'[5] The problem in fact was, how to distinguish analytical relevance from empirical connection.

What was lacking was a theory which would specify what was relevant and what peripheral to the resolution of a particular problem, or to the understanding of an event. For example, Firth spent seven fascinating pages in *We the Tikopia* on sexual themes in conversation, humour, and stories (in addition to a very valuable section on indecency).

One of the Tikopian tales he related was of a woman who tempted her husband's penis outside their house and threw it into the sea. She would scoop it up whenever she wanted sexual gratification, but one day her son came along, took the penis for a sea-slug, and shot it dead with his arrow. Now this Tikopian Oedipus story may be relevant to all sorts of theoretical problems, but it was included only because it dealt with married couples and sex and so was connected to the theme (and presumably because it was entertaining in itself). It did not relate to an overriding issue, but rather raised an irrelevant little problem of its own – something which would better have been treated in a separate paper. Just as the descriptions threw up these disconnected little problems, which gave the monographs a spurious theoretical content, so the material lent itself to moralizing, in the absence of a pervasive theoretical concern. Thus Schapera gave point to his descriptions by showing what a mess the missionaries were making of traditional Tswana morality, and Richards argued the point that the Bemba were not idle, as the colonists thought, but rather undernourished.

The fieldworker searching for criteria for abstraction and selection was conscious of the absence of helpful theoretical orientations. This was the central issue in the anthropology of the late thirties. In 1937 Radcliffe-Brown was setting out his views at length in Chicago, but the value of the sociological option had still to be *demonstrated* in a social anthropological analysis of the sort of material the fieldworkers were bringing home. The experimental works of this period were not exclusively sociological in their interests, but in their emphasis upon frameworks for abstraction they had a marked structural tone. In 1936 Bateson published *Naven*. In 1937 Evans-Pritchard's first book appeared, *Witchcraft, Oracles and Magic among the Azande*, and Radcliffe-Brown's students in Chicago produced a collection of essays, *Social Anthropology of North American Tribes*, and Warner's study of the Australian Murngin, *A Black Civilization* was published. The Chicago studies provided the demonstration of Radcliffe-Brown's methods which had formerly been lacking, and they had their influence in Britain. The other two books, perhaps, are more original, representing spontaneous reactions to the problems of analysis.

IV

Bateson was a Cambridge natural scientist, and he related that 'Dr Haddon first made me an anthropologist, telling me in a railway train between Cambridge and King's Lynn that he would train me and send me to New Guinea.'[6] But Haddon (and Marett at Oxford) had got into the habit of sending their students to be trained by Malinowski for fieldwork. Bateson found Malinowski's notion of function unacceptably ambiguous, but he saw the possibilities of his adaptive theory of culture. 'This method of approach is probably sound,' he wrote, 'and its careful investigation might give a coherent system of anthropology allied to systems of economics based upon "calculating man".'[7] This was the direction in which Firth later developed the theory. Bateson also came under Radcliffe-Brown's influence, and the master accepted his views to such an extent that he usually referred the question of the relation between culture and structural form to Bateson's analysis in *Naven*.

Naven opened with the problem of selection and abstraction. The first chapter began:

If it were possible adequately to present the whole of a culture, stressing every aspect exactly as appears in the culture itself, no single detail would appear bizarre or strange or arbitrary to the reader, but rather the details would all appear natural and reasonable as they do to the natives who have lived all their lives within the culture.[8]

But this was not a practical solution. Malinowski and Doughty might in their different ways approach it, but some sort of abstraction was inescapable. Yet the process of selection and abstraction should not be allowed to impoverish the interpretation. The anthropologist must convey in their proper proportion not only the structural factors but also the emotional tone of the life, which Bateson called the ethos. *Naven* was an experiment with methods of analysis –

'it is an attempt at synthesis, a study of the ways in which data can be fitted together, and the fitting together of data is what I mean by "explanation".'[9]

Bateson distinguished structure in Radcliffe-Brown's sense, meaning a pattern of relationships between persons, and what he called cultural structure, the relations between the premises of a culture, which form a coherent logical scheme. There was also a third system, of relationships between the emotional needs of individuals and the details of cultural behaviour, and between these and the emotional emphases of the culture as a whole. All three frameworks could and should be used to organize the data. But as Bateson developed his argument he came to realize that the various analytical concepts were not somehow inherent in the observed data, as Malinowski and Radcliffe-Brown tended to believe. They were 'labels merely for points of view adopted either by the scientist or by the native'. As he later wrote:

> The final climax of the book is the discovery, described in the epilogue – and achieved only a few days before the book went to press – of what looks like a truism today: that ethos, eidos, sociology, economics, cultural structure, social structure, and all the rest of these words refer only to scientists' ways of putting the jigsaw puzzle together.[10]

The problem on which Bateson experimented was posed by a bizarre New Guinea ceremony, called *naven*, which was mounted from time to time for a sister's child who had done something praiseworthy. The ceremony involved transvesticism and other dramatic reversals of normal behaviour. For example, the mother's brother of the person being honoured dressed in grotesque female attire, offered his buttocks to his sister's son, and acted the female role in a fantastic similitude of copulation with his wife. This was a classical sort of anthropological problem – an apparently absurd ritual which invited the question, what sense does this make? Bateson's 'explanation' involved the abstraction of data from the three dimensions of social relationships, cultural assumptions, and emotional content. Each of these sets of data was shown to make sense – sociological, logical, and psychological sense respectively; and each element in the ceremony was dissected and set in each of these perspectives.

The analysis was richly suggestive, and contained many seminal ideas, such as the notion of 'schismogenesis', basically a rule that oppositions are continually and dialectically heightened once begun. Bateson himself later developed this idea in his 'double-bind' theory of schizophrenia, which was adopted by R. D. Laing. It reappeared in a slightly different form within anthropology, in Evans-Pritchard's analysis of Nuer feuding and in Gluckman's analyses of conflict.

Nevertheless Bateson's book did not 'catch on' among the anthropologists. Partly perhaps this was because he was isolated from the main group of the profession, first in Cambridge and later in the United States. But more fundamentally, he did not convince because his empirical basis was questionable. He admitted frankly the ethnographic weakness of *Naven*:

> It is clear that I have contributed but little to our store of anthropological facts and the information about Iatmul culture which I have used in the various chapters does no more than illustrate my methods. Even for purposes of illustration my supply of facts is meagre, and I certainly cannot claim that my facts have demonstrated the truth of any theory.[11]

This was too much for the British empiricists.

V

Like *Naven*, *Witchcraft, Oracles and Magic among the Azande* was an attempt to make sense of the bizarre, but where Bateson teased out all the aspects of the institution he studied, like some more systematic and analytical Malinowski, Evans-Pritchard was concerned only with the set of premises of the culture, with what Bateson had called the 'eidos'. His problem was one of rationality – 'Is Zande thought so different from ours that we can only describe their speech and actions without comprehending them, or is it essentially like our own though expressed in an idiom to which we are unaccustomed?'[12]

This kind of question had been food and drink to anthropologists for a generation. Malinowski had developed a theory of magical behaviour which asserted that mystical acts make sense in much the same way as more mundane technical procedures – they are attempts to shape the future, to cope with the unforeseeable accidents which may ruin the most carefully-tended garden, to set at rest the anxiety of the man who has done all he can in the usual way to ensure success in an enterprise, but still knows very well that success is uncertain. But beliefs in witchcraft posed a special problem. As Evans-Pritchard remarked, there are no readily apparent parallels in our culture, so we are not tempted to explain the unfamiliar, perhaps misleadingly, in terms of a cognate practice of our own.

Only Fortune had previously published a monograph on witch and sorcery beliefs, on the basis of a professional field-study. This was *Sorcerers of Dobu*, which appeared in 1932. In Dobu, as among the Azande, 'Death is caused by witchcraft, sorcery, poisoning, suicide, or by actual assault. There is no concept of accident.'[13] The Dobuans believe that mystical assaults are motivated by jealousy:

> Jealousy of possession is the keynote to the culture. In social organization this jealousy is found in a conflict between the kin and the marital groupings. In gardening this jealousy obtains between gardeners. All illness and disease and death are attributed to jealousy and provoke recrimination.[14]

Similar motives of jealousy, associated with tense social relationships, have since been found to be a feature of witchcraft and sorcery accusations in many societies. Evans-Pritchard, however, concentrated upon another aspect of the problem, at once more specific and more general – how can rational people actually believe this sort of thing?

Witchcraft, Oracles and Magic analysed four complexes of mystical belief and action among the Zande of the Sudan: involving witchcraft, witchdoctors, oracles and magic. These beliefs are related to each other, and constitute a single, comprehensible and self-sustaining system. In Evans-Pritchard's view, they were mystical as distinct from empirical modes of belief and action because they depend upon objectively false assumptions about the existence of certain supernatural phenomena.

Among the Zande, witches are believed to inherit witch-craft, which is an actual substance, found in their bodies and identified if necessary by post-mortem examination. None-theless one cannot be sure who is a witch. Witchcraft may be dormant. One may even be an unconscious witch oneself. In addition to possessing this material substance of witch-craft, the witch is associated with certain inauspicious and even inhuman familiars and practices. The power to do evil working through the witch cannot operate at a distance, so witches are sought only among neighbours. Equally they are not believed to be political superiors or inferiors.

Evans-Pritchard argued that the point about the belief in these mystical agents of harm is that it provides at once an explanation of misfortune and a means of combating it. Any misfortune may be related to witchcraft, and a serious misfortune generally is. That is not to say that the Zande neglect proximate physical causes. Cutting one's foot causes a sore, but the sore will fester, despite cleansing, only if you are bewitched. As he later wrote:

At first sight it looks absurd to hold that if termites have gnawed away the supports of a granary and it falls on a man sitting in the shade beneath and kills him, this is an act of witchcraft; but the Azande do not suppose, any more than we would, that the collapse of the granary is not the immediate cause of death. What they say is that it would not have collapsed at a particular moment when a particular man was sitting under it unless the man had been bewitched. Why should it not have fallen at a different moment or when a different man was sitting under it? It is easy to account for the collapse of the granary. That was due to termites and the weight of millet in it. It is also easy to account for the man being under it. He was there for shade in the heat of the day. But why did these two chains of events coincide at a certain point in space and time? We say that the coincidence was chance. The Azande explain it by witchcraft. Witchcraft and the granary operating together killed the man.[15]

One cannot combat chance, but witches are vulnerable to certain kinds of counteraction. Thus witchcraft not only explains misfortune, it also provides one with the possibility of redress. It 'is (firstly) a function of misfortune, and, secondly, it is a function of personal relations'.[16] 'Witchcraft is the socially relevant cause, since it is the only one which allows intervention and determines social behaviour.'[17] As among the Dobuans, one seeks the agent of one's misfortunes among one's enemies. The witch is using an illegitimate means to satisfy an unjustifiable grudge. 'Every misfortune supposes witchcraft, and every enmity suggests its author.'[18]

Having suffered a misfortune one may consult a witch-doctor, who divines the witch – often with the unwitting guidance of the sufferer. Witchdoctors are commoners with special knowledge of certain medicines, and they are not regarded as being completely reliable. The Zande rely more particularly upon oracles, which are often controlled by the politically powerful. The most important of these is the poison oracle. A special poison (normally procured in the Congo) is given to a chicken. A question is then put to it, and the question is answered by the life or death of the chicken. The princes own the most powerful poison oracles, and these are normally consulted in cases involving witches and those quasi-witches, adulterers.

Oracles are also used to regulate everyday activities, much as the Romans relied upon auguries. Evans-Pritchard related that:

I always kept a supply of poison for the use of my household and neighbours and we regulated our affairs in accordance with the oracles' decisions. I may remark that I found this as satisfactory a way of running my home and affairs as any other I know of. Among Azande it is the only satisfactory way of life because it is the only way of life they understand, and it furnishes the only arguments by which they are wholly convinced and silenced.[19]

Finally there is magic, which may be used in healing or in vengeance. Evans-Pritchard did not believe that the Zande medicines were in general efficacious. Most of them are magical means of combating the mystical cause of some physical ailment. In addition to healing, one may use

101

vengeance magic to seek out the witch and kill him or her. Vengeance magic is aggressive, but it can only kill malefactors, and so it is essentially just, good magic.

There is also evil magic which can be used to harm those who have not harmed you; and the Zande believe that its use is restricted to 'sorcerers'. In Zande eyes the difference between sorcerer and witch is that one uses medicines, while the other has an innate power to harm. This is not a vital distinction. 'Both alike are enemies of men, and Azande class them together. Witchcraft and sorcery are opposed to, and opposed by, good magic.'[20] Since most misfortunes are attributed to witchcraft, Evans-Pritchard argued, rather weakly, that 'The concept of sorcery appears to be redundant, a fact that invites historical explanation.'[21]

Witchcraft, witchdoctors, oracles and magic are interlocked elements in a single process. 'Thus,' Evans-Pritchard wrote,

death evokes the notion of witchcraft; oracles are consulted to determine the course of vengeance; magic is made to attain it; oracles decide when magic has executed vengeance; and its magical task being ended, the medicine is destroyed.[22]

The book reads as though it is addressed to a sceptic, whom Evans-Pritchard is trying to persuade that these beliefs are in some way reasonable. Several arguments were developed to this effect. First of all, Evans-Pritchard described how easily he himself adopted these ways of thinking and acting. Secondly, he pointed out that they are not articulated in the abstract, or arranged into a developed theory, but are simply invoked piecemeal in specific situations. Hence the Zande can ignore some inconsistencies. But his most powerful argument, repeated at length and in various ways, was that given the initial premise that harm can be caused by mystical agencies, the notion that ill-luck took the form of a person, an evildoer, then the rest of the beliefs follow logically enough. Moreover they are constantly reinforced by experience. Somebody becomes ill, hence witches are active. Oracles confirm this. Vengeance magic is made. Somebody in the neighbourhood dies, and the oracle confirms that he was the witch.

Evans-Pritchard also constantly demanded, whether or not

there are sceptics among the Zande; whether or not there are contradictions and inconsistencies which force them to recognize the absurdity of their assumptions. For example, he pointed out, oracles are sometimes questioned twice about the same matter and give inconsistent answers. In this case the Zande explain that the oracle has been interfered with by another mystical power. The failure therefore actually strengthens their belief in the whole complex of assumptions. Even experiment is possible within the mystical framework. A Zande may test an oracle by posing a ridiculous problem:

Poison oracle, you tell the fowl I am going to fetch the sun. If I will bring it back, kill the fowl. If a great crowd will collect to-day to see the sun in the centre of my homestead; if I will put the sun on the ground and people will see it there, kill the fowl. If it is untrue, if I will not bring back the sun, spare the fowl.[23]

And if it fails the test, they simply resort to another oracle. Zande will agree quite readily that some witch-doctors are quacks, and that some oracles can be – and are – manipulated. But this does not disturb their general beliefs any more than our scepticism about individual doctors or particular remedies shakes our faith in 'medicine'.

Therefore Evans-Pritchard concluded:

I hope that I have persuaded the reader of one thing, namely the intellectual consistency of Zande notions. They only appear inconsistent when ranged like lifeless museum objects. When we see how an individual uses them we may say that they are mystical but we cannot say that his use of them is illogical or even that it is uncritical. I had no difficulty in using Zande notions as Azande themselves use them. Once the idiom is learnt the rest is easy, for in Zandeland one mystical idea follows on another as reasonably as one common-sense idea follows on another in our own society.[24]

But the monograph had a more combative purpose as well. Evans-Pritchard saw it as in part a challenge to Malinowski, and as an example of the type of abstract argument which anthropologists should aim to develop. In the introduction to the book, he wrote:

If any one were to urge that in discussing magic I have made a

103

partial abstraction of the activities with which it is associated, I would reply that I am dealing with only some of its relations. It would be grotesque to describe Zande economic life in a book on Zande magic, oracles, and witchcraft, since agriculture, hunting, and collecting are not functions of these beliefs and rites, but the beliefs and rites are functions of agriculture, hunting and collecting.[25]

This evoked Malinowski's penchant for relating magic to every activity with which it was associated, and his dogma that one cannot understand a custom except by describing all its concomitants. Further, in this passage he pointedly used 'function' in the mathematical sense of something being a 'function of' something else, and not in Malinowski's utilitarian sense.

Nonetheless the book in many ways reflected the theories of Malinowski, and even an earlier orthodoxy. The problem of rationality was the problem of Tylor, Frazer, and Lévy-Bruhl; and the institutional focus was typically Malinowskian, if the method of abstraction was not. Moreover at the heart of the book was an opposition between mystical and empirical beliefs and activities: an opposition which Evans-Pritchard took over from Frazer and Malinowski. He showed that the Zande do not make this contrast, and that they believe mystical forces operate in much the same way as physical forces, but he retained the category opposition in his analysis. This weakened his critique of Malinowski's theory of magic. He wrote, for example,

. . . we shall not understand Zande magic, and the differences between ritual behaviour and empirical behaviour in the lives of Azande, unless we realize that its main purpose is to combat other mystical powers rather than to produce changes favourable to man in the objective world.[26]

It would have been more interesting to examine the total Zande theory of causation, without this extraneous dichotomy between 'mystical' and 'objective' forces. However, the dichotomy was implicit in the rationalist theme of the whole enterprise – to show 'us' that although 'they' believe in magic, they are still capable of logical thought.

The book was not concerned merely to explain apparently

irrational beliefs, it was also, very consciously, a model of abstraction. Evans-Pritchard wrote, many years later,

> Abstraction can mean several different things. It can mean treating only a part of social life for particular and limited problems of investigation, taking the rest into consideration only in so far as it is relevant to these problems, or it can mean structural analysis through the integration of abstractions from social life.[27]

He identified the first approach with the work of Malinowski and anthropologists like Margaret Mead in America. The structural method was the radical feature of *Witchcraft, Oracles and Magic*. It was developed to an even more severe level of abstract discourse in his second book, *The Nuer*, which was published in 1940.

These books lacked the almost debauched abandonment to experiment of *Naven*, but they proved to have a more immediate impact, and also a more fructifying effect in the longer run. This was partly because they succeeded where *Naven* failed, by giving a convincing analysis of a body of data. Also, Evans-Pritchard was the Crown Prince, and he was now reunited with Radcliffe-Brown, who had captured Oxford. In any case, the Zande book stimulated a number of later studies. The analysis of the closed system of thought was generally taken for granted, but the subsidiary arguments of the book became the central themes of later studies. The key was Evans-Pritchard's remark that witchcraft provided the 'socially relevant cause' of misfortune.

VI

The experiments in abstraction by Bateson and Evans-Pritchard produced two of the most worthwhile monographs in social anthropology, but their methods were not taken over by others. In 1937, the year in which *Witchcraft, Oracles and Magic* appeared, Radcliffe-Brown took up the first chair in social anthropology at Oxford. Evans-Pritchard and Fortes worked in his department, and together they developed a type of analysis new to British anthropology.

105

This was concerned with the social structure, and dealt mainly with kinship and political systems. If one is seeking to identify the models for this work, one must look to the studies of the Chicago students of Radcliffe-Brown, but these were without the political dimension which came to be characteristic of the Oxford school; and they lacked the firm basis of Malinowskian fieldwork in functioning societies.

It is a measure of the narrow institutional basis of social anthropology in Britain at that time, that when Radcliffe-Brown came to Oxford his only teaching colleague was Evans-Pritchard, who had joined Marett two years previously as Research-Lecturer in African Sociology on a salary of £300 per annum. Fortes joined the department from 1939 to 1941, with the insecure title of 'Acting research lecturer in African Sociology'. Even after the war, when Evans-Pritchard took over the department in 1946, his staff consisted of himself, Fortes (by then a Reader) and a secretary-librarian.

There were then four centres of social anthropology in England – at the London School of Economics, University College London, Cambridge and Oxford. But social anthropology in the modern sense was firmly established only at the L.S.E. Now, in 1937, Oxford was taken over, and in due course – though only after the war – the other two departments were captured. Since the number of scholars and institutions involved was so tiny, the concentration of Radcliffe-Brown, Evans-Pritchard and Fortes in Oxford was of the greatest importance. This was particularly so at a time when anthropology at the London School of Economics was entering a period of relative decline, following Malinowski's departure in 1938; and when, moreover, University College London was still pursuing its curious diffusionist hypothesis, and Cambridge was still slumbering in the pre-Malinowskian era.

The new balance of power was only briefly significant, for the war soon intervened. Anthropologists were dispersed, most of them engaged in specialized services connected with intelligence and administration. But the brief partnership of Radcliffe-Brown, Evans-Pritchard and Fortes at Oxford produced a series of studies, dealing mainly with politics and kinship, which established a new paradigm. After the war British social anthropology picked up where they had left off.

In 1940 three major works in political anthropology appeared from this group. These were *African Political Systems*, edited by Fortes and Evans-Pritchard, and with a preface by Radcliffe-Brown, and two monographs by Evans-Pritchard, *The Nuer*, and *The Political System of the Anuak*, both of which dealt with societies lacking centralized government, in what was then the Anglo-Egyptian Sudan. These studies were followed by others, which explored further aspects of segmentary political systems, and which also analysed the person-to-person relationships of kinship within such societies. Although these were mainly written before and during the war, they appeared immediately afterwards – Fortes's two monographs on the Tallensi in 1945 and 1949; Evans-Pritchard's study of the Sanusi of Cyrenaica in 1949, and his book on Nuer kinship in 1951. These studies must be considered together. They form a coherent set, and they established the new paradigm which was to guide British social anthropology throughout the fifties.

If these studies are to be appreciated in their proper historical context, it must be remembered that they dealt with relatively novel problems which were thrown up by the new wave of research in Africa. Seligman had carried out survey work in the Sudan, but the first modern studies in Africa, by participant observation, were carried out by Evans-Pritchard and Schapera. Evans-Pritchard's fieldwork in the Sudan and Kenya was carried out between 1926 and 1938. Schapera spent forty-five months with various Tswana tribes between 1929 and 1943. In 1930 Audrey Richards went out to study the Bemba, and then, with the first studies financed by the International African Institute, a number of others followed in the thirties.

These fieldworkers were confronted not with tiny, bounded island populations, but with comparatively huge, extended, dispersed tribes and nations. It was quickly apparent that the sorts of social controls which writers on Oceania had identified – reciprocal obligations, exchanges, magical

107

controls – formed only a small part of the governmental mechanisms of these societies. These problems were particularly urgent, since the colonial authorities were very much concerned with the methods by which these peoples could most effectively be administered, and to the extent that Lugard's principle of indirect rule was adopted, some accommodation had to be made to 'traditional' forms of government. The most acute problem was posed by those societies which lacked centralized political institutions, and it was in the study of these societies – which fortunately included Evans-Pritchard's Nuer (though not the Azande), and Fortes's Tallensi (though not the Ashanti) – that social anthropology was to make perhaps its most original contribution to the social sciences and to political philosophy.

These factors directed attention to the political system and social control. At the same time, the way in which these problems were worked out was modulated by theoretical developments within the discipline. In particular there was the new concern with models for abstraction, and the influential presence of Radcliffe-Brown. It may be necessary to stress the central place of Radcliffe-Brown in this intellectual enterprise, since Evans-Pritchard's later defection has caused some confusion. The facts are clear enough, however. One instance must suffice for the present. In 1937, writing from his field-camp among the Kenya Luo, Evans-Pritchard contributed a programmatic statement to a symposium on the social sciences. He set out three stages in the anthropological enterprise. First the collection of facts – and fieldwork was the first priority. Second came comparison. Criticizing the Malinowskians, he wrote: 'The present habit of anthropologists of generalizing from the facts of a single isolated society, is contrary to the methods of inductive logic which have been found necessary in the natural sciences.' The third and

final stage will be a comparison of all types of societies in order to discover general tendencies and functional relationships that are common to human societies as a whole. Social Anthropology is at present in the first stage and entering the second stage.[28]

This was Radcliffe-Brown's programme, stated in very

similar terms. *African Political Systems* must also be seen as one of the first attempts at the comparison, classification and generalization that Radcliffe-Brown advocated.

VII

Yet these books also represented a departure from Radcliffe-Brown's position – the difference in tone, definition and emphasis between Radcliffe-Brown's preface to *African Political Systems* and the introduction by Evans-Pritchard and Fortes has often been commented upon. The new emphasis was, in a phrase, upon the lineage as a part of the system of political relationships, rather than simply as a mode of organizing personal relationships, which was Radcliffe-Brown's primary conception. The term 'social structure' came to connote the structure of relationships between groups and, in Fortes's work, offices, rather than between persons.

In the introduction to *African Political Systems*, the editors distinguished two types of African polity – the centralized, pyramidal structure, exemplified by the Zulu, Tswana and others, and the 'stateless society'. The latter were subdivided into the band-type systems, such as that of the Bushmen, where (the editors mistakenly believed) the political system was coincident with the kinship system, as Radcliffe-Brown had argued for the Australian aborigines; and the systems based upon segmentary lineages. The editors particularly emphasized the segmentary lineage systems, and one effect of *African Political Systems* was to divert attention from the many stateless political systems in Africa which were not organized in terms of kinship or lineage.

The emphasis in this seminal work was distinctly odd. Evans-Pritchard later explained:

... the tentative typology Professor Fortes and I put forward ... was intended to be no more than a convenient start towards a more detailed classification of types of African society, in which the absence or presence of forms of descent groups and of state institutions were two criteria . . .[29]

The presence or absence of state institutions was an obvious enough criterion, dictated as much by classical philosophy and anthropology as by the difficulties of colonial administration. But why should the presence or absence of descent groups be selected as a primary criterion for the classification of political systems? It is difficult to believe that it would be as readily selected today.

The emphasis upon the segmentary lineage systems had several sources. First of all, Durkheim had defined a broad class of segmentary societies, which were presumed to be typical of 'primitive societies', and which were thought to be based upon divisions of clan and territory. His analysis of the principles of 'mechanical solidarity' which integrated such societies provided a model for the perception of social systems like those of the Nuer and the Tallensi.

Secondly, classical evolutionist anthropology (notably Morgan and Maine) had argued that the great distinction to be understood was between 'primitive' stateless systems, based on kinship, and the state, based on territory. The evolutionary stage which intervened between these two conditions was characterized by a combination of the principles of kinship and territory – 'blood and soil'. Fortes and Evans-Pritchard simply took over this evolutionist classification and, as it were, stood it on its side. They did not present it as a classification of political systems in time, but rather in space.

Thirdly, in the study of lineage-based societies the anthropological expertise in the study of kinship could be used as a bridge into the unexplored terrain of political systems. At the same time anthropology could escape from Radcliffe-Brown's tendentious equation of the kinship system and the social system.

But finally, and perhaps most important, there was the accident that both Fortes and Evans-Pritchard had chanced to study societies of this type, and were engaged, together, in analysing their material. *African Political Systems* set up a general classification, but the implications of their thinking were most clearly seen in their analyses of segmentary lineage-based systems, and in particular in *The Nuer*, the most important and influential anthropological monograph of the period.

VIII

When Evans-Pritchard studied the Nuer, in a series of relatively brief field-trips in the thirties, they numbered about 200,000 people scattered over an area of 30,000 square miles in the Southern Sudan. The Nuer were just recovering from a brutal 'pacification' programme, which had involved bombing their herds of cattle and hanging their prophets, and were in no mood to welcome white visitors. In these inauspicious circumstances Evans-Pritchard first discovered and demonstrated the way in which a political system can exist without rulers in a state of what he called 'ordered anarchy', relations between territorial groups being conceptualized in an idiom of lineage relationships, and regulated by processes of fission and fusion.

The monograph began with a long discussion of Nuer pastoralism and the ecological setting of Nuer society. The Nuer practise agriculture and fishing as well as pastoralism, and all the aspects of their mixed economy are necessary to making a living, but above all they like to see themselves as cattle people. The Nuer place supreme value upon their cattle, even identifying a man personally in terms of his finest ox. Evans-Pritchard remarked that when one tries to understand a Nuer affair, the best rule is *cherchez la vache*. Cattle provide a wide range of the people's needs, and the Nuer must adjust his life to the requirements of his herds.

The year is divided into two distinct seasons, the rains, from May to October, and the dry season, from November to April. The wet season is spent in the inland villages, and the main economic activity is agriculture. The dry season is spent at riverside camps, for water is scarce in the uplands, and the pastures become barren. At the camps fishing, collecting and hunting supplement the pastoral yield. In both these sorts of settlement people are closely interdependent, and 'one may speak of a common economy of these communities, which are . . . the smallest political groups in Nuerland and in which are taken for granted ties of kinship, affinity, age-sets, and so forth.'[30]

The problem of making a living in this environment sets

various constraints upon the Nuer modes of social organization. Social relationships must transcend the village boundaries, for the people must be free to move between villages
and camps; the ecological conditions will not permit
communities to flourish except between certain demographic
limits; the simple technology concentrates the symbolism of
social relationships in a few highly-charged objects – particularly cattle. And so forth. Nevertheless Evans-Pritchard
insisted that these constraints could not explain the structural
relationships between Nuer groups. These must be understood in terms of structural principles.

The argument now moved on to another plane altogether,
the plane of 'social values', which Radcliffe-Brown always
emphasized, and which, he said, was another way of talking
about 'interests'. The famous third chapter of *The Nuer*
explored the people's notions of time and space, and it
formed a bridge between the introductory chapters on cattle
and ecology and the main section of the book, which was
concerned with territorial and lineage relationships. It was
here that Evans-Pritchard developed his idea of what might
be called social relativity, borrowing concepts like 'fission
and fusion', and the relativity of time and space from the
fashionable discoveries of physics.

The Nuer do not have an abstract notion of time, as something that passes, can be wasted, measured, etc. They
perceive time in terms of physical changes, or social relationships. 'Oecological time', as Evans-Pritchard called it, was
related to natural progressions, like the seasons or the phases
of the day. It was not rigidly divided into units, but rather
one period passed imperceptibly into another. The rainy
season, or season of village life, is called *tot*. But the Nuer do
not say, it is *tot*, therefore we must move to the upland
villages; rather, they say we are in the villages, therefore
it is *tot*.

'Structural time', in contrast, was not an abstraction from
man's relationship to the environment, but rather a way of
conceptualizing the periodicity of social relationships, and
the social development of the individual. The units are
births, deaths, marriages; or, for people in less intimate

112

contact, such events as the succession of age-sets. Structural time was also a way of conceiving of lineage relationships. The social distance between a man and his agnate, for example, could be thought of in terms of the distance in time separating them from their common ancestor. If this was great, they were distantly related; and the shorter the time gap, the closer the relationship between them.

Similarly, the Nuer are not concerned to measure the objective distance in space between two places. They are more concerned, on the one hand, with the practical distance – influenced by such factors as the nature of the intervening terrain, the existence of hostile groups on the way, etc. On the other hand, they measure social distance:

A Nuer village may be equidistant from two other villages, but if one of these belongs to a different tribe and the other belongs to the same tribe it may be said to be structurally more distant from the first than from the second.[31]

Now because these notions of time and space are not based upon objective measurement, but depend largely upon structural relationships, they vary relative to the social relationships defining any situation. Evans-Pritchard made this point most clearly with reference to the Nuer notion of 'home', *cieng*:

What does a Nuer mean when he says, 'I am a man of such-and-such a *cieng*'? *Cieng* means 'home', but its precise significance varies with the situation in which it is spoken. If one meets an Englishman in Germany and asks him where his home is, he may reply that it is England. If one meets the same man in London and asks him the same question he will tell one that his home is in Oxfordshire, whereas if one meets him in that county he will tell one the name of the town or village in which he lives. If questioned in his town or village he will mention his particular street, and if questioned in his street he will indicate his house. So it is with the Nuer. A Nuer met outside Nuerland says that his home is *cieng Nath*, Nuerland . . . If one asks him in his tribe what is his *cieng*, he will name his village or tribal section according to the context . . . If asked in his village he will mention the name of his hamlet or indicate his homestead or the end of the village in which his homestead is situated . . . The variations in the meaning of the word *cieng* are not due to the inconsistencies of language, but to the relativity of the group-values to which it refers.[32]

The thrust of the argument was to show that Nuer notions of time and space were a function of their social and economic values. Moreover, the social referents of these notions were not fixed, but varied with the social context in which they were formulated. In this way the analysis of these notions bridged the earlier ecological and economic analysis, and the political analysis which was to come. Firstly, the economic and physical conditions constrained the kinds of political and organizational responses which were possible. Secondly, Nuer values made a connection between ecological relationships of time and space and the structural relationships between groups. Indeed the rest of the book was primarily concerned with demonstrating the way in which group relationships were conceptualized in territorial, spatial terms, and in terms of lineage relationships, based on a genealogy stretching back in time.

Political relationships in Nuerland are basically territorial relationships. The tribe is the largest political community, within which homicide should be settled by the payment of blood-wealth rather than vengeance. The tribal territory is divided into local units, which are again divided and subdivided. At every descending level of segmentation the group is more cohesive and tends more readily to cooperate and to settle disputes amicably. The segments operate only in opposition to other like segments. If a man in one village killed a man in another, the two villages would mobilize to settle the debt. If a man in one of these villages killed a man in another district, the two villages would unite with other villages in their district against the villages of the other district. Evans-Pritchard termed these processes of division and coalition 'fission and fusion'. He wrote, 'fission and fusion in political groups are two aspects of the same segmentary principle, and the Nuer tribe and its divisions are to be understood as an equilibrium between these two contradictory, yet complementary, tendencies.'[33] Alternatively, the structure could be understood as a balance of power at every level of organization.

The structure was expressed most fully in the blood-feud. While feuds were quickly settled between neighbours in the community of the village, who could not afford to set up a cycle of vengeance and counter-vengeance in the small cooperative group, they often led to violent confrontations when they involved members of more distant sections of the tribe. But any feud within the tribe could be settled by mediation and the payment of blood-wealth. This mediation was usually through the good offices of a 'leopard-skin chief', a member of a hereditary group of mediators, respected but effectively powerless. Evans-Pritchard explained, in terms which recall Radcliffe-Brown's analyses of opposition and conjunction,

A feud has little significance unless there are social relations of some kind which can be broken off and resumed, and, at the same time, these relations necessitate eventual settlement if there is not to be complete cleavage. The function of the feud, viewed in this way, is, therefore, to maintain the structural equilibrium between opposed tribal segments which are, nevertheless, politically fused in relation to larger units.[34]

These territorial, political relationships were conceptualized in terms of the lineage idiom. Every tribe had a dominant clan, and the clan was segmented into smaller patrilineal units – maximal, minor and minimal lineages. Everyone in the clan would claim patrilineal descent from the founding ancestor, A. Two of A's sons (perhaps), B and C would be the founding ancestors of maximal lineages. Each maximal lineage would in turn segment into minor lineages, and these into minimal lineages, with reference to a particular pivotal ancestor at an appropriate level of the genealogy. In some contexts, all members of the clan would identify themselves as A's as against members of another clan. In other contexts, members of minor lineages D and E might unite as B's against members of minor lineages F and G, who were C's. And so on, creating a pattern of fission and fusion, but one mapped in lineage terms rather than territorial terms.

This lineage framework worked at a level of values rather than crude demography. Members of one village might belong to various descent groups, and the members of the minimal lineage segment of the dominant clan might be scattered, perhaps constituting only a minority of the inhabitants of a particular village. Nevertheless, when discussing their relationship with outsiders the villagers would identify themselves with the minimal lineage of the dominant clan, and use the clan's genealogy to express these relationships. Every level of lineage formation corresponds to a level of territorial grouping, from the clan, which provided the identity of the tribe, to the minimal lineage, with a depth of only three to five generations, which provided the core of village unity.

As Evans-Pritchard showed, the lineage system worked in terms of genealogical time, the territorial system in terms of structural space. But the lineage framework provided a way of talking about the territorial system:

The system of lineages of the dominant clan is a conceptual skeleton on which the local communities are built up into an organization of related parts, or, as we would prefer to state it, a system of values linking tribal segments and providing the idiom in which their relations can be expressed and directed.[35]

In this way the values of agnatic relationship gave cohesion to the system. 'In the absence of a chief or king, who might symbolize a tribe, its unity is expressed in the idiom of lineage and clan affiliation.'[36] Because the lineage system was in this way a function of the territorial system, 'the lineages are in number and structural position strictly limited and controlled by the system of territorial segmentation.'[37] Moreover, it was often necessary to manipulate genealogies in order to adjust to the political realities, and so the 'lineage structure is twisted into the form of the political structure'.[38]

IX

The originality and elegance of *The Nuer* are beyond dispute, and it still stands as the supreme example in social anthropology of successful abstraction in the analysis of a single society. Of course, the book did not come from no-where. Evans-Pritchard adopted Durkheim and Radcliffe-Brown's view of the character of segmentary societies, based upon mechanical solidarity, and like them he looked for order in the realm of shared values – Durkheim's 'collective consciousness'. The perception of the relativity of social groupings, and the way in which they emerge in opposition to other, like groups, and also the contrast between the internal divisions and external unity of social groups were all important themes in Radcliffe-Brown's work. The notion of segmentary opposition was current, and Bateson had used it most creatively in *Naven*. Indeed, the well-established nature of these notions may be judged from the fact that in 1929 an amateur anthropologist, F. J. Richards, could write to *Man*, commenting on Radcliffe-Brown's suggestions for classifying different kinds of age-sets:

The distinction between 'group' and 'section' is not a mere verbal quibble; the words stand respectively for two funda-mentally different processes, 'fusion' and 'fission', by which a society is 'organized', and the loose use of these and kindred terms obscures the real nature of any social structure.[39]

But *The Nuer* nonetheless successfully developed a complete model which was original as a whole, if its parts were taken from current ideas in anthropology. Its originality lies in part in the compelling nature of the model, and its analytical power, for the Nuer material. It also exemplified the new point of view which characterized its stable-mates, *African Political Systems* and the later books and articles of Evans-Pritchard and Fortes. These works developed a political view of social structure, analysing social relations from the perspective of the total set of public, inter-group relations. At the same time they distinguished this domain of public, lineage-based, political relationships from the domain of personal, domestic, narrowly kinship relationships. In

117

doing this they liberated anthropology from the inter-personal model of lineage relationships.

Naturally enough, *The Nuer* was subjected to considerable criticism from the Malinowskians, and a similar under-current of criticism has continued throughout the years of its greatest influence. The criticism has two prongs. One is that the fieldwork was inadequate – understandably enough in the circumstances – and that therefore Evans-Pritchard did not really know what was happening on the ground. This led him to develop a highly idealized, abstract analysis, which did not allow for the machinations of calculating man.

This argument is not valid. Evans-Pritchard had done several years' fieldwork in the Sudan, and among the Kenya Luo who are related to the Nuer, before undertaking his Nuer study. He was therefore an experienced observer, as well as an exceptionally able one, working in a familiar country and with personal knowledge of related cultures. Furthermore the very arduous nature of his work may have forced him to grapple with Nuer life at a deeper level than anthropologists have commonly to plumb. As Evans-Pritchard himself said, many years later, 'I was a *ger*, what they call a *rul*, an alien sojourner, among them for only a year, but it was a year's relationship of great intensity, and the quality of a relationship counts for more than its duration.'[40]

Evans-Pritchard's other books and papers on the Nuer contain such a range of ethnographic detail that it is clear *The Nuer* operated on a high plane of abstraction from choice rather than necessity. The monograph must be understood in the context of a conscious effort to develop structural abstraction in ethnographic monographs. Fortes stated the programme in the introduction to *The Dynamics of Clanship among the Tallensi*. He contrasted the description of 'whole cultures', *à la* Junod and the pre-functionalists, with descriptions of particular institutions – such as the *kula* or witchcraft – in the Malinowskian manner. Both these approaches were then set against the new kind of study of social sub-systems which the Nuer and Tallensi monographs exemplified. These had the advantage that 'all studies in social structure or political organizations or economic structure, being concerned with the factors of social integration, are necessarily concerned with attributes of the whole society.'[41]

The other, related, critical reaction has a rather injured tone. It feels cheated in some way. Evans-Pritchard began *The Nuer* with a good, earthy account of ecology; in his next book he dealt with real persons in multi-faceted, low-level interaction. Why were these concrete facts not used in *The Nuer*? Why sweep them under the beautiful, but distracting, structural carpet? This was to miss the point. *The Nuer* was an exercise in the abstraction of the social structure. One may abstract on various planes, and Evans-Pritchard chose the Durkheimian level of the 'collective consciousness'. Moreover the model he developed paralleled that of the Nuer themselves. It is no good complaining that Evans-Pritchard's model leaves out individual variation. He was concerned with values, arguing that political relations 'are best stated as tendencies to conform to certain values in certain situations, and the value is determined by the structural relationships of the persons who compose the situation'.[42] One may argue about whether political relations are best stated in this way; but this is a legitimate way of approaching the subject, and there is no denying the illumination it provided in Evans-Pritchard's hands.

x

Despite the disruption caused by the war, the forties was a remarkable decade for British social anthropology. It began with the publication of *African Political Systems*, which established – together with the Nuer, Anuak and Tallensi monographs – the political perspective on social structure. It ended with the symposium, *African Systems of Kinship and Marriage*, published in 1950, which with *The Web of Kinship among the Tallensi* (1949) and *Kinship and Marriage among the Nuer* (1951), marked a breakthrough in the study of kinship systems. The latter development depended upon the former.

Meyer Fortes was the most important figure in the

development of kinship theory in this decade, next to Radcliffe-Brown himself. He has credited Radcliffe-Brown with developing 'the idea of the synchronic system of kinship relations, focussed on Ego, as the centre of an arrangement of kindred, grouped lineally and collaterally by recognized categories of relationships expressed in the terminology'[43] – in other words, Radcliffe-Brown was the first to see kinship systems as functioning structures. But as Fortes has pointed out, Radcliffe-Brown – and his American students – tended to regard the kinship system as being equivalent to the social structure in tribal societies. This was to overemphasize the role of kinship even in societies like those of the Australian aborigines. Moreover, Radcliffe-Brown – like Malinowski – was too apt to assume that kinship relationships derived from the inner core of family relationships. Both writers also laid too much stress on the interpersonal relationships of kinship. In their work, Fortes wrote, 'the kinship system is envisaged as a bilateral network of recognized dyadic relations radiating outwards from the elementary family.'[44]

The missing factor in these writings was the external weight of legal and political arrangements, which shaped the kinship system together with the domestic pressures generated within the family group. Fortes later wrote:

It is my contention that the major advance in kinship theory since Radcliffe-Brown, but growing directly out of his work, has been the analytical separation of the politico-jural domain from the familial, or domestic domain within the total social universe of what have been clumsily called kinship-based social systems.[45]

Evans-Pritchard's Nuer books and Fortes's books on the Tallensi demonstrated this dual context of kinship groups, domestic and political. The point was given concrete form by dividing the studies of Nuer and Tallensi social structure into two volumes. In each case the first volume dealt with clan and lineage relationships, the second with interpersonal relationships of kinship.

Thus the forties began with *The Nuer* and the demonstration of the political significance of lineages. They ended with

The Web of Kinship among the Tallensi, and the analysis of
the interaction between external and internal constraints
upon kinship relations. The work of Fortes and Evans-
Pritchard recognizably derived from Radcliffe-Brown, but
it represented only one of the possible developments of his
theories. In fact Radcliffe-Brown never fully grasped its
implications. In his long introduction to *African Systems of
Kinship and Marriage* (1950), he still treated descent groups
and other kinship corporations mainly from the internal
point of view. But other contemporaries were mostly
converted. A notable instance was Audrey Richards, one of
Malinowski's closest associates, who demonstrated in her
contribution to *African Systems of Kinship and Marriage* the
interaction of familial and politico-jural constraints upon
Central African matrilineal systems, in what was one of the
finest examples of the new approach.

Finally, it is important to note that this movement was
facilitated by the use of a more sophisticated notion of
structure. Evans-Pritchard and Fortes accepted the logic
of Bateson, and moved beyond the naïve realism of Radcliffe-
Brown. Fortes wrote in 1949:

When we describe structure we are already dealing with
general principles far removed from the complicated skein of
behaviour, feelings, beliefs, &c., that constitute the tissue of
actual social life. We are, as it were, in the realm of grammar and
syntax, not of the spoken word. We discern structure in the
'concrete reality' of social events only by virtue of having first
established structure by abstraction from 'concrete reality'.[46]

It was necessary to achieve such a level of abstraction – to
escape from the narrow focus upon interpersonal relations –
in order to make the sort of distinction upon which their
work depended, between external and internal domains,
between inter-group and intra-group relationships, between
politics and kinship.

XI

The movement of British social anthropology in the thirties
and forties may be charted along various dimensions. There

was the shift from the dominance of Malinowski and the L.S.E. to Radcliffe-Brown, Evans-Pritchard and Fortes at Oxford. Oceania, with its small, bounded, apparently simple cultures was displaced as the main area for fieldwork by Africa, with its large, sprawling, and often highly-differentiated societies. In this period, too, anthropologists first adopted and then abandoned the concrete, institution-based functionalism of Malinowski; experimented with various modes of abstraction; and finally adopted a sociological, structuralist position. Finally, there was a change in topical interest from the family, magic and making a living, to political and kinship systems – from the interests of not only Malinowski but also Frazer and Westermarck, to the different concerns of Morgan, Maine, Rivers and Radcliffe-Brown. These various movements were connected at one level, as should be clear by now.

The whole period may be followed best through its central monographs. These not only reflected the current views and preoccupations but also acted as experiments in understanding and explanation. The most successful became models to imitate. For much of the fifties British social anthropologists of the post-war generation were content to repeat the experiments which Evans-Pritchard had conducted in *Witchcraft, Oracles and Magic,* and *The Nuer.*

The Malinowskian tradition remained alive, however, and the contradictions in the new structural approach, and also its limitations, soon led the more adventurous to explore other routes through the jungle, following paths along which some even met, to their surprise, with a faithful disciple of Malinowski, still making a living, slashing and burning in the bush.

Taking the broadest view, the really remarkable feature of this period was simply the creative energy shown by a group of only two dozen or so, in less than two decades. The achievement of British social anthropology in the interwar years warrants comparison with the *Année* school in its heyday.

FOUR

Anthropology and Colonialism

A painting used to hang in the ante-room of former
President Kwame Nkrumah. The painting was enormous,
and the main figure was Nkrumah himself, fighting,
wrestling with the last chains of colonialism. The chains
are yielding, there is thunder and lightning in the air, the
earth is shaking. Out of all this, three small figures are
fleeing, white men, pallid. One of them is the capitalist, he
carries a briefcase. Another is the priest or missionary, he
carries the Bible. The third, a lesser figure, carries a book
entitled *African Political Systems*: he is the anthropologist . . .[1]

'Sequels to colonialism', it is sometimes said of our
investigations. The two are certainly linked, but nothing
would be more misleading than to see anthropology as a
throwback to the colonial frame of mind, a shameful
ideology which would offer colonialism a chance of survival.
    What we call the Renaissance was a veritable birth for
colonialism and for anthropology. Between the two, con-
fronting each other from the time of their common origin,
an equivocal dialogue has been pursued for four centuries.
If colonialism had not existed, the elaboration of anthropology would have been less belated; but perhaps also anthropology would not have been led to implicate all man-
kind in each of its particular case-studies. Our science
arrived at maturity the day that Western man began to see
that he would never understand himself as long as there was
a single race or people on the surface of the earth that he
treated as an object. Only then could anthropology declare
itself in its true colours: as an enterprise reviewing and
atoning for the Renaissance, in order to spread humanism to
all humanity.

– Lévi-Strauss[2]

I

From its very early days, British anthropology liked to
present itself as a science which could be useful in colonial
administration. The reasons are obvious. The colonial
governments and interests were the best prospects of

financial support, particularly in the decades before the discipline was granted recognition by the universities. At the same time, in the heyday of imperial enthusiasm the thought of its possible utility must have sustained some of those who pursued this esoteric and marginal study in Britain. As early as 1856, one author wrote in the journal of the Ethnological Society of London, with more optimism than was warranted,

Ethnology is now generally recognized as having the strongest claims to our attention, not merely as it tends to gratify the curiosity of those who love to look into Nature's works, but also as being of great practical importance, especially in this country, whose numerous colonies and extensive commerce bring it into contact with so many varieties of the human species differing in their physical and moral qualities both from each other and from ourselves.[3]

This readiness to shoulder arms in the colonial cause was widespread in the early twentieth century too, though it was by no means universal. Haddon perhaps represented the muscular colonial anthropologist at his simplest. He went out to British Columbia in 1909 to pursue researches in Indian culture. While he was there the police moved against dissident Chinese labourers, and Haddon was pressed into service together with other white visitors. He excused himself from taking part in the actual raid, pleading short-sight, but volunteered to guard the sixty-six prisoners who were taken. In a letter home he wrote:

This is not exactly what I came out for to do . . . instead of Indian Ethnology I have had a practical lesson in Sociology . . . But I am having a great time, full of new experiences, some of which will be useful for teaching and others for yarning.[4]

One cannot imagine someone like Frazer participating so actively. Indeed, Frazer represented the contrary position, the ivory tower scholar reluctant even to specify the possible uses of his studies. In his inaugural lecture at Liverpool in 1908 he warned his audience:

But if you wish to shatter the social fabric, you must not expect your professor of Social Anthropology to aid and abet you. He is no seer to discern, no prophet to foretell a coming heaven on earth, no mountebank with a sovran remedy for every ill, no Red Cross Knight to head a crusade against misery and want, against disease and death, against all the horrid spectres that war on poor humanity. It is for others with higher notes and nobler natures than his to sound the charge and lead it in this Holy War. He is only a student, a student of the past, who may perhaps tell you a little, a very little, of what has been, but who cannot, dare not tell you what ought to be . . .[5]

Certainly it would be difficult to specify what practical uses the anthropology of the diffusionists and evolutionists – Frazer's 'students of the past' – could have had for the colonial governments.

Still the anthropologists argued the possible uses of their subject, as a means of gaining recognition. The diplomas at Oxford, Cambridge and London were justified in part as providing training for colonial officers. The Royal Anthropological Institute also stressed the uses of the subject in its repeated attempts to gain funds for research and teaching positions in the discipline, sometimes working in collaboration with the Folklore Society and the British Association. At the simplest level, of course, there was a case. Anyone working in the colonies would be better prepared if he knew something about the peoples with whom he would be dealing. But it was difficult to persuade the British government that the anthropologists had anything very specific to offer.

In 1909 a deputation of colonial administrators, members of parliament, and scholars called upon Mr Asquith, then the Prime Minister, with a request for a grant of a mere £500 a year to establish a teaching centre in anthropology for the benefit of colonial officials and traders. They pressed the commercial value of anthropological knowledge, and even tried to persuade Asquith that such an institute would mean a saving in the long run:

The need for this might be illustrated by the case of an official untrained in anthropology, whose action led to a misunderstanding on the part of a border tribe. A military expedition followed, the cost of which was probably ten times as much as the Institute asked for in the next hundred years.

But in their next breath they inadvertently exposed the irrelevance of some of their concerns:

> Professor Ridgeway proceeded to deal with the need of anthropometry, an important branch of the science, whose claims he advocated. Measurements and other details of physical characteristics should be taken in every school.

> *Mr. Asquith:* That would cost a lot of money.

Sir Harry Johnston advanced another argument – 'As a race we were very snobbish and if a grant were made and the institute called "Royal" by permission of the King, anthropology would receive an enormous impetus.'[6] All to no avail. The Anthropological Institute received the title 'Royal' in 1907, but the new teaching institute was never funded, or even established with such a resounding title.

Sir Herbert Risley might spend a speech day at Winchester, as he did in 1910, telling the boys that they should study anthropology before going to India, but they were never to be required to do so. The demand for anthropological instruction was never widespread, and it never became established outside the African empire. Nor were the anthropologists to succeed in getting money and recognition for many years.

They kept plugging on, even during the war, this odd alliance of opinionated administrators and relatively obscure scholars. Today their initiatives seem rather funny, when they were not a little sinister. At one of Sir Richard Temple's endless special meetings, this time of a committee under the aegis of the British Association, in 1914, Colonel Sir Matthew Nathan, representing the African Society, contributed this assessment:

> The application of the study differs somewhat in East and West Africa as compared with South Africa. In the case of East and West Africa we want to know all about the native in order to develop his capacity to the fullest extent, and gradually to increase that capacity so that he may, in the future, assist in the administration of the Government and of the business of his own country.

In South Africa we want the study of Anthropology to assist in dealing with the ever present native problem. I have always felt, and I think I have sometimes said, that the more we look upon the native in South Africa as a scientific problem the less we shall feel that he is a social danger. It is with nations as with individuals, *tout savoir, tout pardonner*.[7]

This analysis seems to have impressed Temple, because when in 1921 he launched yet another of his appeals for a school of applied anthropology it was under the title 'Tout Savior, Tout Pardonner' – and, he added in conclusion, 'Tout Gagner'.[8] But few of the anthropologists were particularly interested in this aspect of things, except as a device for selling their wares. Characteristically, Seligman's comment on one of these lectures by Temple was that the most useful function of a central bureau of imperial anthropology might be in publishing reports, adding – 'I know of at least three pieces of first-class work, two African and one Pacific, held up because no publisher will take them without a substantial subsidy.'[9]

II

If the British government and the public were not easily stirred to a sense of the possible uses of anthropology, the colonial governments were equally unimpressed. In the East the tradition was that administrators would benefit by studying the languages and legal systems of the complex societies they administered, but sociological research was never encouraged. In India, for example, 'ethnology' seems never to have meant more than the development of the census to include some social and cultural data, and, to a limited extent, the study of 'tribal' peoples. For the rest anthropology was used mainly in the African empire, although in 1920 the Australian administration in Papua appointed a government anthropologist.

The record in Africa is not very striking, at least until the thirties. Government anthropologists were appointed in Southern Nigeria in 1908, after difficulties with local administration, but their contracts were not renewed. In

1920 the Gold Coast government appointed Rattray, an administrative officer, to the newly-created post of government anthropologist; one of the really inspired appointments of the time. In the following year the Nigerian government decided that the census should contain substantial ethnological information – on the model, it seems, of the Indian census. Accordingly Meek, another administrator with some anthropological training, was appointed Census Commissioner in the Northern Province. In 1927 he and Talbot were sent to Southern Nigeria in order to carry out investigations following the breakdown of local administration there. These were mainly *ad hoc* appointments, however; and the role of government anthropologist was not institutionalized on any scale in West Africa.

In East Africa, Seligman had been contracted to carry out anthropological researches on behalf of the Sudan government, a brief he passed on later to Evans-Pritchard. No use was made of their expertise. Evans-Pritchard has recalled:

> Professor Seligman once told me that in all the years he had worked in the Sudan or on Sudanese problems he was never once asked his advice and that the only time he volunteered it, in connection with the rain-makers of the Nuba Hills, it was not taken. During the fifteen years in which I worked on sociological problems in the same region I was never once asked my advice on any question at all.[10]

Elsewhere in East Africa only the Tanganyika government set up a post for a government sociologist.

In southern Africa, Schapera worked for many years in close partnership with the Bechuanaland government, and in the Union the government created an Ethnological section of the Native Affairs Department in 1925. The work of this body – later much expanded – has never gone much beyond the routine of making ethnological censuses, advising on the claims of various candidates for chiefships, and, more recently, devising pseudo-traditional forms of tribal administration. The South African government anthropologists have been virtually untouched by mainstream developments in social anthropology, and they have no sociological theory which might assist the South African government in the vicious work of subordination and exploitation. Much of their sort of work was carried out routinely by District officers in the British colonies, who – if conscientious – made ethnological notes in the District notebooks.

Until the mid-thirties, then, there was little in the way of official anthropology in the British Empire and dominions. Taking the Empire as a whole, it is not too much to say that by this time the direct anthropological contribution to administration was nugatory.

On the other hand, there was an indirect effect through the training of colonial officers in anthropology. The colonial governments were not averse to their officers having a smattering of the subject. As a Governor of the Gold Coast remarked, if anthropology 'is to prove of any practical benefit to the administration [it] must be carried on by officers who are enthusiastic over the study of it, and regard it more in the nature of a pleasurable pursuit than that of a duty.'[11]

Relatively few officers could have got more than a smattering of the subject, even after the watershed in colonial policy which the nineteen-thirties represented. The cadet's training was brief, and the emphasis was upon law and the practical techniques such as accounting, surveying and so forth. Languages were encouraged, but few mastered them, and anthropology was only one of the options which competed for their attention. Moreover the anthropology being taught at the time at Oxford, Cambridge, and University College London was largely mistaken and mis-guided – not only by modern standards, but by the standards of the day at the L.S.E. and in America. It was full of diffusionist and evolutionist assumptions, and confused by doses of physical anthropology, still racialist in orientation, technology, and preposterous theories of religion.

Some administrators got something out of their training, but the record of anthropological research by colonial administrators compares unfavourably with that of the missionaries. The journals which some of the colonial governments published contained little anthropology, though more ethnohistory and curious anecdote. They reveal how the more studious of the administrators were drawn rather to the study of the flora and fauna of their territories, an escape, no doubt, from their tiresome contacts with the human inhabitants.

III

British colonial policy in Africa began to change in the thirties. It was decided to 'develop' the colonies economically and administratively, and the hitherto neglected African colonies were stimulated to engage in more positive administrative planning. The depression, and then the war, delayed the implementation of many plans, but the shift in policy had its effect upon the anthropologists. First of all, the International African Institute at last landed enough money to support fellows in the field, so coincidentally swinging Malinowski's seminar round to focus on 'culture change' in Africa. Secondly, the Rhodes-Livingstone Institute was founded in Northern Rhodesia (as it then was). It set the pattern for the colonial social research institutes which were to provide such a stimulus to anthropology after the war. Thirdly, Lord Hailey was commissioned to carry out his African survey. He came up with proposals for spending comparatively huge sums of money on research, and part of this was to trickle in the direction of the anthropologists.

The International Institute of African Languages and Cultures – to give it its full title – was set up in 1926, with the backing of anthropologists, linguists, missionaries and colonial officials from various European countries. The first council, for example, included Lugard, the great colonial figure; Edwin Smith, the missionary anthropologist and the first director; and such scholars as Lévy-Bruhl, Schebesta and Seligman. They were respected, even fêted in a modest sort of way by the various colonial governments – in 1930 when the Council met in Rome its members were granted an audience by the Pope. But the Institute's

130

work was for some years in the field of pure scholarship, perhaps its most notable achievement being the proposals on African orthography.

Although its active members were mainly based in Britain, the international character of the body, and the distinction of its leading members, made it a good vehicle for the funds which were gradually being made available. There was nothing dramatic on this front: the first year's income, from a charitable trust, grants from various metropolitan and colonial governments, and membership fees amounted to little over £3,000. A grant from the Carnegie Corporation helped to raise the third year's income to nearly £7,000, but the income of the Institute was not stabilized at a reasonable figure until in the early thirties the Rockefeller Foundation decided to support fellowships through the Institute, and raised the income to £9,000. It was these research fellowships that made the Institute such a force in anthropology in the thirties.

There were not many of these fellowships and grants; but then there were very few anthropologists in the inter-war years. The impact of these grants was out of all proportion to their number. The first three fellows were Fortes, Nadel and Hofstra. Other anthropologists who were supported in part or entirely by the Institute in the following years were Monica Hunter (later Wilson), Schapera, Forde, Read, Gordon Brown, and Hilda Beemer (Kuper). The small sums of money disbursed for research yielded an extraordinary return in intellectual terms. Moreover the Institute was able to subsidize the publication of the monographs and symposia which followed from this fieldwork, becoming the most important anthropological publisher in the world.

When the Institute received the Rockefeller funds, it worked out a five-year research plan, which was published in 1932. The plan is of interest as a statement of what 'applied anthropology' meant to the new generation of functionalists, for it reflected their interests, and those of the more sophisticated missionaries. The plan's initial assumption was that the limited resources of the Institute should be directed towards the solution of one major problem, and this was defined as follows:

The fundamental problem arising from the inter-penetration of African life by the ideas and economic forces of European civilization is that of the cohesion of African society. African society is being subjected to a severe strain, and there is a danger lest the powerful forces that are entering the continent may bring about its complete disintegration, the results of which must be calamitous for the individuals who compose it and at the same time render impossible an orderly evolution of the community. It is proposed, therefore, that the enquiries fostered by the Institute should be directed towards bringing about a better understanding of the factors of social cohesion in original African society, the ways in which these are being affected by the new influences, tendencies towards new groupings and the formation of new social bonds, and forms of co-operation between African societies and Western civilization.[12]

This formulation suggests the functionalist illusion – which, of course, some functionalists escaped – that because their models of society assumed equilibrium between the parts, change meant disintegration. The image of the pathetic remnants of Australian and North American tribes haunted them. Nevertheless, the plan went on to insist that the Institute was neither for nor against 'change'. It aimed to make an objective and scientific study of the processes of change, without committing itself for or against any particular policy. The administrator would simply be given the information which might help

in determining the right relations between the institutions of African society and alien systems of government, education, and religion, in preserving what is vital in the former and in eliminating unnecessary conflict between the latter and African tradition, custom, and mentality.[13]

But the Institute's fellows did very little in the way of studying 'change'. They spent most of their time and energy on what they considered more academic and more scientific studies of the bases of social cohesion. Some did participate in small 'applied' projects, on the invitation of their host governments. Thus Fortes gave an account of Tallensi marriage law for use in the courts, and was asked for some general advice on reordering the administration of the remote Northern Territories of the Gold Coast. Margaret Read did a study of the effects of migratory labour on village life in Nyasaland. Nadel advised on the setting up of 'pagan courts' alongside the Mohammedan courts in the Nupe area of Nigeria. He also provided economic data for use in reassessing the scheme of taxation. There were a few other limited studies of a similar nature, by-products of more fundamental anthropological research on social structure.

The academic publications of the anthropologists were of little interest to the colonial administrators, and the applied projects were few and unambitious. Sir Phillip Mitchell was speaking for many when he complained that anthropologists,

asserting that they only were gifted with understanding, busied themselves with enthusiasm about all the minutiae of obscure tribal and personal practices [from which studies] resulted a large number of painstaking and often accurate records . . . of such length that no one had time to read them and often, in any case, irrelevant, by the time they became available, to the day to day business of government.

A different kind of development was foreshadowed by the establishment of the Rhodes-Livingstone Institute in 1938. It was founded to direct social research in 'British Central Africa', and it was followed after the war by the establishment of a number of similar centres in other colonial areas. For the first time social research personnel were employed on the same generous terms as senior government officers, but the research-workers were nevertheless allowed considerable autonomy. This was made easier by the fact that although the Institute was sited in Northern Rhodesia, it was concerned with a group of countries and so could avoid domination by the demands of one colonial government. The beginnings were small, and at first only one or two research officers were employed. Here, as elsewhere,

the turning point was the passage of the Colonial Development and Welfare Act in 1940. This act grew in part from
Hailey's *Africa Survey*.

Hailey was a retired senior official of the Indian Civil
Service, who undertook his survey on the suggestion of
Smuts and with funds from Carnegie and the Rhodes
Trustees. His report was concerned mainly with administration, but he was critical also of the anthropologists.
He was not impressed by the claims Malinowski had been
making. The one great achievement of applied anthropology,
which the anthropologists always used to cite, was the
discovery that the Golden Stool of the Ashanti had a ritual
value such that the Ashanti would never accept its abuse by
anyone without war. Hailey's comment on this was full
of common-sense:

> The attempt of the Gold Coast Administration in 1899 to
> take possession of the Golden Stool of Ashanti has often been
> quoted as an instance of . . . misunderstanding, though it was
> perhaps evidence of flagrant disregard of popular feeling rather
> than of ignorance of indigenous custom.[14]

The anthropologists were being excessively naïve if they
thought that conflicts were the result of misunderstandings
as often as they stemmed from fundamental conflicts of
interest.

His scepticism went deeper. Although he accepted that
administrators should try to have all the available information, he pointed out that the British administration in
West Africa had managed to do a great deal before the first
significant inquiry into African institutions was launched –
the West African Lands Committee, which was appointed
in 1912. Moreover, he felt that if the policy of Indirect Rule
was abandoned, as he hoped it would be, the already limited
uses of anthropology would be further restricted. He wrote:

> The problem of the maladjustments in African society created
> by the extension to it of Western economic or political institutions
> is no more amenable to treatment by the anthropologist than by
> anyone else. The most conspicuous field where his studies still
> have a direct application is in the elucidation of customary

rules of law regulating marriage, succession, and land tenure. Here they have a definite use, and their value is not limited to the field in which they can be immediately applied, for it is probably even greater in its illumination of the context of African custom and values within which all administrative action must work.[15]

Hailey's report appeared at a time when colonial policy was being reviewed, in the light of events in India and the Middle East. The war stimulated more radical rethinking of colonial issues, and in 1940 the government published the Colonial Development and Welfare Act. It provided, among much else, for the allocation of up to half a million pounds a year for colonial research. The government explained that this decision was inspired largely by Hailey's report.

The funds provided for research only reached the half million mark in the late forties, but by the early fifties had passed the million mark. However, it must be remembered that these funds were for all research, in all the colonies. The largest portions went on research in agriculture, animal health and forestry (thirty-five per cent), and medical research (sixteen per cent). All social and economic research accounted for only nine per cent of the total. After the war the Colonial Social Science Research Council (C.S.S.R.C.) was set up, with a committee of nine, including Firth and Audrey Richards, to allocate these funds. The anthropologists were the main group of social scientists working in the African field, and so sufficient funds were available to permit a dramatic expansion of the profession after the war. Such was the shortage of trained people to take up these fellowships, that some were given to Americans, a strange reversal of the traditional funding relationship.

The majority of C.S.S.R.C. fellowships in anthropology were given to people working in the African field. Africa remained virtually an academic monopoly of the anthropologists until the fifties. It was also the primary focus of their field research after 1930. In 1943 Braunholtz, then President of the Royal Anthropological Institute, complained about 'The natural tendency of British anthropologists to study the inhabitants of British colonies'.[16] He might well have added '. . . in Africa'.

This concentration on Africa is not easily explained. The Indian subcontinent and the Middle East were increasingly disturbed politically after the First World War, but Africa was by no means uniformly calm – Evans-Pritchard had studied the Nuer shortly after they had been most brutally 'pacified'. Of course, some anthropologists did go elsewhere. In the thirties, for example, Firth went to Malaya and Leach to Burma; but until the fifties few followed them. Nor did many British anthropologists return to Oceania after the mid-thirties – this was left to the Australians. It was not simply a matter of funds. In 1947 the Scarborough Commission, reflecting Foreign Office anxieties on the eve of the Cold War, tried to stimulate research in the strategic areas of the Orient, but the anthropologists in general steered clear. It *is* a puzzle – but we must remember that in the interwar period particularly, we are concerned with the movements of a handful of people, who were very closely involved with one another. In such a milieu the chance influence of a successful example, or the views of a powerful man – or woman – on a particular committee, must have been very important.

IV

When, more or less reluctantly, the anthropologist 'did some applied work', he tended to pick one of a limited range of topics. (I say he, but applied work was often regarded by the more mandarin as less demanding intellectually, and therefore as best suited to women. Malinowski's first student to be despatched to do a study of 'culture change' in Africa was chosen because it was thought she was still too new to anthropology to do a conventional tribal study.) The issues which recur in these studies are land tenure, the codification of traditional law, particularly marriage law, labour migration, the position of chiefs, especially subordinate chiefs, and household budgets. No British anthropologist attempted a study of the way in which a total tribal system might be systematically altered; and only Monica Hunter and Lucy Mair concentrated specifically upon 'change'. The Brown and Hutt experiment in Tanganyika is illuminating in this respect.

Gordon Brown was a Canadian, who had been trained by Malinowski. He had served as superintendent of education in Tanganyika, and through a concatenation of accidents he teamed up with a sympathetic district commissioner, Hutt, in an attempt to discover how the anthropologist and the administrator could cooperate.

Brown and Hutt agreed to separate the roles of anthropologist and administrator as fully as possible. Brown was not to judge policy; Hutt was not to question the anthropologist's facts, but had simply to ask for information on particular topics and use it as he thought best.

What did he ask? His first three questions referred to the registration of marriage and divorce, the extent of polygyny, and the effect of capital punishment as a deterrent to murder. As the experiment proceeded, in 1932, the questions became rather more wide-ranging, but Hutt specifically resisted Brown's attempts to prepare an analysis of the total social situation in the district. He did not want the study to become too academic. The anthropologist was thus treated as merely a source of reliable information on specific and immediate questions. In other districts, the D.C. would put similar questions to a trusted local clerk.[17]

Very few anthropologists presented governments with a significant body of commissioned material. Hans Cory, the Tanganyika government anthropologist was one exception. Another was Schapera, who worked for many years in close alliance with the Bechuanaland government. He recorded Tswana law, for the chiefs and the courts, wrote an account of the various systems of land tenure in the country, and reported on the effects of migrant labour, as well as preparing confidential reports on more specific and delicate matters. More typically, anthropologists prepared piece meal analyses when they were asked nicely, and perhaps the majority did nothing at all in this line.

Godfrey Wilson reported on a typical example of the sort

of bitty work which was occasionally done on behalf of African colonial governments. The Tanganyika government successfully introduced coffee to the Nyakyusa in the early thirties. After initial successes the scheme ran into difficulties, owing to the Nyakyusa habit of moving their homes with great frequency, and deserting their fields, and also their odd customs with respect to land tenure. Under some government pressure to act, the chiefs passed a law that coffee trees should be the 'absolute property' of their planters, but this proved unworkable.

Godfrey and Monica Wilson had done fieldwork among the Nyakyusa, and Godfrey Wilson was in the field in 1938 and was asked for advice. He pointed out that nothing could be done about the instability of the population. The answer must be to produce a more flexible law, perhaps modelled on the Nyakyusa law regarding banana trees. This was that the trees should be given into the care of new settlers, but that the original planter had to be compensated with a proportion of the crop. The officials received this suggestion well, but at the time Wilson was writing – in 1940 – a decision was still being awaited.

Several points should be made about this little story. First of all, Godfrey Wilson was the closest British social anthropology got in this period to producing an expert on 'social change' with a keen interest in applied work. He had recently become first director of the Rhodes-Livingstone Institute, and he and his wife published the first attempt by functionalist anthropologists to produce a theory of social change.[18] Yet in this article on applied anthropology, published in 1940 in *Africa*, the journal of the International African Institute, he could not dredge up any more inspiring story to illustrate the possibilities of such work. If this marginal, perhaps neglected piece of advice was worth boasting about, the performance of British social anthropologists in applied anthropology was clearly not very impressive.

Reviewing the work which was actually done, the scepticism of the colonial administrators is very understandable. Of course, even their contemporaries were appalled by their smugness, their arrogant assumption of omniscience, and their philistine opposition of the 'Practical Man' (as they liked to call themselves) to the scholar. But the anthropologists played into their hands, participating only grudgingly (as a rule) in the little studies dreamt up by the administrators, and accepting the view that they should not speak out on matters of policy, not being 'practical men'. The worst of it was that Malinowski had promised so much. As Audrey Richards confessed, 'the anthropologist often offers his help, but seldom condescends to give it'.[19]

V

The reasons for this failure are not difficult to identify. For one thing, although the anthropologist might often be financed by colonial governments or interests, his future lay in academic life. British universities have traditionally rewarded the pure scholar rather than the technician, and the anthropologist's commitment to theoretical studies almost always overrode his desire, such as it may have been, to concentrate upon applied research. Moreover, doing such applied research was seldom a major condition of fieldwork grants. The grant-giving bodies recognized the priorities of the scholars, and took the longer view that it would benefit Britain to have a store of knowledge, and a body of teachers, who could help perhaps one day in refining policy. Even after the war, when there were several institutes of social research in the colonies, with scholars on comparatively long-term contracts, few did primarily applied studies, although fieldworkers were more often asked to collect material, as a sideline, for a survey someone was doing for government on the level of education of sub-chiefs, or something of that sort.

On his side the colonial administrator was often suspicious. In 1956 a former American government anthropologist, H. G. Barnett, reviewing the progress of anthropology in administration throughout the world, concluded, 'No matter how tactfully it is phrased, the truth is that anthropologists and administrators do not, on the whole, get along well together.'[20] The colonial officer in British

Africa was no exception. He believed that he knew the relevant facts, and suspected the anthropologist's commitment to his own goal of peace and quiet, or, more idealistically, 'evolutionary development'.

Many District Commissioners believed that they 'knew the native', and that their years of experience made them far more expert than the anthropologist with only one or two years' residence. This may have been in part a defensive reaction, a fear of being shown up, but there was more often something in it of the anthropologist's own jealousy about 'his tribe'.

District Commissioners were often suspicious of all outsiders in their territory. The anthropologist, with his unique opportunities for 'making trouble' – particularly if he was a 'do-gooder' at heart – was especially worrisome. Joyce Cary, who had been a District Officer in Nigeria, wrote a novel about this, with the foolish American woman anthropologist stirring up forces she cannot control, and eventually being the indirect cause of the death of the decent, understanding, District Commissioner, who had become her lover.[21]

The anthropologist often upset local white opinion by hob-nobbing with the Africans. The more orthodox District Commissioners – particularly in East and Central Africa – were easily convinced that they were going native, and letting the side down. Audrey Richards was forced to be rather defensive about this, on behalf of the anthropologists:

While it is probably sheer romanticism to suppose that he, or she, is ever really accepted as a member of a native tribe, as has sometimes been claimed, anthropologists do participate in native life much more closely than do other categories of Europeans living in the community. They must, for instance, live in a native village and not in the nearest European settlement. They must share in the work and play of the people and attend their ceremonies. It would be difficult for Europeans occupying positions of high authority, or closely identified with a particular Church, to attend beer drinks or magic ceremonies with the same freedom as the anthropologist does. An African district officer might be equally limited by what it was thought fitting

140

for him to do. For this reason it is inevitable that the anthropologist should quickly acquire the reputation of a 'wild man of the woods', and should be constantly accused of 'going native'. There can be few who have not been described at one time or another as 'dancing round a tom-tom in a loin cloth'.[22]

Although his life-style was so disturbing, the anthropologist was also regarded as a romantic reactionary, who wanted to preserve 'his tribe' from any outside contacts, and to keep them as museum exhibits in splendid isolation from trade, government, and Christianity. Despite the myth of Indirect Rule, the colonial governments were all committed to the extension of the cash economy, to the support of missions and mission education (with some local exceptions), and to the establishment of new forms of law and government.

This caricature of the anthropologist's politics, was, of course, grossly unfair. But it had some relationship to reality. The liberal position on colonial affairs for much of the twenties and thirties was that all 'change' was dangerous; that cultures all have a value, which should be respected, and that tribal cultures are peculiarly vulnerable to corruption, even disintegration, on contact with outside forces; and that therefore, in general, the forces of decency should be ranged against radical changes of any kind. The liberals warred particularly against the changes which had already caused measurable damage to African interests – white settlement, migrant labour, and so forth. Many anthropologists who rejected this position in part or entirely identified rather with the views of the more progressive administrators. Others became advocates for the sectional interests of 'their' tribes. Some took up a revolutionary position. But overall, the anthropologists failed to develop a coherent view of the structure of colonial societies, and so, with their functionalist orientation, they were easily cast into the mould of the stereotype.

The tension in these attitudes emerges in a paper which Fortes contributed to a Fabian symposium on colonial affairs immediately after the war. On the one hand he attacked the myth that anthropologists wanted to preserve untouched African societies as museum-pieces:

Those who put it about merely show their ignorance of modern anthropological research work, as well as a shocking lack of understanding of the historical processes of our times. In fact, nostalgia for the 'unspoiled savage' is usually found among those who get their living from breaking up primitive societies and 'corrupting' the savage – government officials, traders, missionaries, etc.

But on the other hand he wrote that forces from the West were having a revolutionary effect on African societies, and commented that

the centre of gravity of the equilibrium characteristic of a stable and homogeneous primitive society lies in its scheme of cultural values; and that a primitive society undergoing rapid social breakdown is apt to become a rabble of acquisitive or exploited individuals and the prey of irrational mob impulses if they cease to have common cultural values.[23]

In short, he accepted (he said) Furnivall's analysis of the plural society in the colonies, but he did not build this analysis into his particular studies of tribal societies, and he showed no interest in Furnivall's prescriptions for what came to be called 'depluralization'.

The final belief of the liberals, which perhaps more anthropologists shared, was that once the facts were known all men of goodwill would do the decent thing; and so the tabulation of the causes of (say) Bemba idleness or Tswana indecency were a contribution to tolerance and the eradication of conflict. But as Hailey often pointed out, the problem was not one of misunderstanding. The two sides understood each other only too well.

All in all, perhaps the most telling comment on the general colonial and settler attitude to anthropologists in the British commonwealth, as late as the forties, was the reaction of the Union government as soon as South Africa entered the war. It immediately closed all African reserves to anthropologists. So much for the dependence of the colonialists upon the anthropologists.

It is ironical that the great period of financial support for anthropological research, the nineteen-fifties, coincided with Britain's rapid disengagement from colonial responsibilities. The East African Institute of Social Research, under Audrey Richards and, later, Fallers and Southall, and the Rhodes-Livingstone Institute under Gluckman, Colson and Mitchell specialized in anthropological studies. They rapidly provided the best regional ethnographic coverage Africa had yet seen. Their fellows also paid attention to the emerging social trends, in the towns, the trade unions, the new cash-cropping areas. But their advice was still not often sought. Audrey Richards in Uganda worked in close partnership with that most enlightened Governor, Sir Andrew Cohen, but this was exceptional. The economist and the rural development expert were the new gurus. When universities were set up, from Ibadan to Makerere, anthropologists had to squeeze into departments of sociology.

Moreover, as African studies became fashionable – particularly after the independence of Ghana in 1957 – other social scientists crowded in. They found the anthropologists studying every aspect of social life, and made a place for themselves by attacking the anthropologists. It is only now – after a decade and a half – that the political scientists, the historians, and even the economists are recognizing the immense value of the work which the anthropologists have produced, and the scientific advantages of their humble methods, which brought them into prolonged and intimate contact with the rural people and the urban workers. But in many cases it is too late. The institutes of social research, taken over by sociologists or political scientists, crazed by statistics and newspapers, have all failed to provide the creative centres which Audrey Richards and Gluckman provided.

VI

The inescapable conclusion is that there was never much of a demand for applied anthropology from Whitehall or from the colonial governments. Even in the days of the C.S.S.R.C., when committee members talked hopefully about relevant research, the anthropologists in general went their own sweet academic way. Perhaps a different sort of colonial power might have been greatly helped by anthropologists – as some claim the Americans are in South America and South-East Asia. The U.S.A. has always been far more ready to believe the claims of social scientists than the British have been, but while some anthropologists have sold out to sinister interests, it is not often easy to see how their researches could be of much assistance. In any case, the reality is that British anthropologists were little used by the colonial powers, and despite their rhetoric when in pursuit of funds, they were not particularly eager to be used.

But perhaps this is to take too narrow a view of the sort of support anthropology might have given to colonial régimes and imperial policy in general. The Belgian anthropologist Maquet has written:

> Although many exceptions could certainly be pointed out, it seems not unfair to say that during the colonial period, most anthropological studies were – unwillingly and unconsciously in many cases – conservative: first, in that Africans were described as so different from 'civilized' peoples and so 'savage' just at the time that Europe needed to justify colonial expansion; and second, in that later on, the value of the traditional cultures was magnified when it was useful for the colonial powers to ally themselves with the more traditional forces against the progressive Africans. We do not believe that these parallels are mere coincidences.[24]

The point is worth making, even though the progressive African politicians were even more determined to stress the traditional African values, and to exalt traditional cultures. Many anthropologists shared their motive: the desire to remove the philistine stigma from the cultures of people who simply happened to lack certain post-industrial techniques of production.

This suggests another, more difficult question, but one more relevant to the theme of this book. What effect did the colonial environment have on the development of British social anthropology? The colonial situation did not simply generate academic anthropology. The other European colonial régimes failed to produce schools of anthropology of a similar kind, and the Spanish and Portuguese produced hardly any anthropology at all, of any kind.

Nor can the policy of Indirect Rule be isolated as the progenitor of anthropology, functionalist or other. This policy was applied only to some British territories, and never in the sense of the myth. It is generally recognized by historians that the contrast between the 'indirect rule' of the British and the 'direct rule' of the French diminishes to vanishing point 'when one considers the situation on the ground, and individual British territories differed greatly from each other. In virtually all the colonies local African leaders, recruited on neo-traditional grounds or not, had to be used to administer local divisions according to a more or less home-grown system because the alternative was simply too expensive to contemplate. Moreover, whatever was said about 'indirect rule', major forces of social change were deliberately unleashed in all British colonies from a very early stage – notably the decisions to impose cash taxes, stimulate migrant labour, and regulate force. From the nineteen-thirties all British colonies began to introduce planned developments in the fields of government and economy which simply made no sense in terms of any doctrine of indirect rule.

Yet was functionalism not peculiarly apt as a theory for colonial anthropology – as Maquet, for example, suggested? This is a question which one cannot hope to answer definitively, but a few points may helpfully be made. First of all, the theory which most British colonial administrators accepted more or less without question was an evolutionist one. They were trained in their public schools in the traditions of the Roman Empire, and they saw themselves as bringing the benefits of civilization, with a minimum of the ills, to backward peoples who might – after centuries of 'evolution' – reach the stage when they could be entrusted with their own fates.

Secondly, diffusionism was also quite a good candidate in the circumstances. Malinowski himself defined the business of the new African anthropology as the study of the diffusion of European culture to Africa, and he gave courses on 'culture contact' as the foundation of the new discipline. This was also the line of approach advocated by Americans like Herskovits. It is significant that Malinowski's functionalism was greatly altered when he developed his ideas on contemporary Africa. His point of view was theoretically vacuous and politically absurd: but it was not anything like the caricature of the functionalist.

And, most significantly, it was precisely the crude functionalist view which was immediately abhorrent to the administrators, who scoffed at the anthropologist's supposed reluctance to countenance even gradual change, or to accept the presence of the trader, the missionary and the administrator. The functionalist failure to cope with change was *not* something which endeared anthropologists to colonial administrators – quite the contrary. The colonial administrators also recoiled from the implicit relativism of the functionalist position. They mocked the – perhaps mythical – anthropologist in New Guinea who argued that head-hunting was very good for his tribe, and said that it should not be judged by inappropriate western standards of morality. The colonial administrator was firmly committed to an evolutionist theory, which included an evolutionary scale of values up which he felt bound to chivvy his charges.

Yet it has been plausibly argued that functionalism can be seen as an implicit refusal to deal with the total colonial reality in a historical perspective, and this has been attributed to the colonial situation, which may have inhibited, or even blinded the anthropologist. This line of argument underplays the broader context of functionalist theory in sociology. Functionalist-type studies were not peculiar to interwar British social anthropology in the colonies. Studies of a similar sort were carried out by sociologists in Europe and America, and by the few British social anthropologists working outside the colonies. The functionalist approach was an experiment with synchronic analysis which made sense in terms of the intellectual history of the discipline, and it justified itself to the extent of producing better ethnographies than any previous approach – it was for this reason that Whyte adopted the method in his study of Boston's Italian slums, and Arensberg and Kimball adopted it in their studies of Irish rural society in the thirties. Equally it should be emphasized that it was quite possible to write historical studies without considering the colonial context, as many American and German ethnologists demonstrated. The refusal to consider Marxist theory – with a few notable exceptions – is also something which cannot be held against colonial social anthropology alone. This was an omission which characterized most of the social sciences in their academic guise in the West.

Although a number of the arguments currently fashionable are crude and based upon misinformation, it is nevertheless inescapably true that the colonial situation hindered the free development of British social anthropology at the theoretical level, while no doubt facilitating access to funds and to field-sites. The acid test is, what happened to British social anthropology after the loss of the Empire? The rapid changes in the discipline after the mid-fifties must be attributed in part to the changes in the political environment, and while social anthropology is, of course, not free today from an implicit political content, the changes it has undergone indicate the pressures which have been released since decolonization.

Two effects stand out. First, the anthropologists did not treat the total colonial situation in a scholarly fashion. Few studied settlers and administrators, for example, and this robbed their work of a vital dimension of reality. This is perhaps why the great studies of the colonial period dealt with kinship, with political constitutions of tribes, and with cosmological systems. It was in these fields that the restrictions of the colonial setting became the anthropologists' strengths.

Secondly, British social anthropologists were inhibited from discarding the racialist and evolutionist adhesions of their pre-functionalist past. The functionalists did not really feel that their subject was concerned with a special type of person, the 'primitive' or 'savage' – or at any rate

147

ANTHROPOLOGISTS AND ANTHROPOLOGY

leading figures like Radcliffe-Brown rejected this idea.
But they slipped into accepting that their speciality was the
study of the colonial subject, and they allowed him to be
identified with the erstwhile 'primitive' or 'savage' of the
evolutionists. This was an easy assumption, a convenient
blurring of definition, but the consequence has been to
identify anthropology with the mass-humiliation of colonialism. The British social anthropologist is so often an object
of suspicion in the ex-colonial countries because he was the
specialist in the study of colonial peoples; because, by
identifying his study in practice as the science of
coloured man, he contributed to the devaluation of their
humanity.

But there were numerous exceptions to these generalizations, and indeed to the broad picture I have described so
sketchily. It is not too misleading to talk of a liberal functionalist anthropology, dominant in the interwar years, but there
was a considerable amount of valuable work which burst
the constraints of the paradigm. In South Africa Gluckman
and Hilda Kuper examined the racial set-up in dynamic
and radical terms, and Hellman pioneered the study of
urban African workers. At the Rhodes-Livingstone Institute
Gluckman published an account of Lozi land tenure and
included for comparative purposes the constitution of a
Soviet collective, an action which the settlers considered
little short of sedition. As a group – with a few
exceptions – the Rhodes-Livingstone fellows were politically
on the left, and not backward in showing it. Worsley's
analysis of cargo cults in New Guinea became a superb
critique of colonial policy and an account of the
beginnings of a nationalist movement. Kenyatta, Busia and
Z. K. Matthews were trained in anthropology, as were other
future nationalist politicians, and they learnt through it
new respect and understanding for their cultural heritage.
One could go on, but my point is simply that in treating this
complex and diffuse problem all generalizations must be
qualified.

In conclusion, one characteristic of British functionalist
social anthropology should be stressed. After Malinowski,

the anthropologists based their methods upon participant-observation, which required intimate and free contact with the peoples they studied. They therefore had to break down the barriers of the colour bar, which existed in most colonies, and they had to challenge the basic, unspoken assumptions of all colonial régimes. Their individual examples of how sophisticated Europeans could happily adopt many tribal habits and live on a basis of friendship with illiterate and poor peoples constituted a constant irritation to settlers and many colonial officers. To us today this example still has its point.

FIVE

From Charisma to Routine

... Andrew Lang once said to me on a memorable occasion,
when I walked back with him, after a dinner-party, to
Merton where he was staying: 'If I could have made a
living out of it, I might have been a great anthropologist!'
                                                    – Marett[1]

I

The hiatus caused in the development of British socia
anthropology by the Second World War was not complete.
Some anthropologists were drafted as colonial administrators, notably Evans-Pritchard and Nadel, and Audrey
Richards went into the colonial office. Others served in
intelligence units, or on special missions, and Leach had an
adventurous war with guerilla units in Burma. But the Royal
Anthropological Institute maintained a centre for lectures
and meetings for several years, and the handful of
anthropologists kept in touch with one another. Further,
some young men serving in the armed forces had their first
experience of Africa or Asia, which decided them to study
anthropology when peace came.

With peace, British social anthropology entered a period
of relatively spectacular expansion. At last money was
plentifully available for research, new departments were
established, and new institutes of social research staffed in
the colonies. For the first time social anthropology offered a
career structure in Britain. The graduate student was no
longer taking a crazy gamble, he was entering a profession.

With the establishment of the Colonial Social Science
Research Council, the previous dearth of funds was
succeeded by a glut. It was a struggle to find enough
trained students to take up the new fellowships. Teaching
positions also began to open up. African and Oriental
studies began to enjoy public favour. The potency of
nationalist movements in India and the Middle East stimu-

lated new thinking about colonial problems, particularly in the Labour Party, which came to power at this time. All this provided a favourable environment for the expansion of teaching in anthropology. New chairs were created at University College London, the School of Oriental and African Studies (which expanded greatly after the Scarborough Report), the University of Manchester, and Edinburgh University. Anthropologists also found niches in some other departments, or in universities which did not have fully-fledged departments of anthropology. In 1953 (when Forde published a survey of the position) there were thirty-eight teachers of social anthropology in British universities. Some sort of instruction in the subject was available in twelve universities. About 160 students were reading for degrees in social anthropology, roughly half of them post-graduates, and perhaps 500 students were taking subsidiary courses in anthropology.

There was therefore a rapid increase in the numbers recruited into the profession after the war. One good measure is membership of the professional association, the Association of Social Anthropologists of Great Britain, founded, significantly, in 1946. It began with fourteen members based in the United Kingdom, and seven based overseas. By 1951 membership in both categories had doubled. In 1953, when Forde found there were thirty-eight teaching posts in social anthropology in Britain, there were sixty members of the association, over a third of whom were based outside the United Kingdom. By the end of the decade there were over 120 members, and in 1968, when the Social Science Research Council reviewed the situation of British social anthropology there were 240 members, although probably only a third were employed as social anthropologists in Britain. At the same time there were about 150 British postgraduate students in training, perhaps half of them proceeding to the doctorate.

Many of the new wave of recruits found employment abroad, in the U.S.A., the new colonial universities of Africa and Asia, and the 'white commonwealth'. Others found opportunities in the institutes of social research which

151

were established in the colonies after the war, particularly the Rhodes-Livingstone Institute, the East African Institute of Social Research, which was founded in 1950 at Makerere, in Uganda, and the institute attached to the growing university at Ibadan, in Nigeria. A few positions in 'applied anthropology' also opened up in Britain. The base of the profession, however, remained the teaching departments in Britain itself. There was not to be another dramatic increase in the number of departments, and the 'plateglass universities' of the sixties preferred to open departments of sociology. Nonetheless the established departments expanded, and social anthropologists found openings in departments of sociology. Such was the shortage of trained sociologists during the great expansion in the teaching of the subject in the sixties, that a number of sociology chairs went to social anthropologists.

Research funds became available from a number of sources, and the winding up of the C.S.S.R.C. did not have much impact. In the period 1961–6 the eighty British-based members of the Association of Social Anthropologists spent nearly a quarter of a million pounds on research. Only thirty-five per cent of this came from government sources. Thirty-five per cent came from foundations (often based in America), and the balance from universities, international organizations, industry, etc.[2]

Thus in the years following the war the resources of British anthropology, human and financial, expanded greatly. The discipline was entrenched with a reasonably broad university base, and a flow of students was available. One consequence was to make social anthropology a recognized profession in Britain, and this was reflected in organizational developments.

The structure of the profession was influenced by its odd demographic characteristics. It remained small enough to be a cohesive group throughout our period, and recruitment had been concentrated in three distinctly marked phases. The first phase was the late twenties and the thirties, when Malinowski's students came into anthropology. There was then a lull, until after the war when there was a comparatively huge influx. As the Ardeners concluded from a survey of the A.S.A. 1961 register, 'the striking "bulge" in members born between 1915 and 1929 may be taken as real evidence of a great expansion of intake into the discipline which occurred after World War II.' But this group

included as its core persons of various ages who shared in common the circumstance that they had had opportunity for little or nothing but a war-service career by 1945. Some read for new qualifications in social anthropology in the succeeding years, others completed previous partial qualifications. Since for practical purposes those born between 1915 and 1929 entered social anthropology almost within the same university generation, the age-group pattern alone is not a fair guide to the relative abruptness of the post-war expansion.

And comparing the pre-war and post-war groups, they went on:

The latter move with steady progression from qualification to field-work and then to publication: the group were in the field within a year or two of qualification, and within five years its publications follow. The pre-war group tended frequently to do its field-work before it gained its first anthropological or socio-logical qualification (at least in the 'twenties and early 'thirties) and seems to have published, on the whole, more quickly.

Their conclusion was that 'The "professionalization" of the discipline for which the pre-war generation worked, was overwhelmingly realized in the post-war "bulge" group.'[3] The third group was recruited from about 1963, when the rate of increase in the membership of the A.S.A. suddenly doubled. This group – born after about 1938 – was the product of the great post-war boom in higher education, particularly after the Robbins report.

Until recently these three generations coexisted in the profession. The pre-war intake held the professorships and senior appointments; the war-veterans filled the middle-range teaching positions; and the young intake of the sixties filled the junior positions and held posts in some of the new departments of sociology. This age-grade structure

153

(elders, warriors, youths?) was dramatically evident when the first generation reached retiring age in a group between 1969 and 1972, vacating the senior positions and bowing out in a shower of *Festschriften*, to be replaced by those warriors who had not moved into departments of sociology or been seduced by North American universities.

II

The pioneer generation achieved professorial rank as a group in the years immediately following the war. In 1944 Firth was appointed to the chair vacated by Malinowski at the L.S.E. In 1945 Daryll Forde was appointed to University College London, where he had to build up a department virtually from scratch, since little had been done since Perry's retirement before the war. In 1946 Evans-Pritchard succeeded Radcliffe-Brown in Oxford. In 1949 Gluckman went as Professor to Manchester, to start a new department. In 1950 Fortes was appointed Professor at Cambridge, and Schapera moved from Cape Town to join Firth at the L.S.E. (where students began to call the department 'We the Tikopia and I. Schapera'). Nadel had gone to Durham as Reader and first head of the department of anthropology in 1948; in 1950 he too became a professor, travelling to Canberra to take up the new Chair in Anthropology and Sociology in the Research School of Pacific Studies. In 1951 von Fürer-Haimendorf was appointed Professor of Asian Anthropology at the School of Oriental and African Studies.

These men controlled the profession for two decades, only Nadel dying before the end of the period. Few new chairs were created and where they were established they were usually personal or auxiliary chairs, which did not carry with them departmental headships. The power of this professoriate was impressive. Like most British professors, the leading anthropologists had the decisive voice in the appointment of staff and often in the choice of students, particularly graduate students. The professor could effectively withhold or grant promotions, leaves, and other privileges; and his recommendation was crucial in any application for a research grant or for a position elsewhere. He was generally the only effective channel of communication with the university authorities and grant-giving bodies.

This formidable base was reinforced by appointments to the bodies which dispensed patronage. The small group of anthropology professors held the relevant positions on government grant-giving committees, and in the major institutions, such as the International African Institute, the Association of Social Anthropologists, and the Royal Anthropological Institute (though here power was shared with the physical anthropologists and some archaeologists). This monopoly of influence had its comic side, as the professors solemnly succeeded one another as Presidents of the Royal Anthropological Institute and office-holders in the A.S.A.; and disbursed to one another the various prize lectureships and honours at their disposal. But it was a serious matter, since whatever their personal or academic differences the professors formed an effective cartel, presenting a united front to the grant-giving agencies and to their juniors.

The A.S.A. was set up in 1946, partly in reaction to the plethora of amateurs and non-social anthropologists in the Royal Anthropological Institute. It was explicitly a professional body, and its first committee reflected the power structure in the profession. The president was Radcliffe-Brown, an honorific post reflecting his continued dominance of theory. The chairman and secretary was Evans-Pritchard, and the committee consisted of Firth, Forde and Fortes. The only notable omission was Gluckman, who soon became chairman and secretary in his turn. This was the power map and it remained the same for twenty years.

The outstanding man outside this magic circle was Edmund Leach, who never became head of a department, choosing rather in the late sixties the public honour of being Provost of King's College, Cambridge. In 1972 Cambridge awarded him a personal chair. Despite the prominence of women in Malinowski's seminars, none became head of a department of anthropology. This is perhaps less surprising when one sees how rare it is for women to be appointed heads of departments in any subject in universities, but the position outside Britain was different. Monica Wilson and Eileen Krige became professors in South Africa, and Elizabeth Colson and Audrey Richards were directors of institutes of social research in British African colonies.

I have stressed the power which office gave to the new professoriate after the war. This power also had its non-material side, for the men and women who came into the field were in general ready to accept the intellectual leadership of at least some of the professors. For most of their period in office, they dominated the theoretical debate as well.

This is not to say that the professors were in complete agreement on theoretical matters. Far from it, although they did share certain fundamental assumptions about the nature of their study. There were frequent conflicts on theoretical questions, between professors, or between individual professors and others, and polemical exchanges were a favourite sport. Each professor had a distinctive set of interests, and specialized in a particular area. In this situation, given the power of the professor, there were what amounted to distinct schools. Most of the professors developed departments in their own image, appointing staff and producing students who shared their orientations. The theoretical map of British anthropology between about 1950 and 1970 was largely, though never entirely, the same as the map of the major departments.

The key points on the map were the three London departments, and Oxford, Cambridge and Manchester. Firth was the most powerful influence at the L.S.E., where he was joined by Richards, Nadel, Schapera, Mair, Leach and Freedman, at one time or another. The department did not have a firm 'party-line', but it inclined towards the Firthian recension of Malinowskian functionalism. Of all the English departments, it was perhaps here that the structuralism of Radcliffe-Brown was least important. Despite his great originality, one can identify Leach as a typical product of the L.S.E. The central concerns were with individual manipulation of political systems, the context of economic choices, and the sphere of optation in kinship systems.

Forde came to University College London with an unusual background. He had worked under Kroeber and Lowie in California, and was professionally competent in geography and archaeology as well as in social anthropology. He shared with the Americans a traditional view of anthropology, embracing not only social anthropology but also human biology and archaeology, and he had a strong interest in problems of evolution and ecology. His department specialized in providing an all-round anthropological education, but some of his most successful graduates made their mark in the study of political development, notably M. G. Smith and the Belgians Jan Vansina and Jacques Maquet. Forde also became director of the International African Institute, and most of his students did fieldwork in West Africa, as he had done.

Von Fürer-Haimendorf could claim to be the only cultural anthropologist in the major British departments, and his department at the School of Oriental and African Studies placed great emphasis upon ethnographic and linguistic competence. For many years it was the only anthropology department in Britain with a strong interest in India, and the recruitment of Adrian Mayer and F. G. Bailey strengthened this commitment. However, there was no particular theoretical emphasis associated with the School.

The three leading departments outside London were all more firmly dominated by the views of their professors. At Oxford Evans-Pritchard abandoned many of Radcliffe-Brown's dogmas and moved increasingly towards a historicist position. The main job of the anthropologist, as he came to see it, was the translation of cultural values into the language of the anthropologist's culture – an essentially humanist rather than a scientific pursuit. He also came to insist upon the necessity for a historical perspective. These orientations came to dominate the Oxford school which he built up, and, referring always to the classics of the *Année* school, the Oxford anthropologists began to develop an idealist position which marked them off from their colleagues elsewhere in Britain. These tendencies may have been related to the odd fact that several of the members of the department were converts to Roman Catholicism, including Evans-Pritchard himself. In many cases students coming to Oxford were converted first to the vogue theoretical position, and subsequently to Roman Catholicism; and the professor acted as godfather at their baptism. Four of the dons – Evans-Pritchard, Pocock, Lienhardt and Beattie – wrote introductions to social anthropology, with the peculiar consequence that for some years anyone consulting a text-book on social anthropology was likely to be faced with the Oxford viewpoint. The department (or as it was called, almost by accident, the 'institute') at Oxford never offered an undergraduate degree in anthropology – although Evans-Pritchard once tried to persuade the university authorities to provide one – and so it concentrated upon the training of graduate students, most of whom were recruited from other disciplines.

Meyer Fortes took over a weak, pre-functionalist department in Cambridge in 1950, and he set about its transformation with great energy. For several years he did much of the teaching himself, assisted by visiting professors of social theory – Radcliffe-Brown, Talcott Parsons and George Homans. A number of his early students became professional anthropologists, and he also drew in many of the ablest graduate students in the country. In 1953 he brought Leach to Cambridge, and Audrey Richards, who held a university readership in Commonwealth studies, was also closely associated with the anthropologists. Goody, the student closest to Fortes's theoretical interests, also joined the department.

Unlike most other departments, Cambridge came to have two main theoretical prongs, the neo-Radcliffe-Brown line which Fortes represented, and the shifting but always exciting line of Leach. This divergence was intensified by their different regional interests. Fortes and his students were predominantly concerned with Africa, while Leach and his students worked mainly in South Asia. However, all the members of the department shared a central interest in the study of kinship, and this was the major field in which Cambridge made its mark on modern anthropological theory. When people talked loosely of the Cambridge school in this period they referred to a central focus of interest, in problems of descent theory particularly, rather than to a specific theoretical stance.

Manchester was different again. Max Gluckman had built up a research school at the Rhodes-Livingstone Institute, and he brought a number of its alumni with him to Manchester. They came to write up their theses, returned as visiting Simon Fellows, or joined the department as lecturers. Far more than anywhere else, a single line dominated the department. As they used to joke, 'We are all Maxists here.' The main regional interest continued to be Central Africa, to such an extent that the few people who had not worked there felt at a serious disadvantage. The theoretical issues were also carried over from Gluckman's days at the Rhodes-Livingstone Institute – particularly problems of conflict, process, and ritual integration; and the methods were the extended-case study, and later, network analysis. The department had close links with some departments abroad and, later, in the north of England, which became part of the Manchester 'empire'. As soon as a member of the school was appointed to a post elsewhere, he tried to surround himself with his fellows.

The school was so solidary that in many typical publications only other members of the school were cited. Collections of essays edited by one member of the school normally included only essays by other members. A characteristic recent example is Epstein's *The Craft of Social Anthropology*, published in 1967. Its list of contributors reads like a roll-call of the Manchester school – Gluckman, Colson, Mitchell, Barnes, Turner, Van Velsen, A. L. and T. S. Epstein, and Marwick. Other prominent members of the school who did not work in Central Africa (and so, perhaps, were judged to be lacking in the essentials of the craft of social anthropology) were Frankenberg, Peters and Worsley. As might be expected in such a situation, deviants and turncoats were treated with great ferocity internally, but no criticism was tolerated from outsiders.

III

The theoretical position to which British anthropology returned at the end of the war was that of Radcliffe-Brown and his Oxford adherents. The key texts had all appeared in 1940: Radcliffe-Brown's lecture 'On Social Structure', Fortes and Evans-Pritchard's *African Political Systems*, and Evans-Pritchard's *The Nuer*. The movements which developed in the following years had to define themselves with reference to this orthodoxy; none more so than the reactions against it. Fieldwork continued to be done in the Malinowskian manner; but if fieldwork was still functionalist, analysis and theory were dominantly structuralist.

Fortes remained closest to the orthodoxy, though he developed it in his own way, but most of his professorial colleagues soon reacted against it. The reaction took various forms – one might almost say that the attacks came from the right and from the left. First, Evans-Pritchard repudiated Radcliffe-Brown's scientific pretensions, and adopted an idealist position, with historicist implications. Secondly, Firth and to some extent Nadel and others revived Malinowskian theory, reacting against the formalism of the structuralists, and demanding that greater attention be given to the irrepressibly selfish, manipulative individual. Thirdly, there was the conflict theory of the Manchester school. And finally, in the fifties, but increasingly in the sixties, Lévi-Strauss's radical development of the *Année Sociologique* tradition was received into British social anthropology.

This is a first rough sketch of the position, and it must be said right away that a number of the most interesting anthropologists in the period cannot be so neatly pigeonholed. Leach, for example, transcended the barriers between the schools; M. G. Smith drew heavily on Weber, and Furnivall, and moved beyond the preoccupations of his contemporaries; Fallers, Colson and Paul and Laura Bohannan were all Americans who came into British social anthropology for a while and then returned to the very different milieu of American anthropology. Others too escape ready classification. Nevertheless, let us accept this broad plan for the time being, and explore the contours after getting a first orientation.

In this chapter I shall discuss the positions taken up in the fifties by Evans-Pritchard, Firth, Fortes and Nadel, and what might be called the mainstream of 'normal science' In the next chapter I turn to the two key mavericks, Leach and Gluckman. Finally, I shall attempt in a separate chapter to summarize the impact of Lévi-Strauss's structuralism on British social anthropology. This plan involves a departure from the straightforward chronological presentation that was possible earlier. This is unfortunate, but the complexity of the situation in the post-war decades makes it necessary. Yet there is an element of sequence in the presentation. The early fifties saw the publication of the main orthodox monographs of the post-war generation, and also the statements of position from the leading professors. In the mid-fifties Leach and the Manchester writers began to dominate the scene, and the Lévi-Straussian movement achieved its greatest momentum in the early and mid-sixties.

IV

Evans-Pritchard accepted Radcliffe-Brown's theoretical position at least until the war, but shortly after succeeding him at Oxford in 1946 he issued a manifesto of rebellion. In the following years some of his closest associates have attempted to represent his career as a unity, without a sharp break, despite Evans-Pritchard's irrefutable observation that 'consistency is surely the worst of all vices in science'.[4] It is therefore necessary to make something of an issue of what might otherwise be simply taken as read. The point might be made by a close analysis of his earlier works, particularly perhaps *The Nuer*, but there is more direct evidence.

I have already cited the programmatic statement he published in 1937, in which he laid out the future of social anthropology along the lines which Radcliffe-Brown had defined. In conclusion he stated the basic assumption underlying this programme:

I am assuming that there are functional interdependencies in culture. If there are not, then Social Anthropology will have a position as an art, like History, in humanistic studies. In this case, much of what I have written in this paper will be irrelevant. Some social anthropologists indeed, would be willing to accept this position, and I admit that those who, like myself, believe that social interdependencies exist and can be established, base their beliefs on faith rather than achievement.[5]

In his Marett lecture, delivered in 1950, he made precisely the contrary assumption, and drew the opposite conclusions. He told his audience:

The thesis I have put before you, that social anthropology is a kind of historiography, and therefore ultimately of philosophy or art, implies that it studies societies as moral systems and not as natural systems, that it is interested in design rather than in process, and that it therefore seeks patterns and not scientific laws, and interprets rather than explains. These are conceptual, and not merely verbal, differences.[6]

Clearly there has been a complete reversal. The 'faith' in the existence of 'functional interdependencies in culture' on which he based his stand in 1937 was now abandoned. Acceptance of it had led to an acceptance of the natural science model for anthropology; rejection led to the view that social anthropology was ultimately 'an art, like History'. One may speculate that the reversal was not caused simply by disappointment with the achievements of social anthropology between 1937 and 1950. It has been suggested that the crunch came with Evans-Pritchard's conversion to Catholicism during the war, and that may well explain his concern with freedom of choice, and with the internal integrity of cosmological systems.

Still, one may question whether this reversal on basic principles had much immediate effect on Evans-Pritchard's practice. At the level of the monographic analysis, which was his forte, he still argued that one should proceed by the isolation of the structural pattern of the culture, with the help of comparison. The difference he stressed was in the use of history. The functionalists had turned their backs upon history as misleading or at best unnecessary; but in line with his belief that social systems should be studied by the methods of the humanities rather than those of the natural sciences – a view difficult to define more precisely – Evans-Pritchard insisted upon the use of history. He argued that there was little essential difference between the techniques and aims of social anthropology and those of history, particularly social history.

The insistence upon a historical perspective was a move against the stream, but Monica Hunter (Wilson), Gluckman and Schapera had been using historical methods for some time previously, and in the years after the Marett lecture several others were to do the same, without, however, abandoning the scientific claims of social anthropology. Indeed, Evans-Pritchard's historical study of the Sanusi, published in 1949, produced a structural analysis strongly reminiscent of that which emerged from the ahistorical book on Nuer politics. It was written in such a way as to bring out the structural principles Evans-Pritchard had described with reference to Nuer prophets – that segmentary societies faced with an external threat may join and organize behind a religious leader. Thus Evans-Pritchard's conversion to the humanist and historicist position did not reflect itself immediately in his work, and did not at once alter the work of his contemporaries. The great revolution in the historical study of African societies came in the next decade, when Vansina and others showed how oral tradition could be tapped – something Evans-Pritchard never did to any extent, preferring to rely upon published and documentary sources.

But Evans-Pritchard has always published his material piecemeal, over many years, before drawing it together in a book, and so it probably took some time before the implications of his new position were fully exposed; or, perhaps, he became more anti-sociological as he went on. In any case, he increasingly came to describe himself as an ethnographer rather than a social anthropologist, the implication being that he regarded the role of observer and interpreter as more important than that of sociologist. In the sixties he published more ethnographic texts and historical material, and his papers on theories of religion and the French and Scottish masters expressed a scepticism about the value of sociological analysis and generalization.

Evans-Pritchard was the greatest social anthropologist of his generation. His elegant analyses, developed in pellucid prose, influenced everyone who read them. While his pessimism about the sociological enterprise had a particular effect within Oxford, as did his idealist bias, his colleagues elsewhere were more deeply impressed by his earlier monographs, and in particular *Witchcraft, Oracles and Magic*, and *The Nuer*. A surprising number of the books written in the decade after the war were virtually local recensions of these masterpieces.

v

In 1951 Evans-Pritchard published a series of semi-popular lectures in which he expounded his views on social anthropology. In the same year Nadel and Firth presented ambitious attempts to synthesize a theoretical basis for the discipline. Both Firth and Nadel challenged the old Oxford orthodoxy, but on lines different from Evans-Pritchard. They were both in their fashion neo-Malinowskians.

Nadel's dense, rather Germanic book, *The Foundations of Social Anthropology*, reflected his discovery of Weber, and also his earlier training in psychology; nevertheless its central thesis was distinctly Malinowskian, although he was much more concerned with social systems than Malinowski had been in his later period. Beneath the philosophical flourishes the old message emerged – institutions are mutually adjusted to fulfil the basic needs (or in Nadel's terminology, 'innate action potentials') of individuals. He went beyond Malinowski, in his concern with the

logical interconnections of institutions, and with psychological theory, but in the end the book must be judged
'sub-Parsons'. It may be that he was writing as a
Parsonian, although he did not say so, but Talcott Parsons
took the same elements of theory and constructed an even
denser and more tortuous version of functionalism, with
the same bias towards the integration of psychological
analysis into sociology.

In 1955 Nadel visited the L.S.E. on leave from
Australia, and delivered a series of lectures later published
(posthumously) as *The Theory of Social Structure*. This book
served even more clearly to define his opinion of the two
traditions of modern British anthropology. The bulk of the
book is a critique of the utility of the notion of 'social
structure'. In conclusion he wrote that

the 'structuralist' judges his own frame of reference to be not only
heuristically useful and promising, but to be more useful and
promising, and indeed more important, than the other frame of
reference, resting on the concepts of utility, purpose, or 'function'.
. . . I cannot accept this judgement, and . . . I feel it is not enough
merely to acknowledge the two ways of analysing social existence.
As I see it, social existence belongs to a universe of discourse
governed by the concepts of purpose and utility; the approach
through structure cannot but be subordinated to them.[7]

For the rest, in this book and in the *Foundations*, he developed
the tool of role analysis beyond anything previously
attempted by anthropologists, and he gave his support to
the experiments being made in the development of social
psychology (as it would be called now), and network and
mathematical models. However, his central argument was
simply that the structuralist orthodoxy was inadequate by
itself – it had to be wedded to a functionalist perspective
which would incorporate psychological theories.

Firth's book, *Elements of Social Organization*, constituted
an even more direct attempt to graft something of
Malinowski's theory back on to the main growth of British
social anthropology, but his emphasis differed from that of
Nadel. He preferred to concentrate upon the 'calculating
man', the figure Bateson discerned as the most promising

member of Malinowski's conceptual team. Firth may have
been ready to use this approach since it fitted in with the
pre-Keynsian economics he had learnt, with its obsessional
interest in individual choice-making. In any case, such
an approach was certainly subversive of the rather idealist
structuralism in vogue at the time.

In perhaps the key passage of *Elements of Social Organization*, Firth wrote:

Social organization has usually been taken as a synonym for
social structure [*sic*]. In my view it is time to distinguish between
them. The more one thinks of the structure of a society in abstract terms, as of group relations or of ideal patterns, the more
necessary it is to think separately of social organization in terms of
concrete activity. Generally, the idea of organization is that of
people getting things done by planned action. This is a social
process, the arrangement of action in sequences in conformity
with selected social ends. These ends must have some elements
of common significance for the set of persons concerned in the
action . . . Social organization implies some degree of unification,
a putting together of diverse elements into common relation. To
do this, advantage may be taken of existing structural principles,
or variant procedures may be adopted. This involves the exercise
of choice, the making of decisions.[8]

Or – as he summed it up in a sentence – 'The fulfilment of
the moral obligations laid down by structural requirements
is conditioned by individual interests.'[9] It is not clear how
structural requirements can impose moral obligations, but
the gist is clear enough: social anthropologists must bring
back the individual interests which the structuralists had
ignored. With this major thesis went a (late Malinowskian)
concern with social and cultural change, though not with
history in Evans-Pritchard's sense. In 1957 Firth edited
an evaluation of Malinowski's work, *Man and Culture*,
'because some of us have thought for a long while that too
little attention has been paid to the work of Bronislaw
Malinowski'.[10] His whole effort was directed, in short, to
reintroducing the concerns of Malinowski which the
followers of Radcliffe-Brown had pushed aside.

While his professorial colleagues set out their reservations, or raised banners of revolt, Fortes continued to develop the central tenets of the original Oxford structuralists. In 1953 he published several statements of position, in which he defended the orthodoxy, stressed the role of 'social structure' as a central organizing concept, relegated the study of 'culture' and individual variation to a subsidiary position, and energetically attacked Evans-Pritchard's lapse from purism.

VI

Despite these sounds of conflict, the outstanding feature of British social anthropology to outsiders was its cohesiveness; and when faced with a challenge from outside the British drew together. It is worth considering one of the most influential of these challenges, Murdock's critique of 1951, for it dramatized the parameters within which all British social anthropologists operated in the fifties.

Murdock, a leading figure in American anthropology, published his attack in the *American Anthropologist*. It was sparked off by the symposium, *African Systems of Kinship and Marriage* (1950), and expressed a mixture of admiration and dissatisfaction which was widespread among American anthropologists at the time. He wrote that

the descriptive and analytical writing of the British social anthropologists attains an average level of ethnographic competence and theoretical suggestiveness probably unequalled by any comparable group elsewhere in the world. This explains and justifies the respect so widely accorded them. Offsetting these merits, however, are a number of special limitations which many professional colleagues abroad find difficult to understand and impossible to defend.[11]

He listed these limitations as their 'exclusive' concentration 'on kinship and subjects directly related thereto, e.g., marriage, property and government [*sic*]'; and their geographical concentration on British colonial dependencies, and, consequently, their lack of a broad ethnographic range. Further, they 'are as indifferent to the theoretical

167

as to the descriptive writings of their colleagues in other lands', and ignored their interests in history, culture change, and psychology. Murdock laid the blame unambiguously – 'These various limitations reflect the overwhelming influence of Radcliffe-Brown.' The consequence of all this, Murdock said, was that the British social anthropologists were not anthropologists at all. Ignoring the notion of 'culture', they had become sociologists, of a rather old-fashioned sort.

Stripped of its polemical trimmings, the description was reasonably accurate. Firth and Fortes both accepted it, more or less, but answered that given the limited resources of British social anthropology a limitation of ambition was reasonable. Or, to put it more positively, British social anthropologists had decided to concentrate on a limited set of issues, and their work had all the strength of these self-imposed limitations. Actually the dialogue was in a sense between social anthropologists and cultural anthropologists – between the course British social anthropology had followed under Radcliffe-Brown and that which had been charted by Frazer, or Tylor, or Boas. Murdock had failed to see that the success he granted British social anthropology in ethnography was intimately related to the theoretical assumptions which guided fieldwork. Conversely, the comparative poverty of American ethnography at the time reflected the muddled theoretical situation there. In a social science one cannot applaud the results and reject the framework which produces them.

In short, the British anthropologists felt no regrets in ignoring the culture and personality work so fashionable at the time in America, or the continued 'salvage' ethnological studies of American Indians, or the rather uncritical statistical cross-cultural studies of Murdock himself. They believed not only that they were bound to concentrate their energies, but, even more, that the results proved that they had chosen rightly in concentrating upon the structure of social relationships. Their post-war students were trained to follow suit, and they did.

VII

The monographs produced in the fifties by the post-war intake certainly had a great deal in common. Two issues predominated. First there was the study of politics more or less in the terms laid down by *African Political Systems*. The key problem was the political role of lineages in segmentary systems and in states, and virtually every monograph which appeared in this period tackled this question. The fine late Malinowskian studies of African states were admired but did not generate comparable theoretical interest. These were Nadel's *A Black Byzantium* (1942), the Kriges's *The Realm of a Rain-Queen* (1943), and Hilda Kuper's *An African Aristocracy* (1947). All of them were more or less centrally concerned with the organization of the ruling class in African states, and this was a problem – obviously central to any political understanding – which did not particularly interest those who derived their inspiration from the Oxford studies.

The orthodox studies followed on each other's heels throughout the fifties. In 1954 Barnes published an account of the Ngoni state, showing the way in which it had marched through southern Africa, segmenting and accreting in classical form. In the same year Leach published a radical analysis of Kachin political systems, but despite its great originality the central problem was defined in the same terms – the Kachin political communities embraced segmentary and state systems, and Leach concentrated upon the problem of how the one type was transformed into the other. In 1956 Fallers produced a monograph on the Soga of Uganda, in which he investigated the way in which the bureaucratization of the Soga state affected traditional political roles and the functions of clans and lineages. In the same year Southall published his analysis of another Ugandan society, the Alur, and made a great issue of the fact that they were neither a classical segmentary society, based on lineages, nor a centralized state, but something in between, a combination of the two classical types, which he described as a 'segmentary state'. Mitchell's *The Yao*

Village, which also appeared in 1956, investigated the way in which competition for authority in this centralized Malawian tribe occurred simultaneously within the matrilineages and the system of offices, the two arenas of competition being closely interlinked. Also in 1956, M. G. Smith's essay 'On segmentary lineage systems' attempted to raise the issues of the day to a more general level of significance, demonstrating that segmentation is a feature of all political action, although the fact that segmentation occurred in some systems on a lineage basis had significant consequences. In *Government in Zazzau* (1960), he produced the most sophisticated of the orthodox studies, but one of his central concerns was still the relationship between centralized administration and lineage-based competition and fission. In 1958 Middleton and Tait edited a new symposium on African political systems, *Tribes Without Rulers,* which was even more restricted than its prototype to problems of lineage organization. Its contributors were all members of the post-war cadre, and the book reflected the dominance that lineage theory exercised in the work they carried out.

There were two important differences between these studies and the monographs published by Evans-Pritchard and Fortes in the forties. The first was in the very general use of historical materials, a development which owed something to the influence of Evans-Pritchard. The second was a shift towards a concern with bureaucracy. This interest was suggested partly by the problems of 'states within states' in the late colonial period, but it was fostered also by the discovery of Weber, at least in the case of Fallers and M. G. Smith. But the theory of bureaucracy did not become of prime concern to the bulk of their contemporaries in the field, and indeed it was largely irrelevant to many of the uncentralized societies.

The second major concern of the period was with 'magico-religious' systems, to use what was already a rather dated term. This kind of study usually treated one of two main issues, both of which had been stated in monographic form by Evans-Pritchard. First there was the whole problem of witchcraft. The studies in the fifties took up Evans-

Pritchard's observation that witchcraft was a way of identifying a socially relevant cause of misfortune. They examined the way in which accusations of witchcraft and sorcery dramatized social tensions, and transformed them. This analysis often appeared as a subsidiary theme in the monographs of the period – for example in Mitchell's study of the Yao, or Turner's *Schism and Continuity in an African Society*. It was often integrated with a conventional study of a segmentary lineage system, witchcraft accusations being seen as an aspect of the process of lineage fission. Marwick's study of the Cewa was an analysis of the stresses of the lineage system seen through the prism of sorcery accusations. In due course this field of studies generated its own symposium, Middleton and Winter's *Witchcraft and Sorcery in East Africa* (1963).

The other problem was a larger one, the study of religious systems proper, which had been neglected by Malinowski and his students. The key texts here were Radcliffe-Brown's essay on 'Religion and Society' (1945), and Evans-Pritchard's essays on Nuer religion, pulled together in a monograph in 1956. Radcliffe-Brown's position was essentially determinist – ancestor-worship, for example, was to be understood as a functional requisite of certain kinds of lineage system. Evans-Pritchard accepted the fact that religions are conditioned by their social environment, but as in his study of Zande witchcraft he was more concerned to explore the logical interrelations of their cosmological notions. Both these positions had their adherents, but the difference between them was really only one of emphasis. Middleton's *Lugbara Religion* (1960) treated ancestor-worship in a Ugandan tribe in much the same way as some of his contemporaries treated witchcraft – as a function of lineage structure, and, in action, as a reflection of the processes of lineage segmentation. Lienhardt's *Divinity and Experience: The Religion of the Dinka* (1961), was rather more similar to Evans-Pritchard's *Nuer Religion* – and the two tribes were neighbours in the Sudan.

Gluckman's analyses of rituals of conflict surrounding the office of kingship in African states were congruent with

171

the studies treating witchcraft and ancestor-worship as modes of conducting and adjusting tense social relationships. Here once again Evans-Pritchard had provided the paradigmatic analysis, in his essay 'The Divine Kingship of the Shilluk' (1948).

The Malinowskian preoccupation with myth was not much in evidence in this period, except in terms of the evaluation of historical evidence. An exception was Leach's neo-Malinowskian analysis of the political functions of myth in *Political Systems of Highland Burma* (1954), although his analysis was also influenced by the work of the lineage theorists on the manipulation of genealogies. The revolution in the analysis of myth which Lévi-Strauss was to bring about was in no way foreshadowed in the work being done in Britain in this period.

Perhaps unexpectedly, the study of kinship was relatively neglected after the publication in 1950 of *African Systems of Kinship and Marriage*. Contrary to Murdock's view of the position, political organization was the primary interest, and problems of kinship theory were investigated mainly in relation to descent theory. There was, for instance, a flow of studies emerging from Fortes's essay 'Time and Social Structure' (1949). These were concerned with the developmental cycle of the domestic group, but in terms of the constraints imposed by the politico-jural system, paradigmatically concerned the lineage. This sort of analysis featured as a minor theme of many monographs, and was the centrepiece of the first volume in a new series of papers in social anthropology which the Cambridge department began to publish in 1958. Another issue which commanded attention was raised by Gluckman in *African Systems of Kinship and Marriage*, where he argued that the divorce rate is a function of the lineage structure. The classical, purely kinship topics were neglected – kinship terminology, marriage rules, incest and exogamy, interpersonal roles of kinship. They came into prominence again only at the end of the decade, when the debate between Leach and Fortes directed attention to the theories of Lévi-Strauss, and when Firth, Freeman and Leach raised the problem of non-unilineal kinship systems, and the question of the role of choice in the formation of kinship groups.

Of course there were other problems being written about and studied in this period. The C.S.S.R.C. commissioned reports on land tenure, budgets, and other economic matters, and some colonial governments requested studies of labour migration. Some of these studies had an impact on contemporaries – perhaps most notably the demonstrations by Schapera and Watson that labour migration was not necessarily disruptive of the social structure. But in general the economic reports were of restricted interest, and there was little development in economic anthropological theory. Firth alone made this a central preoccupation, and a few students influenced by him tried to apply economic theory in exotic circumstances. However, it was not until the sixties that economics, and ecology, began to re-emerge as issues of primary importance, as Malinowski had seen them to be.

Law was another field which concerned colonial governments, and a number of studies in legal anthropology or 'social control' appeared in this period. Some, like the work of Goody and Bohannan, were really aspects of the study of segmentary lineage systems. Others, particularly the work of Gluckman and Schapera, were more concerned with problems of jurisprudence. Once again, however, law was not a field which attracted great interest in its own right.

If Murdock was broadly correct in picking out the limited range of interests of contemporary British social anthropologists, however wrongly he specified them, he was certainly correct to remark upon the geographical limitations of their work. The fifties continued this trend. To a certain extent it was a function of departmental specialization, and of connections set up by 'old boys' with institutes and universities in the colonies. The Oxford anthropologists continued to travel to the Sudan, though some also explored the Middle East and Catholic Europe. Cambridge set up a strong link with the East African Institute of Social Research, under the directorship of Richards and, later, Southall and Stenning, but a number of Fortes's students continued to work in Ghana, while Leach directed his own students to South-East Asia. Manchester continued its close association with the Rhodes-Livingstone Institute, and its students overwhelmingly worked in Central Africa. The London professors also tended to send their students to the areas which they had opened up – Forde's students went to Nigeria, and Firth's to Malaya and Oceania. Elsewhere, the Australian departments naturally concentrated on the aborigines, but in the fifties they moved into the new ethnographic region of highland New Guinea. In South Africa studies were done increasingly in the British High Commission territories, as the political situation in the Union deteriorated.

I shall be coming shortly to consider the cross-currents of the fifties and early sixties, but it is remarkable how consistent and how sharply focused on a small range of issues modern British social anthropology was in the fifties. This was a function of the small size of the profession and the overwhelming power of the professoriate. The rapid expansion of the early post-war years gave a new impetus to the discipline, but it did not displace the theoretical dominance of the point of view which had been established at Oxford in the years immediately before the war.

SIX

Leach and Gluckman –
Beyond Orthodoxy

Law and order arise out of the very processes which they
govern. But they are not rigid, nor due to any inertia or
permanent mould. They obtain on the contrary as the
result of a constant struggle not merely of human passions
against the law, but of legal principles with one another.
– Malinowski[1]

I

The last chapter was concerned primarily with the mainstream, the developments within the orthodoxies established
by Radcliffe-Brown and Malinowski. Throughout the fifties
and sixties there were eddies and currents which moved
against the main flow, and in this chapter I shall discuss the
two leading mavericks, E. R. Leach and Max Gluckman.
Although both published their first important essays in
1940, they came into their own in the nineteen-fifties.

There may be some resistance to considering Leach and
Gluckman in one breath. Leach has described Gluckman as
'my most vigorous opponent in matters theoretical',[2] and
represented him as one of the least repentent adherents of
the kind of organic equilibrium theory which Leach himself
rejected. Furthermore, despite his recent apostasy, Leach is
often thought of primarily as the English prophet of Lévi-
Strauss, as Radcliffe-Brown was of Durkheim, while Gluckman has never shown any interest in the preoccupations of
the neo-structuralists. Yet it is probably more accurate to
see Leach's Lévi-Straussian period as a secondary development, which never really jelled with his major work. As he
recently said:

I myself was once a pupil of Malinowski and I am, at heart,
still a 'functionalist' even though I recognise the limitations of
Malinowski's own brand of theory. Although I have occasionally

175

used the 'structuralist' methods of Lévi-Strauss to illuminate particular features of particular cultural systems the gap between my general position and that of Lévi-Strauss is very wide.[3]

In the next chapter I shall deal with the impact of Lévi-Strauss's work on British anthropologists; and Leach will figure prominently there. Here my concern is with the broadly political topics which are the subjects of Leach's monographs. It is in this field that the convergences, and divergences, with Gluckman are of interest.

Leach and Gluckman only just belong to the senior age-grade of British anthropologists. Leach was born in 1910, Gluckman in 1911. Both came into anthropology in Britain in the mid-thirties, after the majority of the first generation had completed their doctoral training, and at a time when Malinowski's influence was giving way to that of Radcliffe-Brown. Both men attended Malinowski's seminars in this period, but Gluckman was commuting from Oxford, where he was formally under the supervision of Marett, while Leach was a student at the L.S.E. Gluckman later came under the influence of the new structuralism in Oxford, being particularly impressed by the early work of Evans-Pritchard. Leach was never greatly influenced by either Radcliffe-Brown or Evans-Pritchard, and after Malinowski's departure he was closest to Firth at the L.S.E.

They were the brilliant new recruits of the two main schools. Both set out to develop the insights of their masters in novel ways. But although Leach remained recognizably a Malinowskian in much of his writing, and Gluckman was always an Oxford structuralist at bottom, there was a real convergence of interest. Both were drawn to problems of conflict of norms and the manipulation of rules, and both used an historical perspective and the extended-case method to investigate these problems. (By a sad coincidence, they also both lost the field-notes of their most important studies during the war!) Their students took up similar problems, if one excepts those of Leach's students who pursued the interests of Lévi-Strauss. Barth, Barnes and Bailey – three of the liveliest anthropologists of the fifties and sixties –

demonstrated in their work the ultimate convergence of Leach and Gluckman.

A fuller and more nuanced comparison might well wait until the work of these two scholars has been reviewed in detail. At this stage it is sufficient to note that Leach and Gluckman, the figures intermediate between the pioneer generation and the post-war generation, were primarily concerned with advancing the range and sharpening the bite of the theories which had been established in the thirties. Following their work new options were realized, and, at last, their contributions can be seen to have supported each other. If one had to sum up in a sentence the message both propagated it was this – that the central dynamic of social systems is provided by political activity, by men competing with each other to enhance their means and status, within the framework set by often conflicting or ambiguous rules.

The reader should also know that both are 'charismatic' figures, large men, emphatic, committed, outspoken. Both have attracted strong personal loyalties, but, intolerant and even overbearing at times, they have also alienated some colleagues.

II

Gluckman was born in Johannesburg, of Russian-Jewish parents. He first studied social anthropology at the University of the Witwatersrand under Mrs Hoernlé. She was a successful teacher. A number of her pupils went on to become professional anthropologists, and Gluckman's class included Ellen Hellman, Hilda Beemer (Kuper), and Eileen Jensen (Krige). Gluckman has suggested that Winifred Hoernlé developed his interest in conflict theory, but there is nothing in her work, or in that of her other students, to suggest this. She was a follower of Radcliffe-Brown, and Gluckman's generous tributes to her may be read as in part an attempt to individuate his genealogy with reference to a maternal ancestress. However, Mrs Hoernlé did instil in her students the values of scholarship, which were not strongly represented in South African universities. As a group these students also saw their commitment to anthropology partly in political terms. At a time when their British-based contemporaries tended to avert their eyes from the realities of power and deprivation in the colonial societies, they never forgot the context of the systems which they investigated.

In 1934 Gluckman went to Oxford as a Rhodes scholar, taking his D.Phil. in 1936. He did fieldwork in Zululand between 1936 and 1938. In 1940 his first major essays appeared: a chapter on the Zulu in *African Political Systems*, and the first part of the brief monograph, *Analysis of a Social Situation in Modern Zululand*. In these papers he dealt with the kind of segmentary opposition which was the great focus of Oxford theory, but he introduced also a concern with other forms of opposition and conflict, which were to preoccupy him more in the years to follow.

In his contribution to *African Political Systems* Gluckman described two stages of pre-colonial Zulu society, and argued:

The essence of both the systems described is the opposition of like groups and the potentially conflicting loyalties of the people to different authorities. The nation was a stable organization, for this opposition was principally between the tribes which were united in the king's position and his regiments . . . In actual administration, the loyalties of the people and the competition of officers did not often conflict, since the administrative machinery worked through the heads of groups of different type: the main opposition was between similar groups, co-operating as parts of a larger group.

This type of segmentary opposition produced coherence and equilibrium. The conflicts which occurred were even positively functional – like the Nuer feud. However, Gluckman went on to contrast these stable systems with the situation he found in the field:

Today the system is not stable, for not only is Zulu life being constantly affected and changed by many factors, but also the different authorities stand for entirely different, even contradictory, values . . . The modern political organization of Zululand is the opposition between the two colour-groups represented by certain authorities . . . The opposition between the two groups is not well-balanced, for ultimately it is dominated by the superior force of Government . . . The threat of this force is necessary to make the system work, because Zulu values and interests are so opposed to those of the Europeans that the Zulu do not recognize a strong moral relationship between themselves and Government, such as existed, and exists, between themselves and their king and chiefs. They usually regard Government as being out to exploit them, regardless of their interests.[4]

This was the only realistic piece of political analysis, which dealt with the context of racial domination, to be found in the whole of *African Political Systems*.

The *Analysis of a Social Situation in Modern Zululand* went further in showing how the plural political society formed by colonial or settler domination must provide the framework for the understanding of local 'tribal' systems. Using a novel form of presentation, Gluckman described in great detail the scene at the opening of a new bridge in Zululand – the comings and goings, the speeches and comments, the taking of tea – always drawing attention to the social allegiances of the actors, from the white magistrate and his entourage, to the chief and his followers, even to the anthropologist himself. Gluckman's point was that although the members of the different colour groups were symbolically and actually divided and opposed at every point, yet they were forced to interact in spheres of common interest. He concluded:

To sum up the situation at the bridge, one may say that the groups and individuals present behave as they do because the bridge, which is the centre of their interests, associates them in a common celebration. As a result of their common interest they act by customs of co-operation and communication, even though the two colour-groups are divided according to the pattern of the social structure. Similarly, within each colour-group, feasting unites the members though they separate according to social relationships within the group.[5]

This did not mean that the situation was stable; on the contrary, despite the cross-cutting ties which existed contemporary Zululand represented the type of social system in which conflicts could not be properly resolved without radical structural changes. This type of system was contrasted

179

with the pre-colonial Zulu societies where, despite changes, often radical enough, there were long periods of comparative stability when the conflicts generated by the system could be absorbed by it. Gluckman argued that the social anthropologist should study these periods of comparative stability, when the social system approached a state of equilibrium.

The essence of Gluckman's position, as it developed, was that social equilibrium is not a simple affair, resulting from the neat integration of groups or norms. On the contrary, it emerges through the balancing of oppositions in a dialectical process. As he and Colson once wrote, social groups have 'an inherent tendency to segment and then to become bound together by cross-cutting alliances . . . conflicts in one set of relationships are absorbed and redressed in the countervailing relations'.[6] Equally, the norms governing social life are often critically ambiguous, or even conflicting. For example, the rules of succession to a chieftaincy are often so phrased that there will inevitably be several 'rightful' claimants who will compete for the office. But since it is in the interests of all the claimants to unite in boosting the central value of the office, the very competition generated by the rules will strengthen the consensus about the value of the office. In ritual, too, Gluckman saw conflict and not merely some sort of transcendent unity being expressed; but in the expression of its conflicts the society was temporarily purged. He came to see ritual, that is,

not simply as expressing cohesion and impressing the value of society and its social sentiments on people, as in Durkheim's and Radcliffe-Brown's theories, but as exaggerating real conflicts of social rules and affirming that there was unity despite these conflicts.[7]

This sort of theory, focusing on the achievement of equilibrium through the contained expression of conflict, is familiar to sociologists in the work of the German scholar Simmel (1858–1917). Gluckman has, however, stated that he developed his views in ignorance of Simmel's work, and there is no reason to doubt this. Even Weber was virtually unknown to British anthropologists until after the Second World War. One may also detect in some of Gluckman's work the influence of Freud's notion of ambivalence, and he was certainly familiar with Freudian throught, and sympathetic to it. There is an even more direct appeal to Bateson's analysis of schismogenesis. Nevertheless the immediate inspiration was closer at hand, in the work of the Oxford structuralists.

Radcliffe-Brown had expressed his 'principle of opposition', and Evans-Pritchard had developed the idea in his analysis of segmentation and feuding among the Nuer. Evans-Pritchard went even further in his analysis of Anuak politics, and in his outstanding essay, 'The Divine Kingship of the Shilluk', published in 1948. There he wrote, in terms Gluckman was to use also,

Shilluk rebellions have not been made against the kingship. On the contrary, they were made to preserve the values embodied in the kingship which were being weakened, or it was believed so, by the individual who held office. They were not revolutions but rebellions against the king in the name of the kingship.[8]

In their attempts to rewrite history, and to detach him from his British sources, some of Evans-Pritchard's followers have also tried to disown much of the work which derived from his major analyses, and particularly Gluckman's work. Pocock, for example, has argued that Radcliffe-Brown and Gluckman confused two meanings of the notion of 'opposition' – antagonism, and structural juxtaposition. In discussing Evans-Pritchard, Pocock (and Dumont) tried to bring him into line with the modern French structuralists, for whom 'opposition' is a process which occurs at the level of the classification of groups rather than at the level of the confrontation of two bodies of people. Thus Pocock argued that Gluckman vulgarized Evans-Pritchard's model, and imposed upon it a distorting functionalist emphasis.[9]

This is not the place to argue whether Gluckman's development of Evans-Pritchard's ideas was legitimate or not, and in any case it is not a question of importance. It is clear enough that the line of development he followed differed from that followed by the majority of Evans-Pritchard's post-war students, but then after the war Evans-Pritchard's own views altered fairly drastically. My point is simply that Gluckman's theories were one possible development of the orthodoxy he imbibed at Oxford from Radcliffe-Brown and Evans-Pritchard.

The most vulnerable feature of Gluckman's theory, as it evolved, was the concentration upon what he had identified as repetitive as opposed to changing social systems. This sometimes led him to ludicrous extremes, and he later modified his position. Discussing the views he advanced in the forties and fifties he wrote, in 1963, 'I was still thinking in crude functional terms of institutions – even civil war, which after all can be an institution – contributing to the maintenance of a rather rigidly conceived social structure.'[10] This emphasis, he explained, grew out of his study of white-ruled Zululand, 'which, despite its many unresolved and irresoluble conflicts, "worked" ', thus forcing him to consider 'how social systems could contain the deep conflicts which are present in all of them'.[11]

III

Gluckman's essays on the Zulu set out the sociological ideas which he carried over to Central Africa when he joined Godfrey Wilson at the Rhodes-Livingstone Institute, in 1939. He became acting Director in 1941 and served as Director from 1942 to 1947. This was a period of intense activity at the Institute, and Gluckman's ideas were taken up by the fellows who now came to do fieldwork. Although Gluckman's views represented a shift of emphasis rather than a total divergence from the position of the pre-war Oxford structuralists, their adoption had significant consequences. The fieldworkers who were influenced by Gluckman came to conceive of social reality in a way which differed markedly from the more conventional views of the students of Evans-Pritchard and Fortes, and consequently the work of the Rhodes-Livingstone fellows in Central Africa is distinctive, and stands in sharp contrast to much of the work of the Oxford and Cambridge anthropologists in East and West Africa.

The characteristic features of the Rhodes-Livingstone studies in Gluckman's days should emerge in the following pages. A few points might be noted at the outset, however. Gluckman's concern with the total context of the plural society was of vital importance. Outlining the research plans of the Institute in 1945, Gluckman stressed his interest in the total social structure of the region, including whites and Indians. He wrote:

I must emphasize that I do not view the social processes at work as entirely disintegrative . . . My whole formulation of the problem depends on recognizing that there is a Central African Society of heterogeneous culture-groups of Europeans and Africans, with a defined social structure and norms of behaviour, though it has many conflicts and maladjustments.[12]

Following from this, it was necessary to study urban as well as rural areas, and to see African workers in the towns not simply as displaced peasants but as workers, operating within an industrial, urban social system. This ambitious programme contrasted sharply with the research plan which the International African Institute had published a decade earlier. While the promised studies of white and Asian communities unfortunately never materialized, the settlers and administrators are present in the Rhodes-Livingstone studies in a way distinctly unusual in the anthropological reports of the period.

One of the problems which this orientation raised concerned the role of the village headmen, the N.C.O.s of district administration, caught between the demands of the alien authorities and those of their own people. This was a situation in which the inherent conflicts of colonial administration were dramatically evident, and it was one Gluckman had explored in his Zulu studies. Most of the Rhodes-Livingstone fellows tackled it at one time or another.

Gluckman's detailed analysis of a single 'social situation' in Zululand had indicated a dissatisfaction with conventional modes of presenting illustrative ethnographic material. It represented a reaction against the selectivity of the Malinowskian technique of 'apt illustration'. Mitchell used the 'social situation' approach in *The Kalela Dance*, but other fellows searched for alternatives. Their experiments came to fruition in Turner's use of 'social dramas', later termed 'extended-case studies', a technique particularly well suited to the study of processes of conflict and conflict resolution. The members of the Institute also used statistical methods more successfully and conscientiously than did most of their contemporaries, and Barnes and Mitchell made advances in the refinement of statistical methods to meet the exigencies of anthropological research. Finally, Gluckman's example of the use of historical data to identify stages of comparative stability and equilibrium which could be analysed and compared to the contemporary situation also inspired imitation and development, particularly in the hands of Barnes.

Thus Gluckman brought to the study of Central African societies not only his theories of the role of conflict in the social process, but also an insistence that the total political situation should be taken into account, and an openness to methodological innovation. He passed on his ideas at the Institute through close and constant interchanges at seminars, and visits in the field, and also in his review articles and contributions to the Institute's journal.

His own major research in this period, however, was at a tangent to the work he inspired. This was his study of Lozi law. He had some legal training, and his main interest was in the principles of jurisprudence used by the Barotse, and in their convergence with the principles of European law. This work was scholarly and influential in the development of legal anthropological theory, but except in some of Epstein's work in the Copperbelt it did not have much effect on the studies of the Rhodes-Livingstone fellows.

IV

In 1947 Gluckman left the Rhodes-Livingstone Institute to take up a teaching appointment at Oxford, and after a couple of years he moved again, to open a department of anthropology at Manchester University. But throughout he maintained close connections with the Institute, now under

the control of his associates, first Elizabeth Colson, and later
Mitchell. A number of the fellows of the Institute were
later associated with the Manchester department, some
closely and for many years, and even those who were not
remained committed for a considerable period to the tenets
of the 'Manchester school'. Perhaps the best known of these
fellows were Barnes, Cunnison, Epstein, Marwick, Turner,
Van Velsen and Watson. Others who worked in Central
Africa were drawn into the circle – the administrator C. M. N.
White and the agronomist Allan were two of the more
sympathetic.

The studies they published exhibit a remarkable degree of
uniformity. With the occasional exception of Cunnison,
their work is almost always readily identifiable as 'Manchester' in theme and inspiration. Perhaps this is because
they represent a special case in the formation of anthropological schools. Most develop in a university, through the
intellectual domination of the professor. This emerged in the
field, and in conditions of greater camaraderie and equality,
with all the members engaged in similar, demanding
inquiries. Certainly the cohesion which developed was
unusual – though not, of course, without the undercurrent
of conflict.

Virtually all the monographs on Central African rural
societies which members of the school produced concentrated
upon village structure, and analysed the processes of
conflict and conflict-resolution inherent in the structure of
the community. They also examined the position of the
headman as an 'inter-calary' figure in the local administration, studied witchcraft and ritual as channels for the
expression, and resolution, of social conflicts, and experimented with statistical and extended-case material. Each of
the monographs had its particular focus – village fission
for Turner, vertical political integration for Mitchell on the
Yao, labour migration for Watson, sorcery accusations for
Marwick, and so forth. Yet each can be read as a particular
projection of the fundamental model they all shared, and
which they took from Gluckman.

Less work was done in the tense urban areas, but

Epstein and Mitchell produced studies of the Copperbelt and Watson contributed his analysis of labour migration seen from the rural end. Here too the characteristic preoccupations of the school were evident. The analyses brought out the situationally defined structural oppositions, overridden at times by shared interests, which had been analysed in the rural communities.

Turner's study of the Ndembu, *Schism and Continuity in an African Society* (1957), was the most satisfying of these studies, and I shall briefly describe it as a good example of the work that was produced. Turner began with a problem which Malinowski had raised and which Richards had analysed some years earlier for the matrilineal societies of Central Africa. This was, how do matrilineal societies reconcile the conflicting interests of men as members of a matrilineage, brothers, husbands and brothers-in-law? The Ndembu village is built around a core of male matrilineal kin. They normally bring their wives to live at their homes, and their sisters move away to live with their husbands. But every man is succeeded by a sister's son, who must therefore be brought in at some stage to the core community of matrilineally-related men. The ambitious men try to build up their communities, and to this end they try to keep their own children at home as well as recovering their sisters' children. The resulting conflict between the pulls of family and matrilineage was a basic problem for the Ndembu – 'Thus both marriages and villages are inherently unstable and in-laws struggle continually for control over women and their children.'[13] In this situation the only solidary unit was the matricentric family, the group formed by children of one mother. It was this unit which was pulled between the competing father and mother's brother.

There were other structurally-generated conflicts as well, between men and women, with their different economic roles and different functions within the matrilineages; and between the men of the core matrilineal community itself, competing for authority and property within the village. Turner analysed the resulting pattern of relationships both in broad terms, by a statistical survey of the composition of a number of villages; and in depth, by analysing the conflicts within one village.

Turner used what he called 'social dramas' to present his analysis of the way in which these conflicts worked themselves out in the village. He argued that overt conflicts brought out the underlying strains of the social system; they therefore dramatized the inherent stresses within the structure. By dealing with a series of confrontations involving the same actors one could look at the way conflicts developed and were resolved, and also test the fundamental analysis. The result was a new kind of monograph, with a long story of quarrels, tensions and resolutions running through it. Barnes has compared this sort of study to a Russian novel, in its diversity of actors and complexity of motives – not to mention its proliferation of impossible names.

The theoretical analysis was cast in Gluckman's mould; for example:

> People live together because they are matrilineally related, but just because they are matrilineally related they come into conflict over office and over the inheritance of property. Since the dogma of kinship asserts that matrilineal kin participate in one another's existence, and since the norms of kinship state that matrilineal kin must at all times help one another, open physical violence between them seldom takes place. Their struggles are phrased in the idiom of sorcery/witchcraft and animistic beliefs . . . Conflict is endemic in the social structure but a set of mechanisms exist whereby conflict itself is pressed into the service of affirming group unity.[14]

Turner himself freely acknowledged his debt to Gluckman, and like many of the works of the school, the book carried an approving introduction by Gluckman. Turner's analysis also referred back directly to the work of the Oxford structuralists, and particularly to Fortes's Tallensi study, in his analysis of lineage fission and the operation of ties of kinship outside the lineage.

Although it is fair to say that Turner's analysis was not theoretically innovative (as his studies of Ndembu ritual were to be), the quality of the case material and the care with which it was presented and analysed put the monograph in a class of its own. The reader was given a fresh look at the cut and thrust of interpersonal relationships in an exotic social context. He got to know the protagonists, saw them acting out their roles, appreciated the conflicts which faced them, and came away with an understanding of Ndembu village life which carried a conviction that was never so fully achieved by the disorderly books of Malinowski, or the excessively orderly books of the structuralists. Because the focus was upon the individuals – in their prescribed roles – the path from this sort of study was to lead to network analysis, game theory, and other modes of conceptualizing the strategies of everyday life. The Rhodes-Livingstone fellows were beginning to move away from the structuralists and towards what has been called 'methodological individualism'; but this was not yet apparent in the fifties.

v

In the urban studies of Epstein and Mitchell the central structural opposition was, of course, between whites and blacks, as it had been in Zululand. The Copperbelt towns were organized around the mines. They were divided into white municipality and African township, and the Africans were separately administered by government officials. The Africans were drawn from several countries and over seventy tribes, and they were in turn divided in two ways – by tribal origin, and by occupation, or urban prestige.

The whites, drawing upon their experience of rural administration, reinforced by their stereotype of the African, believed that Africans should be governed on a 'tribal' basis, even in the towns. Urban administration should operate through 'tribal elders' of some kind. But although Africans were fairly willing, in general, to consult these 'elders' on some matters, they did not accept their leadership in the industrial context. The 'elders' were accused of selling-out to the whites, and when the workers rioted on the Copperbelt in 1935, the 'tribal elders' who had been elected had to seek refuge with the whites, in the same way as the hated black policemen.

The fact was that in some contexts occupational ties overrode tribal loyalties. But the structure of employment generated its own tensions. The whites occupied the highest positions of power and prestige, and they set the standards for individual aspiration. The educated, westernized Africans held the highest-paid 'white-collar' jobs below the colour line. This group naturally provided much of the African leadership, but their style of life separated them from their fellows, and their position of comparative privilege put them in a dilemma when the lower-grade workers went on strike. Therefore although they built up the trade unions which took over the leadership of the Africans after the 'elders' had been ditched, they were in turn displaced from the leadership in favour of more militant if less educated underground workers.

This situation was further complicated by other factors. First, there was considerable overlap between tribal origin and 'class' position. Some 'tribes' were disproportionately represented in certain occupations, and certain groups were particularly favoured by educational advantages in their home areas. This served to confuse the lines of division in some situations, in others to reinforce them. Secondly, the meaning of 'tribal' identification was very different in the town and in the rural areas. In the towns it did not connote acceptance of whole series of ascribed positions of authority, but rather served as a primary mode of grouping people into possible friends and probable foes. Finally, Epstein and Mitchell demonstrated that the form of identification which was selected varied in different situations in urban life. Sometimes a man would side with, say, Bemba against non-Bemba; at other times with clerks against underground workers; and then again line up with fellow-Africans against the white mine authority or the government.

Many of the subsidiary themes developed by Epstein and Mitchell were simple transformations of the themes they and their colleagues had investigated in the rural areas of

Central Africa. But the conflicting norms and competing interests of the rural society became alternative types of action and utterly opposed racial blocks in the towns. This led them to concentrate particularly upon the situational selection of allegiances and hence of modes of behaviour, choices generated by the organization of 'class' and 'tribe', and, ultimately, by the overarching structure imposed by the dominant white group.

One cannot readily separate the development of Gluckman's ideas and the work he inspired at the Rhodes-Livingstone Institute. They fused in the productions of the 'Manchester School', which in the fifties became a recognizable mutation of British structuralism. At the same period Leach was working alone, from a different starting-point, but my argument is that his development converged with 'Manchester' to a degree that can be appreciated only now, in retrospect.

VI

Leach is one of the few British anthropologists of the pre-war vintage with a 'conventional' upper-middle-class background. After an appropriate schooling he went to Cambridge where he read for a degree in engineering. He then spent some years in the East, in China, before abandoning his first career and entering the L.S.E., in the mid-thirties, as a student of Malinowski. In 1938 he spent a few weeks doing fieldwork among the Kurds, but although he had envisaged a return the war found him engaged in a more ambitious field-study of the Kachin in Burma. The war was spent in irregular military units, often with Kachin. He lost his field notes, but eventually, after the war, prepared a thesis based largely upon published materials. He became a Reader at the L.S.E. under Firth, where he was for some time regarded as an expert on material culture. In 1953 he went to Cambridge as lecturer, and a few years later did a further field-study, in Ceylon. Although his old college, Clare, refused him a fellowship on the grounds of his militant atheism, he was elected to a fellowship at King's, and later became Provost. In 1972 he was belatedly awarded a professorship by personal title.

Leach's first monograph, *Social and Economic Organisation of the Rowanduz Kurds*, appeared in 1940. This was a tentative piece of work, based on only five weeks in the field, and it was rather neglected at the time. After all, the same year saw the appearance of Evans-Pritchard's political studies of the Nuer and the Anuak, and of *African Political Systems* (which contained, with much else, Gluckman's first essay on the Zulu). Yet it was a suggestive little book, and set out many of the ideas Leach went on to develop in later years. The book also provides a solid link between the neo-Malinowskian position which Firth was setting out and the explorations with which Leach was later to dazzle his colleagues.

Leach's central observation was that the Kurds were passing through a period of rapid change, as a consequence of external administrative interference. He pointed to 'powerful and perhaps irresistible forces at work tending not so much to the modification as to the total destruction and disintegration of existing forms of tribal organization'.[15] This was a state of affairs which presented a problem to the functionalist, whose basic premise was that the system he was studying was well-integrated and in equilibrium. Gluckman had recognized the dynamism of social systems, but had posited the existence of periods of comparative calm and equilibrium of forces which could be studied in more or less conventional terms. Leach rejected this. All societies maintain only a precarious balance at any time, and are really in 'a constant state of flux and potential change'. The norms which exist are neither stable nor inflexible. 'There can never be absolute conformity to the cultural norm, indeed the norm itself exists only as a stress of conflicting interests and divergent attitudes.' This is where one may identify the source of the dynamism. 'The mechanism of culture change is to be found in the reaction of individuals to their differential economic and political interests.'[16]

This being the case, Leach argued,

191

in order to make the description intelligible at all, some degree of idealisation seems essential. In the main therefore I shall seek to describe Kurdish society as if it were a functioning whole and then show up existing circumstances as variations from this idealised norm.[17]

Analysis must therefore operate at two levels. First the anthropologist builds up a model of how the society might be expected to work *if* it were in equilibrium, if it were well-integrated. But this is an idealization of limited value. To get back to the historical reality one must look at the interplay of personal interests, which can only temporarily form a balance, and which must in due course alter the system.

The emphasis on change, and on the creative force of individual demands, and the view of 'norms' as unstable ideals based upon temporary configurations of interests, all went back to the late Malinowskian position. What Leach added was his use of a model, an ideal type, abstracted for limited heuristic purposes. Gluckman had seized upon the part played by competing interests and conflicting norms which were present, but secondary in Radcliffe-Brownian structuralism. Leach brought a highly-sophisticated structural approach to the aid of Malinowskian analysis, which was too much obsessed with the vagaries of 'calculating man'.

After the war Leach wrote his doctoral thesis on Kachin society, and in 1954 published perhaps his most outstanding book, *Political Systems of Highland Burma*. This grew out of the thesis, and the comparatively crude arguments of 1940 re-emerged in a more mature and elaborate form. The communities of highland Burma, roughly classified as Kachin and Shan, form a bewildering variety of linguistic, cultural and political units. Leach argued that the notion of a bounded 'tribe' was of no use in understanding the situation. The whole set of interacting communities had to be seen as comprising in some sense a single social system. But it was not a system in equilibrium. As he had argued in 1940, so now he insisted that equilibrium could be assumed only for purposes of analysis at a certain level. One had to remain aware of the fictional nature of this assumption, and recognize that 'the reality situation is in most cases full of inconsistencies; and it is precisely these inconsistencies which can provide us with an understanding of the processes of social change.'[18]

If the anthropologist needed an ideal pattern to provide an orientation, so did the people themselves. In their case this was set out in ritual, which from time to time expressed symbolically 'the system of socially approved "proper" relations between individuals and groups'; rituals 'momentarily make explicit what is otherwise a fiction'.[19] Ritual expression – broadly understood as an aspect of all behaviour – and the cultural symbols through which it worked did not correspond, however, to normative rules of behaviour. They were too ambiguous, and evoked too spasmodically. Indeed the ambiguity of ritual and symbol, the levels of uncertainty inherent in ritual and cultural communication, were necessary. They permitted the actors a range of legitimate choices.

The structural analysis of the anthropologists and the rituals of the people are therefore both idealized abstractions, attempts to impose an *as if*, fictional but comprehensible order upon the flux of social life. Beneath these attempts at formalization lies the reality of individuals in pursuit of power. In this continual competition the actors make a series of choices which collectively may alter the structure of their society.

There were three basic types of political system in the Kachin Hills area – the egalitarian, almost anarchic system of the *gumlao* Kachin; the unstable, intermediate *gumsa* form, a sort of mini-state; and the Shan state. These were ideal types, but useful to the people and the anthropologist in classifying real communities. Communities swung from one type to another, and the *gumsa* communities were particularly unstable. Leach examined in depth the categories used by the people to describe these systems, and showed that they were represented in terms of the same set of symbols, in different combinations. When a community swung from one type to another, as a result of political activity, the people might then weight the value of the various symbols differently, while still in a sense speaking the same ritual language.

The difference between these systems is reminiscent of the classical anthropological opposition between kin-based societies and states. This was the basis of Fortes and Evans-Pritchard's opposition between states and stateless societies organized by a segmentary lineage system. Leach's conception was related to theirs, as he said, but his analysis was particularly concerned with the mechanisms by which one 'type' of system was transformed into another.

The Kachin lineages differ from the normal African pattern in that they are ranked relative to each other. Their rank is fixed by a system of marriage alliances. One cannot give a wife to a lineage from whom one takes a wife, and vice versa. This permits an ideal ranking of lineages, with wife-givers superior to wife-takers who are their vassals. This combination of lineage and rank is at the root of the instability of the *gumsa* system. As Leach summarized the position:

The *gumsa* ideal order consists of a network of related lineages, but it is also a network of ranked lineages. As the process of lineage fission proceeds there comes a point at which choice has to be made between the primacy of the principle of rank or the principle of kinship. Rank implies an asymmetrical relationship ... Kinship implies a symmetrical relationship ... The weakness of the *gumsa* system is that the successful chief is tempted to repudiate links of kinship with his followers and to treat them as if they were bond slaves. It is this situation which, from a *gumlao* point of view, is held to justify revolt.[20]

There is an equivalent structural defect at the heart of the *gumlao* system. Leach wrote that

a *gumlao* community, unless it happens to be centred around a fixed territorial centre such as a patch of irrigated rice terraces, usually lacks the means to hold its component lineages together in a status of equality. It will then either disintegrate altogether through fission, or else status differences between lineage groups will bring the system back into the *gumsa* pattern.[21]

194

In both cases the dynamic for change is provided by individuals competing for power. The dissatisfied man with some inherited status might decide to seek office in a hierarchical system or to repudiate hierarchy; to be a rebel against the incumbent chief, or a revolutionary against the *gumsa* system. The influential figure in a *gumlao* system may choose to repudiate democracy and swing his community towards a *gumsa* structure. Each system carries within itself the seeds of its contrary, and communities swing between the *gumlao* and *gumsa* extremes.

When Leach came to demonstrate his thesis that the Kachin Hills communities exemplified something like Pareto's succession of lions and foxes, he was faced with serious difficulties. He used two methods. First he presented a detailed analysis of one small and unstable *gumsa* community as it was in 1940, concluding that

Hpalang in 1940, in my view, was probably in process of changing from a *gumsa* to a *gumlao* type of organisation. It was restrained from completing the change over only by the arbitrary dictates of the paramount power whose officers objected to the *gumlao* system as a matter of principle.[22]

This was by no means conclusive. His second test was historical, but the historical sources were unsatisfactory. They provided a clue to the forces making for instability and change – in myths the *gumlao* leader is presented as 'a minor aristocrat of ambition and ability who might himself have been a chief if the accident of birth order had not dictated otherwise. The myth is a description of the real man.'[23] But so far as his thesis as a whole was concerned, Leach could show only 'that there is nothing in the history of the area which conflicts with my interpretation'.[24]

Yet it is difficult to see how this thesis could have been disproved by historical materials. In a preface to the 1964 reprint of the monograph Leach remarked that 'my own attempt to find systemic ordering in historical events depends upon the changing evaluation of verbal categories and is, in the final analysis, illusory.'[25] For what changes when a community swings from *gumlao* to *gumsa*? Discussing his community of Hpalang, he had remarked that

> while the kinship composition of the community had remained more or less unaltered over the past 40 years, there had been radical changes in the internal authority structure. The leaders of the community still used *gumsa* categories to describe the respective status of groups and persons; they attached importance to the notion of aristocracy, the title of chief, and to the rights of chiefs . . . But all this was largely pretence. Had the community been organised on *gumlao* principles with no aristocrats, no chiefs and no tributary dues, the de facto situation would have been almost the same. This is an illustration of the fact that the contrast between *gumsa* and *gumlao* is a difference of ideal order rather than empirical fact.[26]

This suggests the central problem which the book raises. If there is such a difference between 'ideal order' and 'empirical fact' – presumably, a difference comparable to that between ideology and action – with which level is Leach concerned? Or is he engaged in an attempt to analyse the complex and dynamic interaction of these two levels? Presumably the latter, and the book can be read in this way. But the uncertainty is there, and it is significant. Leach's subsequent writings swung between the extremes of an idealist view of social structure and a perception of social structure as a sort of map of power relations on the ground. He generally maintained that political relationships were in some way primary, but the distance between his later neo-structuralist essays and, say, *Pul Eliya*, is at first blush very striking.

If there is a higher unity in his work it lies in the Malinowskian premise that the people's model is a sort of screen behind which the actual competitive relations of community life are worked out. But since the people's model is expressed in inexact and symbolic terms, they can manipulate alternatives with an easy conscience, and resolve apparent contradictions at the ideological level. The anthropologist's model is also, necessarily, at several removes from the empirical facts. It is an equilibrium *as if* model, differing from the sort of model used by the people themselves only in the precision of its categories. But this necessary precision freezes the model, and it cannot accommodate change. To understand the actual flux of social relations the anthropologist must consider the anomalies and contradictions, and see how ambitious individuals are manipulating political resources.

Political Systems of Highland Burma was, then, a difficult monograph but daring and experimental, particularly in its model of cyclical change. Nonetheless it lacked the aggressively revolutionary tone of Leach's next book, *Pul Eliya*, which appeared in 1961. This was an explicit frontal attack on those he called 'Oxford structuralists', represented (in Leach's summary) by Radcliffe-Brown, Fortes, and Evans-Pritchard.

Leach defined social anthropology as the study of the way in which 'custom' constrained individual behaviour. He identified three approaches to this issue, all deriving ultimately from Durkheim. First there was the Oxford model, which was used to analyse society as an assemblage of roles, the occupants of the roles being under moral and jural constraints to fulfil them. The second approach, deriving from the Durkheim of *Suicide*, took the statistical norm as the basic datum. This was the Malinowskian position — 'Custom is what men do, normal men, average men.'[27] Both these approaches were deficient, but in different ways. The first did not begin to cope with individual variation, while the second evaded the problem of how the norm established itself and was institutionalized.

Leach derived the third approach rather more shakily from Durkheim's notion of collective representations:

Here the thesis is that 'the sacred' and the 'profane' are distinct categories of verbal and non-verbal behaviour and that the former is, as it were, a 'model' for the latter. In some developments of this argument, ritual is looked upon as providing an 'outline plan' in terms of which individuals orientate their day-to-day behaviour. The divergencies of individual behaviour from any standard norm are not then the result of moral error or of unenlightened self-interest, but arise simply because different

197

individuals, quite legitimately, fill in the details of the ideal schema in different ways.[28]

This was basically the line Leach had taken in *Political Systems of Highland Burma*, while stressing that 'ritual' was an aspect of everyday behaviour, not something restricted to 'sacred' contexts. In *Pul Eliya* the set of symbols which the people use to orientate their lives are based on kinship. But now he went further, and looked for an objective basis for the orientation. In the Kachin study this was provided by power relations; in the Singhalese village of Pul Eliya the basic constraints were even more down-to-earth. The lay-out of the village fields and the irrigation arrangements, which could not easily be changed, presented a set of objective constraints in terms of which the villagers had to adapt their behaviour. For purposes of analysis, 'custom' is still the statistical norm, while the ideal norm becomes the gloss upon it, but the ecology provides the ultimate determinant.

The thesis was sharpened by taking 'kinship' as the central issue. Kinship theory was dominated by Fortes at this time, and Fortes operated in terms of an equilibrium model of the kinship system, which was perceived in jural terms – as a system of rules, rights and duties pertaining to particular kinship roles. The emphasis on descent theory had added a vital rider: the continuity of the social system may be maintained by the perpetuation of corporate lineage groups, that is, enduring assemblages of rights and duties focused on a particular 'estate'.

To this Leach opposed the view that at least this one village in the dry zone of Ceylon was ordered above all by material factors. It was 'locality rather than descent which forms the basis of corporate groupings'.[29] Indeed,

> The group itself need have no rules; it may be simply a collec-
> tion of individuals who derive their livelihood from a piece of
> territory laid out in a particular way. The continuing entity is
> *not* Pul Eliya *society* but Pul Eliya itself – the village tank, the
> *gamgoda* area, the Old Field . . .[30]

Kinship was an epiphenomenon of property relations, an

elastic and fairly ambiguous idiom in which people talked about property relations. The 'kinship system' did not constrain behaviour: it was a mode of describing choices which were constrained rather by material factors.

The argument was demonstrated by way of the extended-case method which had been developed by the Manchester school (though Leach seemed to imply that this was all his own invention). The detailed land-tenure records of the village, which had been preserved for decades, allowed him to examine specific manipulative operations and their consequences over time. His conclusion was always that the kinship rules were bent or reinterpreted to permit the villagers to make the adaptive, economic choices. For example, discussing the *variga* ('sub-caste'), he wrote:

Ideally the cardinal rule is that land should never be allowed to pass outside the *variga*. Sales and gifts of land should only be between members of the same *variga*. If these rules were always maintained *variga* heirs would necessarily be within the *variga*. ... in the past, the operations of the *variga* court were such as to ensure that all tolerated spouses of *variga* members were themselves treated as *variga* members whatever their actual origin. Thus by a legal fiction the rule of *variga* endogamy was maintained and inherited land necessarily stayed within the *variga*.[31]

Compare the argument with that of the Burma monograph. There the actors made choices in terms of a power model of the community, and tried to maximize power. The cultural symbols defined gross alternatives, and permitted the actors to make a traditional sort of sense out of whatever real structure emerged. In Pul Eliya the actors' choices were constrained by the actual lay-out of the agricultural resources, and they attempted to maximize wealth. (In both societies, one might argue, the ultimate goal was the improvement of social status. Power and wealth may be converted into each other.) The cultural symbols in Pul Eliya, and specifically 'kinship', provided the idiom within which choices could be talked about and, ultimately, legitimized.

In *Pul Eliya* the 'ritual' dimension was granted less

autonomy than in the Kachin study. This was in keeping with the polemical tone of Leach's attack on Oxford 'idealism', but it served to weaken the interpretation. As Fortes was able to show in his counter-attack, Leach's own data indicated the ways in which the kinship categories and rules in themselves served to constrain choices.[32] Nonetheless the argument was consistent, both internally and with regard to Leach's own earlier works. The basic argument remained the same, a development of Malinowski's position. The 'reality' of the social situation is the statistical pattern created by individuals maximizing satisfactions. The 'ideal' norms are no more than a rough and ready mode of conceptualizing or orientating action, and their utility depends upon their ambiguity.

I have so far concerned myself with only one aspect of Leach's writing. Particularly in his essays, he was often more concerned with the 'ritual' dimension itself. This concern led to his prolonged flirtation with Lévi-Strauss's structuralist methods, at first sight so foreign to his basic approach. Leach had defined the issue as early as 1945, in his essay on 'Jinghpaw Kinship Terminology', and the terms he used then were echoed in *Pul Eliya*, sixteen years later. He wrote:

In my own field work, I have found the determination of sociological norms extremely difficult . . . The field worker has three distinct 'levels' of behaviour pattern to consider. The first is the actual behaviour of individuals. The average of all such individual behaviour patterns constitutes the second, which may fairly be described as 'the norm'. But there is a third pattern, the native's own description of himself and his society, which constitutes 'the ideal'. Because the field worker's time is short and he must rely upon a limited number of informants, he is always tempted to identify the second of these patterns with the third. Clearly the norm is strongly influenced by the ideal, but I question whether the two are ever precisely coincident. In the study of kinship this is an important distinction, because any structural analysis of a kinship system is necessarily a discussion of ideal behaviour, not of normal behaviour.

But while the ideal statements did not simply reflect the

actual norms, they could usefully be treated as an internally consistent system. Therefore, one could for example, show that Jinghpaw kinship terminology

which is superficially extremely complex, would appear simple and consistent to a man living in an ideal society, organized according to certain very simple rules. These rules constitute the ideal pattern of Jinghpaw society, to which the actual society is now, and probably always has been, a somewhat remote approximation.[33]

In his essay on Jinghpaw kinship terminology Leach made up his own methods for the analysis of the system. When he later adopted Lévi-Strauss's methods this was because he saw them as a superior means of analysing ideal systems. With very few lapses he remained what he called a functionalist, since, in contrast to Lévi-Strauss, he never believed that the structure of the ideal system was congruent with the structure of the statistical pattern which emerged as the sum of individual choices in a dynamic social and ecological context.

But this is still only part of the story. Leach has also consistently been a hammer of orthodoxy, ready to challenge any received ideas. He urged his colleagues to rethink their basic category assumptions, to dare to reconsider familiar facts, and to abandon their established procedures. In 1959, delivering the first Malinowski memorial lecture, which he provocatively entitled 'Rethinking Anthropology', Leach challenged his audience to think mathematically about society. They should abandon their obsession with typologies – this was just an anthropological version of butterfly-collecting. They should drop comparison in favour of generalization. This could be achieved *'By thinking of the organizational ideas that are present in any society as constituting a mathematical pattern'*;[34] in other words, by building real models. In the course of his lecture he characteristically singled out three living anthropologists as exemplars of folly. They were Fortes, Goody and Richards, his three senior Cambridge colleagues! For at least a decade he brandished Lévi-Strauss's reputation as a weapon in these polemics, arguing that his colleagues were being parochial, smug and backward in ignoring the significance of the French scholar's work.

One might suggest a sociological correlate of Leach's iconoclasm. He was, like Gluckman, a figure intermediate between the generation of Malinowski's first students and the post-war generation. He was also the most prominent senior anthropologist in Britain never to become a professorial head of department (no doubt from choice). He has himself pointed out that his eminently gentle social background was rather unusual among the social anthropologists of his time. He was, then, structurally something of an outsider, though an outsider who could very smoothly become Provost of King's College, Cambridge. He clearly relished this position, and his self-confidence permeates his polemics and allows, perhaps, his bold departures from the easy and conventional route.

VII

Have I exaggerated the parallels between the work of Leach and the Manchester school? To some extent the similarities, such as they are, must have been the product of working at the same time in the same professional environment; and the dissimilarities are certainly striking enough. Yet at the heart of all their work there was a shared concern with the ways in which social systems somehow recognizably persist despite their inherent contradictions, and despite the fact that individuals are always pursuing their self-interest. Leach always tended, like Malinowski, to stress the individual's manipulation of the rules, while Gluckman, like the Oxford structuralists, placed greater emphasis upon the coercive force of rules and values, yet each edged away from the position he inherited and perhaps unwittingly moved closer to the other. It is certainly interesting that where Leach studied 'ritual' aspects of social relations, Gluckman preferred to emphasize 'legal' aspects, but the convergence was there. Perhaps it was simply that this area of tension between man's interests and the values propagated by the 'society' was obviously the area to investigate after the massive, dichotomous statements of Radcliffe-Brown and Malinowski had been assimilated.

Turner was perhaps the most creative of the Central Africa/Manchester group which formed around Gluckman. In the sixties he developed his analysis of Ndembu ritual, which he saw in the way Leach saw ritual, as a language for communicating statements about structural relationships, but a language infinitely suggestive and ambiguous; a language fitted to the transformation of social conflict. Barth, one of Leach's most original students, developed another theme, directing attention to individual strategies and the manipulation of values, and elaborating 'transactional' models of social relationships. Gluckman's student Bailey – another intermediate figure, since he worked in India, the terrain of Leach and the neo-structuralists – developed a different thread of Manchester theory until it converged with Barth. These and other convergences between some of the students of Gluckman and Leach suggest that the parallels I have drawn between their work are not merely surface coincidences.

Leach, Gluckman and their students were among the dominant forces in British social anthropology in the late fifties and the sixties. Together (though not in partnership) they formulated the basis of a new synthesis from the thesis of Malinowski and the antithesis of Radcliffe-Brown.

But this is to ignore the Pandora's box Leach opened with his advocacy of the methods of Lévi-Strauss. That is the subject of the following chapter.

SEVEN

Lévi-Strauss and British neo-structuralism

> In anthropology as in linguistics . . . , it is not comparison
> that supports generalization, but the other way around. If,
> as we believe to be the case, the unconscious activity of the
> mind consists in imposing forms upon content, and if these
> forms are fundamentally the same for all minds – ancient
> and modern, primitive and civilized (as the study of the
> symbolic function, expressed in language, so strikingly
> indicates) – it is necessary and sufficient to grasp the un-
> conscious structure underlying each institution and each
> custom, in order to obtain a principle of interpretation
> valid for other institutions and other customs, provided of
> course that the analysis is carried far enough.
>
> – Lévi-Strauss[1]

I

The three levels of social reality which Malinowski identified
demand different strategies of social inquiry. People are
observed to pursue their interests competitively and in
alliances; they tell one another what to do, and they explain
to the ethnographer how things should be done; and they
think – as Lévi-Strauss says – socio-logically, in terms of the
categories and images presented by their cultures.

The Malinowskian obsession with 'what really happens'
survived the Oxford structuralist movement and continued
as a central thread in British social anthropology. The
Oxford school of the forties was primarily concerned with
the rules of the game, the explicit code of social behaviour.
But the interest in how people think, in what used to be
called psychological problems, in the logic of belief and myth,
so central in the work of the British pre-functionalists, had
been virtually absent from British social anthropology for a
generation. As Murdock had noted, this was the price of
the sociological orientation which had been chosen, and the
consequent neglect of the tradition of Tylor and the 'culture

concept'. The most recent monograph of importance which could be directly related to that tradition was Evans-Prit-chard's classic, *Witchcraft, Oracles and Magic among the Azande* (1937). Lévi-Strauss reintroduced this range of concerns to British social anthropology. He revived an appropriate theoretical tradition, stemming from the later Durkheim and from Mauss; and he drew also on the work of the American cultural anthropologists, with whom he had worked in New York immediately after the Second World War.

British anthropology had always drawn its facts from the Empire, but its theories traditionally came from France. Radcliffe-Brown had transplanted the theories of Durkheim, although it can be argued that Durkheim's ideas had suffered a certain impoverishment in their journey across the channel. Radcliffe-Brown created a rather British Durkheim, a no-nonsense, down-to-earth sort of chap with a sound theory about how social groups in 'primitive societies' cohered through the dramatic recreation of appropriate sentiments and the enforcement of norms. Religion and perhaps all aspects of cosmology were ultimately epipheno-mena of group structure.

Lévi-Strauss's Durkheim (of whom he was, he said, rather wistfully, 'an inconstant disciple') and even more his Mauss were very different figures, though there was, of course, a certain family resemblance to the British Durkheim. Perhaps this made the intrusion of the disturbing new Gallic figure a little easier.

The tradition of the *Année* school which Lévi-Strauss developed was concerned with 'primitive classification' and 'primitive logic'. It was this, with Mauss's theory of exchange, which provided Lévi-Strauss's initial impetus. (The connection between these two theories may emerge later.) He married these strains with others which he picked up during his American exile in the forties – the structural linguistics of Jakobson and the Prague school, and the Boasian tradition of cultural anthropology which he learnt from Lowie.

My purpose here is to examine Lévi-Strauss's impact upon

British social anthropology, not to present a rounded picture of his total contribution. His influence in Britain was at its height around 1960, though it had begun to grow in the fifties, some time between the partition of India and the independence of Ghana. The time was ripe. Not only was there a certain boredom with conventional theory, but the Empire was falling apart – and with it, some felt, the traditional laboratory of the discipline. Many were ready to shift their interest from norms and action to symbolic systems; and they were prepared to make the necessary shift in theoretical orientation.

The leaders of the new British 'structuralism', as it emerged, were Leach, Needham, and, later, Mary Douglas. Their success in converting some of the brightest students of the period was facilitated by the almost religious enthusiasm of some of the proponents of Lévi-Strauss's ideas. 'Structuralism' came to have something of the momentum of a millennial movement, and some of its adherents felt that they formed a secret society of the seeing in a world of the blind. Conversion was not just a matter of accepting a new paradigm. It was, almost, a question of salvation.

I remember attending Lévi-Strauss's Huxley Memorial Lecture in London in 1965. The general public in Britain was then becoming aware of structuralism, the post-Sartre influence from Paris, and the hall was packed. Lévi-Strauss delivered a brilliant but highly esoteric lecture on the future of kinship studies to a rapt audience. Leach was called upon to give the vote of thanks, and he prefaced it by remarking that he had no idea why so many people had attended the lecture, since only he himself and a handful of others could possibly have understood it. In the same vein, he introduced a collection of papers by British social anthropologists, dealing with Lévi-Strauss's theories of totemism and myth, with the comment that some of the contributors did not appear even to have read Lévi-Strauss, and that their criticism depended 'either on English arrogance or straight misinformation'.[2]

Lévi-Strauss's first major work, *The Elementary Structures of Kinship*, appeared in French in 1949. Its reverberations

206

continued to be felt in British social anthropology until, ironically, the English translation appeared in 1969. In the early sixties Lévi-Strauss published his two volumes dealing broadly with what he termed *la pensée sauvage* (untamed thought – wild pansies?). Finally, in the mid-sixties he published the first of his series of volumes on South American myths, the fourth and final volume, *L'Homme nu*, appearing in 1971. The absorption and development of Lévi-Strauss's stimulating and contentious theories of kinship engaged the attention of a number of talented anthropologists in Britain, as elsewhere, throughout the fifties and early sixties. His analyses of structures of thought also set a number of new studies in train, though it has been argued that in this field Evans-Pritchard's work was equally germinal. So far as the study of myth is concerned – that classic field, which still attracts the first interest of the amateur – Lévi-Strauss's work has had little perceptible influence in Britain. Perhaps it will be absorbed slowly. In any case, Leach is the only British anthropologist who has so far made a creative effort to develop Lévi-Strauss's mytho-logic.

II

Durkheim provided Lévi-Strauss with a model of society built up of like or unlike segments, which must be integrated to create mechanical or organic solidarity. From Mauss he learned that this solidarity may be best achieved by setting up a structure of reciprocity; a system of exchanges binding the segments in alliances. Exchanges may involve one of three media: goods and services, language and symbols, and the super-gift, women. Underlying any system of exchange is the rule of reciprocity, the rule that every gift demands a return. The return may be direct, in which case one has a system of restricted exchange; or it may be indirect, in which case one has a system of generalized exchange.

Lévi-Strauss argued that the principle of reciprocity was the key to understanding kinship systems, for a kinship system was a mode of organizing the exchange of women in marriage.

The precondition of such a system was a rule banning incest. Once men are forbidden to enjoy their own women but must exchange them for others, they are forced to set up a system of exchanges which provides the basis for the organization of society. In this sense, the incest taboo is the beginning of culture.

The bulk of *The Elementary Structures of Kinship* was concerned with what Lévi-Strauss saw as the obverse of the incest taboo, that is, the rules specifying which women a man *should* marry. In some societies one may marry any women not barred by the incest taboo, but in others the category of possible wives is precisely specified. A man *must* marry a woman who falls into a particular kinship category – for example, a 'mother's brother's daughter' – or a women who belongs to a specific class from which one's group takes its wives. Societies with such a 'positive marriage rule' (to use Dumont's phrase) have what Lévi-Strauss called *simple* kinship systems. Societies which have only prohibitions but no positive marriage rule have *complex* kinship systems. Some very simple societies, like the Bushmen, have complex kinship systems in this sense, and Lévi-Strauss insisted that he was not making a crude evolutionary antithesis. (Nevertheless, in its implicit reference to Durkheim's *Elementary Forms of the Religious Life*, in the use of the Australian aborigines as the crucial case-study, and in other ways too, Lévi-Strauss's sophisticated structuralist machine moved easily enough in the old evolutionist tracks.)

If a positive marriage rule exists, it can take one of two main forms, corresponding to the distinction between generalized and restricted forms of exchange. In a system of generalized exchange, A gives his sister to B as a wife. B gives his sister to C, and so on until at some stage (to be rather formal and simplistic) someone along the chain gives a woman to A, so closing the circle. This is a supple, highly efficient form of integration through exchange, since any number of groups may be included in the circle, and new groups can always be slotted in without disturbing the arrangement. Now, this form of marriage exchange may be conceived of as being equivalent to a system in which men marry their mothers' brothers' daughters. If every man were to do so, a system of generalized exchange would result; and societies which practise such a positive system of marriage tend to describe it in terms of a rule specifying marriage with a mother's brother's daughter. In formal terms, however, the only rule which is necessary for such a system to develop is that no man can give a woman to a group from which men of his group take wives, and vice versa.

Restricted exchange, by contrast, is a transaction involving two groups only, and it is symmetrical. A gives a woman to B, B gives a woman to A. Such a system of 'sister-exchange' is typical of societies divided into exogamous moieties, but it can occur without them, and it may be conceived of as marriage with the 'double cross-cousin', that is, marriage with a woman who is both one's mother's brother's daughter and one's father's sister's daughter.

Poised uneasily between these two major forms of exchange, Lévi-Strauss identified a bastard form, involving delayed reciprocity. A gives a wife to B, and in the next generation B returns a wife to A or to his son. This may be represented as a form of father's sister's daughter marriage. Later commentators sometimes argued that such a form of marriage rule could not work, unless there was another rule sharply dividing the generations into separate classes. Otherwise this type of system would collapse into a system of direct, symmetrical exchange.

Lévi-Strauss identified different problems. The trouble with delayed reciprocal exchange was that it bound together only two groups, and thus was less efficient in establishing relationships of solidarity throughout a social system. But generalized exchange had its dangers too: it was essentially speculative, since A gives a woman to B on the assumption that he will get a wife in return from C, or D, or E – *or from all of them!* This meant that some groups might become rich in wives to the exclusion of others, and in his analysis of the Kachin – Leach's own tribe – Lévi-Strauss suggested that this was the sad pass to which they had come. The egalitarian assumptions of generalized exchange had been eroded by its aristocratic consequences. If *Political Systems of Highland Burma* had appeared, he might have suggested that this was responsible for the swing from a *gumlao* to a *gumsa* structure (and it is clear that Leach took some hints from this analysis). Another, related, problem with a system of generalized exchange was that those who felt their return in doubt might abandon this method in favour of the less integrative but more secure direct exchange.

There are thus three types of marriage exchange, and each may be represented in genealogical terms as a mode of cross-cousin marriage. Even in the stark and simplified terms in which I have described the model, some questions might suggest themselves. Is this the way in which the actors conceptualize the system, or formulate the rules? Or is it the observer's model? Do the people follow the rules? And what are the units which are making these exchanges of women? A good deal of the publications which Lévi-Strauss's monograph stimulated are engaged with such questions as these, and with examining what he really meant. In the later editions of *The Elementary Structures*, and in his Huxley lecture, Lévi-Strauss returned to some of these questions, and, incidentally, repudiated the interpretations of Leach and Needham.

I shall not attempt to unravel the extremely complex and technical debates on these issues, but shall rather concentrate upon the larger question – what was the aim of Lévi-Strauss's long, brilliant and often baffling exploration of Australia, the Far East and India in pursuit of simple marriage systems? In particular, to return to the Malinowskian question, was he concerned with what people say or with what they do?

Despite the assertions of some of his commentators, Lévi-Strauss did not believe that he was dealing only with sets of linguistic categories and their interrelations in his theory of kinship. He was convinced that his theory applied also to the actual marriage choices which could be collected in the field and analysed statistically. This was not because the actual pattern of choices was directly constrained by the rules. Rather, both the rules and the statistical pattern were more or less independent refractions of the single underlying, unconscious grammar of opposition and reciprocity. Given this assumption, one could get at the basic grammar either through an analysis of the people's model, or through an analysis of the statistical distribution of marriage choices. But the actual marriage choices are also influenced by extraneous political, economic and demographic factors, which have to be abstracted out before the underlying pattern becomes clear. It is therefore easier to tackle the model of the people.

These assumptions have a further consequence. If the rules and the choices are independent expressions of the basic grammar, then it is possible that a pattern of choices might be discovered in the absence of explicit rules. This permits Lévi-Strauss to suggest how his analysis of simple kinship systems may be used to illuminate complex kinship systems, in which there are no marriage prescriptions. One must assume that as any marriage system is based on reciprocity it will reflect one of the formulae of exchange; and since we would be concerned here with a complex and diffuse pattern of exchanges it would be a system of generalized exchange. One might find, for example, that in a large sample of French marriages the tendency to marry distant kin on the mother's side is greater than would be expected if the pattern were random. If so, the objective rate of certain marriage choices

of which members of the society may remain unaware, expresses certain structural properties of the system which I assume to be isomorphic with those which are directly known to us in societies showing the same 'preference' more systematically, that is, in prescriptive form.

This would be 'sufficient to place the society in question in the same group as a theoretical society in which everyone would marry according to rule, and of which the former can best be understood as an approximation'.[3]

Although Lévi-Strauss feels he can identify the major structural features in statistical patterns of actual marriage choices, he is more concerned to get 'behind' the flux of real behaviour to the unconscious generating structure. This is the level he believes one must penetrate if one is to understand how misleading the surface appearances are, but it is also just one stage of the enterprise. Beyond the unconscious models lies the human mind, and the final goal is to uncover the universal principles of human mentality. Kinship systems were above all a way to approach this goal, as languages were to be for Chomsky.

Lévi-Strauss later came to believe that the study of kinship may not be the royal road to the understanding of human mental universals. But before going into that problem, let us consider the impact of his theory of kinship on British social anthropologists.

III

Needham developed what he considered to be an orthodox interpretation of the 'alliance' theory of kinship, as Lévi-Strauss's theory came to be known. His persistent search for simple systems, and his mastery of the literature resulted in a series of ingenious interpretations of various systems of 'prescriptive alliance'. However, Needham insisted upon a dichotomy of 'prescriptive' and 'preferential' systems, on the basis that the theory applied only to systems in which there was a prescriptive marriage rule, and not to those in which there was merely a statistical tendency for marriages to occur more frequently between particular categories of kin. This was to limit the range of application of the theory, for the properly prescriptive systems admittedly embraced only a tiny proportion of all known systems. Indeed, as Needham's analyses proceeded, this proportion showed a marked tendency to shrink. Needham also showed a rather literal faith in the ideal model, and assumed that it corresponded to some actual societies in a direct fashion. When the ethnography was at variance with his assumptions, he either turfed the society in question out of the sacred range of prescriptive systems, or questioned the validity of the observations. As David Schneider, one of his most persistent critics, pointed out, not without justice:

Needham expects to find, free in nature, a concrete system which precisely replicates his type. If the type has characteristics X, Y, and Z in that order, then Needham expects to find that the Purum or the Lamet have characteristics X, Y and Z in that order. Needham works with this type as if it were a kind of

212

LÉVI-STRAUSS AND BRITISH NEO-STRUCTURALISM

'missing link', a real entity which a really good ethnographer who is a good hunter will be able to find – on Sumba perhaps, or among the Old Kuki. Once it is found we will *see* '. . . how the system really works' (Needham).[4]

After a decade of polemical publications from Needham, Lévi-Strauss repudiated his interpretation, on grounds similar to those which Schneider had adumbrated. Lévi-Strauss insisted that the 'model' was in the minds of the native and the anthropologist. Empirical realities would always diverge from it. The dichotomy between so-called prescriptive and preferential systems was unnecessary. All systems were prescriptive at the level of the rules and preferential at the level of actual choices. Therefore the model had wider relevance than Needham allowed it, for it should apply even to those societies which did not have positive marriage rules.

The other development of the theory was quite happily heterodox. This was the work of Leach and some of his students, particularly Yalman. They took over Lévi-Strauss's view of society as a system of 'communication'. Women were 'exchanged' as a sort of message between groups, and these exchanges were linked up with other forms of communication, particularly the communication of goods and symbols of status. The central issue was not what was communicated, or who made the communication, but rather the structure of the system of communication as a whole.

Leach departed from Lévi-Strauss in arguing that the forms of exchange in society, particularly the system of marriage choices, were adapted to political and economic circumstances. If wife-givers were systematically of higher status than wife-takers (or vice versa), this would correlate with differences in the political and economic status of the groups concerned. This emphasis reflected Leach's primary interest, which was not in psychological universals, but in particular social systems. Where Lévi-Strauss was interested in Man and Society, Leach preferred to investigate men in specific societies. The model of marriage exchanges must therefore be used to illuminate a total social situation, not purged of non-kinship elements in order to provide clues to human mental universals. Leach also anchored the model

213

more firmly to the ground. What were the units, so vaguely specified by Lévi-Strauss, which exchanged women? In a curious implicit reference to Radcliffe-Brown's Australian studies, Leach suggested that they were universally local groups of adult males recruited by descent.

IV

It was in this form that 'alliance theory' clashed directly with the orthodox British 'descent theory'. Particularly in the hands of Fortes, this had become a highly refined system, but like alliance theory it derived ultimately from a widespread actors' model, and like alliance theory again, it was processed in a Durkheimian mould. The peoples' models (in many parts of Africa at any rate) posit the existence of perpetual corporations, recruited and internally organized on the basis of unilineal descent. These groups are political and legal units. How do they cohere in societies? Mauss's solution, in terms of exchange and reciprocity, was neglected in favour of Durkheim's notion of mechanical solidarity. Integration emerged from the opposition of like segments, balancing each other, at every level of structure. This was the point of view that had dominated *The Nuer*. Fortes stressed that another mechanism was also at work, but at the level of domestic, interpersonal relationships. This was the web of kinship relationships that cross-cut descent groupings. Even in societies which made a great deal of use of the principle of unilineal descent, kinship is reckoned bilaterally. The integrative principle is thus 'complementary filiation' – the use of relationships traced through the mother in a patrilineal system or through the father in a matrilineal system.

To this the alliance theorists opposed the idea of kinship systems providing solidarity through a series of exchanges of women. What was the crucial factor – alliance and affinity, or the distribution of rights in persons and in things, and so descent? This question preoccupied Leach and Fortes in a series of widely-read polemical exchanges in *Man* in the late fifties. Leach argued that Fortes 'while recognizing that ties of affinity have comparable importance to ties of descent, disguises the former under his expression "complementary filiation" '.[5] Fortes countered:

> Leach thinks that it is the relationship of marriage and its concomitant relationships of affinity that form the 'crucial' link between corporate descent groups in the Kachin-type systems. I would put it the other way round and say that marriage and affinity are *the media through which* structurally prior politico-jural alliances and associations are expressed and affirmed, and I would contend that they are effective as such media because they give rise to matrilateral kinship bonds. This is an argument from first principles, not from the data presented by Leach.[6]

Some critics suggested that the differences between Fortes and Leach arose from their concern with different ethnographic regions. Descent theory may work in much of Africa; alliance theory seemed to fit in many South-East Asian societies.

Leach pursued the controversy with characteristic vigour, but his attitude to alliance theory was essentially pragmatic. It helped to explain various systems, and in particular it illuminated his Kachin material. But his commitment to alliance theory did not prevent him from experimenting with the optative models of non-unilineal kinship systems developed by Firth and Murdock; and at a very early stage of the game he was raising the fundamental problems of definition which Needham was belatedly to revive after his repudiation by Lévi-Strauss. Thus when Leach was denied by Lévi-Strauss in his turn, he could quite happily counter with an attack on Lévi-Strauss's methods, even comparing him to that archetype of folly, Frazer.

But more serious and consistent attempts were made by others to use Lévi-Strauss's methods in the interpretation of field-data. Dumont in India and Yalman in Ceylon both showed the power of the theory with reference to rich ethnographic material.

v

Lévi-Strauss never abandoned the theory of kinship he had published in 1949, though he implicitly accepted criticisms of some particular formulations and analyses. But in the sixties he moved towards a more direct concern with systems of thought. As he later remarked, in the 'Overture' to *Le Cru et le Cuit* (1964),

> In *The Elementary Structures* we had disentangled a small number of simple principles from the apparently superficial contingency and incoherent diversity of the rules of marriage. Because of those principles a very complex ensemble of usages and customs was drawn together into a meaningful system, though at first they seemed absurd and had generally been so judged. There was nothing meanwhile to guarantee that these constraints were of internal origin. It was quite possible that they only reflected, within the minds of men, certain demands of social life which had been objectivized in institutions. Their reverberations on the psychic level would then have been the effect of mechanisms whose mode of operation alone remained to be discovered.

So kinship was too embedded in social action to provide a sure guide to mental processes. The next step had to be to look for a purer expression of social thought. This was mythology, where 'the mind, freed for conversation with itself and rescued from the obligation of dealing with objects, finds itself reduced in some way to imitating itself as an object'.[7]

But in between the two major projects, on kinship systems and on myths, Lévi-Strauss paused, as he has said, to consider for a moment what had been achieved and what remained to be attempted. In this brief period of assessment he published his two comparatively short volumes on systems of classification – *Totemism*, and *La Pensée Sauvage*, both of which appeared in 1962. In these he examined the way in which man orders his social and natural environment through verbal categories, building up a 'logic of the concrete' using the homely elements of his everyday life. These were the most Durkheimian of his books, and provided the most straightforward entry to his world for those British social anthropologists who had absorbed the theories of the *Année* school. The structuralist method was exhibited in operation but free of unfamiliar assumptions about marriage or tendentious summaries of selected myths.

In these two monographs Lévi-Strauss argued that the most general mode of human thought is analogical rather than logical. This was true of all non-scientific or mathematical thought, and not only of 'primitive mentality'. Man imposes a pattern on his world by classifying the objects in the natural and social environment. The boundaries of these categories are arbitrary. He may, for example, group living creatures into flying things v. earth-bound things, or mammals v. non-mammals, or meat-eating v. vegetarian species, etc. The categories may be formed on the basis of any set of superficial resemblances or oppositions. But if the terms are arbitrary, the relationships between them have a more universal character. The terms of the systems are grouped as pairs of oppositions, and these pairs are then related to each other to form a system of oppositions. For example, in an imaginary society people may oppose men and women, the sky and the earth, flying things and earth-bound things, right hand and left hand ... and then use these terms in a dialectical fashion, so that male things, 'up' rather than 'down', right hands, are all connected and opposed as a set to female things, 'down', and left hands. In this way the oppositions provide the elements of a system which can be used to 'think about' other kinds of relationships, such as the relationships between social groups.

In this imaginary society, let us say, the people are grouped into 'clans'. Each 'clan' may then have a particular natural species as a totem, so that the relationships which the culture has asserted between the species it has defined become a way of thinking about the relationships between the social groups.

The basic notion is that man thinks through making a series of basic oppositions, each with a concrete reference, and then relating these oppositions. This approach, Lévi-Strauss always says, came to him through the work of Jakobson and the Prague school of structural linguistics. It is also related to the approaches used in cybernetics. However, it is a method with a long history in the social sciences and philosophy, and we have seen that Radcliffe-Brown used a similar approach in his second major paper on totemism. Commenting on that paper Lévi-Strauss wrote:

217

The ideas of opposition and correlation, and that of a pair of opposites, have a long history; but it is structural linguistics and subsequently structural anthropology which rehabilitated them in the vocabulary of the humane sciences. It is striking to meet them, with all their implications, in the writings of Radcliffe-Brown, who, as we have seen, was led by them to abandon his earlier positions, which were still stamped with the mark of naturalism and empiricism.

The naturalist error was one from which he felt Radcliffe-Brown never completely freed himself, however, for Radcliffe-Brown always tended to assume that the associations and oppositions which people seized upon were somehow presented to them by their environment. Lévi-Strauss insisted that on the contrary, 'it is this logic of oppositions and correlations, exclusions and inclusions, compatibilities and incompatibilities, which explains the laws of association, not the reverse.'[8] Nevertheless, the basic method was one which the British structuralists operating in the tradition of the pre-war Oxford school could accept fairly easily. And using this method Lévi-Strauss was able to elaborate the most daring hypotheses.

An illustration is appropriate, and I shall summarize the argument of a lecture he delivered in England in 1962, in which he covered some of the same ground as in *Totemism* and *La Pensée Sauvage*. The theme of 'The Bear and the Barber' is that totemic, equivalent, exogamous clans, of the Australian type, and specialized, ranked, endogamous castes, of the Indian variety, are not completely unrelated forms of social organization. They are rather to be understood as different transformations of the same basic structure.

In a totemic system one finds clans, each of which may be identified with a particular natural species, its totem. Thus the relationships which have been posited between natural species become a way of talking about the relationships between social groups. In some systems, members of a clan should abstain from eating the totemic species so that it becomes more freely available to members of other clans. In other societies members of a clan are held to be responsible for the fertility of the totemic species. In these ways totemic prohibitions and rituals may become part of the reciprocal exchanges which bind the clans into a society.

In the totemic systems, therefore, social groups are first contrasted with other social groups, and natural species are in the first instance set against other natural species. They are then related to each other in a sort of horizontal system of classification. But an obvious alternative would be to make the initial connection between a social group and a natural species, and then to contrast this pair with another pair comprising a social group and a natural species. This would represent a vertical mode of classifying social groups and natural species. The consequence would be to represent the differences between social groups as natural differences. Members of other social groups would be regarded as belonging virtually to different species, with whom, therefore, intermarriage would be unthinkable. This, Lévi-Strauss suggested, was the basis of the caste model.

This fundamental shift in the mode of conceptualizing the relationships between groups has its implications for the kinds of exchanges which will be set up between them. In a totemic system, based on clans, women are exchanged between groups, but the exchange of services is restricted. In the caste system women are kept within the group, but the groups each provide specialized services for the others. So in a system of totemic groups, there are exchanges of natural objects – women. In a caste system, where the groups are conceived of as being distinguished in nature, cultural artifacts are exchanged. 'In other words,' Lévi-Strauss wrote,

both the caste system and the so-called totemic systems postulate isomorphism between natural and cultural differences. The validation of this postulate involves in each case a symmetrical and inverted relationship. Castes are defined after a cultural model and must define their matrimonial exchange after a natural model. Totemic groups pattern matrimonial exchange after a cultural model, and they themselves must be defined after a natural model. Women, homogeneous as regards nature, are claimed to be heterogeneous as regards culture, and conversely, natural species, although heterogeneous as regards nature, are claimed to be homogeneous as regards culture, since from the

219

standpoint of culture, they share common properties in so far as man is believed to possess the power to control and multiply them.[9]

The basic opposition on which the whole system rests is that between Nature and Culture, an assumption which runs through much of Lévi-Strauss's work, notwithstanding his recent admission that 'the appearance of certain phenomena has made this line of demarcation, if not less real, then certainly more tenuous and tortuous than was imagined twenty years ago.'[10] In his theory of kinship it was the introduction of the incest taboo, forcing men to exchange their women, that marked the movement from nature to culture; and in his writings on systems of classification, and on the myth, the various modes of exchange are represented as being implicit in the acts of classification, opposition and association. Thus the total social system rests upon a single structural framework, and the social anthropologist cannot detach the cosmology from the social structure.

Lévi-Strauss's creative impact on his British colleagues has been particularly apparent in this field, in tempting them back to the study of systems of thought. He taught them to see cultural sub-systems as 'codes', media of communication susceptible to the same sort of treatment as language. Behind the manifest content of the sentence lies the grammatical form, the structure which generates the whole variety of possible sentences, and constitutes the essential reality. This grammar of symbolic communication is based upon a series of binary oppositions, of the kind Eaglehawk/Crow; Priest/Barber. These are in turn related to each other to form a total system.

He took the argument further in his volumes on myth. The *story* of the myth is only superficially what the myth is about. One must decode it, treating it as a single statement rather than a linear series of statements. The real message is contained in the system of relationships with which the myth concerns itself, and these must be broken up into their opposed, paired elements: Nature/Culture, Raw/Cooked, Honey/Tobacco, Silence/Noise, etc. Using these terms, myths attempt to provide logical models capable of resolving, at this level at least, some of the insupportable contradictions and problems of man's world – such as the problem of mortality, or the more specific contradictions of matrilineal forms of social organization. The aim is to show – as Lévi-Strauss said in his first statement on the subject – that

the kind of logic in mythical thought is as rigorous as that of modern science, and that the difference lies, not in the quality of the intellectual process, but in the nature of things to which it is applied . . . man has always been thinking equally well; the improvement lies, not in an alleged progress of man's mind, but in the discovery of new areas to which it may apply its unchanged and unchanging powers.[11]

VI

Leach has been the most enthusiastic and original of the British social anthropologists who have experimented with this method. His particular contribution has been to extend the range of applications, and to rationalize the method in some ways. There are not only binary oppositions – one needs a third term to define a binary set, a term which is neither A nor B. Because of its anomalous nature it will become hedged around with taboos. For example, one may classify people as relatives, friends, neighbours, strangers. Animals may be classed as pets, farmyard animals, wild animals, and so forth. There may be a homology between such sets of categories. Moreover, just as one cannot marry a woman who is too closely related, and should not marry one who is too foreign, so one does not eat pets, and in general one eats game only in special, heightened situations. But Leach is particularly interested in the anomaly, the creature which does not fit neatly into any of these categories. For example, the rabbit. It is not quite a pet, not quite a farm animal, not quite a wild animal. It does not quite fit, and so it is the source of ambivalence, and is likely to be tabooed in some contexts. And in fact the various idiomatic terms for rabbits quickly become 'indecent' – cunny, bunny, etc.; and the rabbit (under one name or another) becomes the symbol of various kinds of improper or ludicrous sexual behaviour.

Mary Douglas was also particularly interested in the anomalies, which became sources of impurity and danger. Her interest in these problems antedated Lévi-Strauss, deriving partly from her teacher at Oxford, Franz Steiner, whose lectures on taboo were edited and published after his premature death. Nevertheless her work on the sociology of perception shows the impact of Lévi-Strauss's structural method, which she used to great effect, for example demonstrating the way in which the food prohibitions set out in Leviticus can be understood in terms of the Hebrew system of classifying animals, the misfits being taboo. Leach was influenced by this analysis.

Arguments of this kind became familiar in anthropology seminars in the sixties in Britain. The journals were full of controversies about such matters as what the Nuer meant when they said twins were birds, problems which most British social anthropologists had neglected for thirty years. The new structuralism made its appearance in the monographs and papers of the younger generation, particularly in the work of Yalman, Beidelman and Rigby.

But, it was objected from Oxford, Evans-Pritchard had been doing this all the time! And from America came news of the re-emergence of the linguistic tradition in cultural anthropology in a radically different form. Perhaps this was also to carry a message for the British anthropologists. So how significant was Lévi-Strauss's intervention for the development of British social anthropology? And what were the consequences?

VII

Lévi-Strauss's impact can be better understood by contrasting the reception of his work to the British reaction to the 'new ethnography', an American movement which gathered steam in the late fifties. A group of American scholars, including Goodenough, Lounsbury, Conklin and others, working parallel to Lévi-Strauss, defined the mental life of peoples, and particularly their classifying activity, as a major focus of anthropological research, and developed essentially linguistic techniques to pursue this study. These concerns had deep roots in the American tradition. It is not too far-fetched to place Goodenough and Lévi-Strauss together, as the successors to the tradition of Boas, Kroeber and Lowie. (Who but Boas would have bothered to publish pages and pages of Kwakiutl gooseberry pie recipes, in the vernacular? And who but Lévi-Strauss would be interested in reanalysing such material?) The novelty of the 'new ethnography' lay in its methodological rigour and its cultural purism.

Although Lévi-Strauss occasionally referred approvingly to the work of this school, it failed to commend itself to a single British social anthropologist of consequence. Why not? Precisely for the reasons which made it such a force in the United States – its super-scientific pretensions, together with its limited range of applications. British social anthropologists felt that – like pretentious experiments in 'mathematical anthropology' – the methods of componential analysis were unnecessarily cumbersome, and yielded no new insights. In what way were their endless analyses of Crow-Omaha kinship terminologies an advance on the work of Radcliffe-Brown, Eggan and Tax? They were not even definitive, since several convincing componential analyses could be made of a single system. And above all, they were so pedantically unwilling to go beyond limited semantic domains.

The publications of the 'new ethnography' abounded in ambitious programmatic statements about getting into the minds of the natives, etc., but the analyses which followed provided no support for the claims that were made. Componential analysis was a good way of formulating rules which permitted the ethnographer to use words in the way the natives did, but when the exponents of the method tried to relate these rules to principles of social organization they came horrible croppers. Lévi-Strauss scored because he did not look at cultural facts as somehow expressions of social forces; rather both were analysed within a single frame of reference, as transformations of one underlying structure. In short, Lévi-Strauss provided dynamic analyses of total systems, while the 'new ethnography' only produced intricate statements about the structure of isolated semantic domains. The British anthropologists were not interested in culture as a thing in itself; they remained firm in their determination to connect what people said and what they did.

Lévi-Strauss had to be taken into account not only because of his towering genius; but because he talked directly to the interests of British social anthropology. A few even argued that he was hoeing the same row as Evans-Pritchard, Steiner, and their Oxford students. They had been involved throughout the fifties in the analysis of systems of thought. They had treated ideological systems as being ultimately conditioned by the social structure, but as nevertheless exhibiting considerable internal coherence and independence. It was true that Evans-Pritchard, and Lienhardt, had been concerned with particular social systems, while the new structuralism demanded the simultaneous consideration of several systems – but then the British never took Lévi-Strauss's more cosmic ambitions very seriously. Moreover they had always drawn on some of the sources which Lévi-Strauss used. Indeed it had been the younger Oxford anthropologists who translated the key essays of Durkheim, Mauss, Hubert, Hertz, etc.

This tradition of cultural analysis also persisted in some places outside Oxford. Radcliffe-Brown's structural analysis of totemism had been preceded by his analysis of Andaman ritual, in which symbols were treated as 'words' which had to be defined by examining the contexts in which they were used. Victor Turner used this technique in his analyses of Ndembu ritual and symbolism. He never even genuflected in Lévi-Strauss's direction, but he was also using an ultimately para-linguistic technique to analyse a symbolic system, if his concern was with 'semantics' rather than 'phonetics'. One can trace a direct line of descent from Radcliffe-Brown on ritual to Turner. It runs through Monica Wilson, who influenced Turner at a critical stage in his development.

Turner was interested in both the emotional resonance of symbols, and their social content. His theoretical approach combined elements from Freud, Radcliffe-Brown and Gluckman. But the distinctive feature of his writing on ritual, which has been so influential, is his analysis of the function of ritual and symbolic statements in the development, severance and repair of ongoing social relationships.

Mary Douglas had criticized Lévi-Strauss at an early stage for his intellectualist bias, his failure to take into account the emotive force of symbolic action. Now, citing Turner's example, she developed a more radical critique of Lévi-Strauss's paradigm. Her reaction constituted an interesting insight into the different priorities of Lévi-Strauss and the British neo-structuralists. Turner had understood the psychic content of symbols, while Lévi-Strauss assumed that the content of the symbol was arbitrary. Further, Turner's painstaking ethnography, his deep personal insight into Ndembu life, was contrasted favourably with Lévi-Strauss's less humane understanding. And finally, and most significant, Turner had provided 'a convincing demonstration of how the cultural categories sustain a given social structure'. Douglas went on, 'It should never again be permissible to provide an analysis of an interlocking system of categories of thought which has no demonstrable relation to the social life of the people who think in these terms.'[12] She now judged her own analysis of animal categories in Leviticus XI to be inadequate on this test, however successful as an example of Lévi-Strauss's methods.

Leach has specified the ultimate contrast between the concerns of the British neo-structuralists and Lévi-Strauss himself:

Most of those who at present call themselves social anthropologists either in Britain or the United States claim to be 'functionalists'; broadly speaking they are anthropologists in the style and tradition of Malinowski. In contrast, Claude Lévi-Strauss is a social anthropologist in the tradition though not in the style of Frazer. His ultimate concern is to establish facts which are true about 'the human mind', rather than about the organisation of any particular society or class of societies. The difference is fundamental.[13]

But even though there was an indigenous British tradition of cultural analysis that could assimilate the methods of Lévi-Strauss; and despite the very general reaction against Lévi-Strauss's intellectualist perspective, and his often rather cavalier treatment of the mesh of particular social systems, the impact of Lévi-Strauss was very great. The work which showed his influence most clearly was quite distinct from the general run of British or American studies, so much so that in a recent lecture Ardener felt able to catalogue the assumptions of this 'school', contrast them to the functionalist assumptions, and dub the product 'the new anthropology'.[14] The adoption of a new paradigm involves an almost physical sense of changing one's view of the world; and on this test Lévi-Strauss provided a new paradigm for several senior British anthropologists, and many of those who entered the profession in the sixties. Lévi-Strauss insists that structuralism is a method rather than a philosophy or even a theory. The method is being adapted: but it is more than a method, for Lévi-Strauss has also directed (or redirected) attention to a particular range of problems. This has resulted in a fresh interest among some British social anthropologists in the ways in which people use verbal categories to order their worlds; and the ways in which systems of exchange order social relationships.

EIGHT

1972

What, in heaven's name, are we trying to find out?
                                                   – Leach[1]

I

'British social anthropology' is not merely a term for the work done by British or even British-trained social anthropologists. The phrase connotes a set of names, a limited range of ethnographic regional specialities, a list of central monographs, a characteristic mode of procedure, and a particular series of theoretical problems. In short, it connotes an intellectual tradition. It may be silly to talk about the substantive nature of 'British physics' or even, today, of 'British economics', but at least between 1922 and 1972 everyone concerned with anthropology knew what was meant by 'British social anthropology'. In the preceding chapters I have tried to show how Malinowski and Radcliffe-Brown established this distinctive tradition, which continued under its own momentum for over a generation.

Has this 'British social anthropology' reasonable prospects in the future? Will the qualification 'British' soon be dropped, except for organizational purposes?

These questions have a peculiar urgency in 1972, for arbitrary historical reasons. Malinowski's seminar flourished in the thirties. Its leading members took up the available chairs in the discipline between 1945 and 1950, and they ran British social anthropology for twenty years. They all reached retiring age between 1968 and 1972. They had provided the fixed points on the map. Each major department was built around one of these professors, and reflected his theoretical and regional interests. Even in retirement they will exert an influence, but the powers of the professoriate are now in new hands, and in most cases the new professors have come from outside the departments.

227

Malinowski and Radcliffe-Brown were prophets, obsessed with their messages, incapable of accepting criticism, dominating their followers. The next generation institution-alized their charisma, and succeeded in making the discipline into a profession. The present senior generation, trained after the war, are the professionals. They are often more concerned with the minutiae of regional scholarship, more sceptical of general theory, less daring, perhaps; but more open to suggestion, more flexible, more willing to explore neighbouring disciplines. But the social sciences progress through prophetic pronouncements rather than discoveries, and even in the present rather staid generation there is the odd bid for grandeur. None has yet succeeded. Impudent Malinowski Memorial Lectures are defused by scepticism, and apocalyptic foreigners are greeted with the polite inattention of the specialists.

If the professoriate retains effective power over appoint-ments, grants, and public anthropological bodies, the new men will have the greatest opportunity to influence the developments within the discipline in Britain. On the other hand, in the last two decades Leach exerted great influence despite his lack of a professorial base, and there may be more people in this position in the years to come, particularly if the number of departments remains fairly static, while the departments themselves continue to grow. Non-professors, of course, have the advantage that they are not bogged down in administration; and if the rather bland face which the majority of the new professors present to the world is not misleading, then sheer boredom will drive many of the younger generation to look elsewhere for inspiration.

'Elsewhere', more than ever now, includes abroad. Travelling all over the world in search of material, British anthropologists have been notoriously parochial in admitting theoretical influences. But the shock of Lévi-Strauss's challenge has jolted many into a state which makes them more receptive to trends in other countries. The current developments in the United States, including the work of the neo-evolutionist school, with their interest in ecology and ethology, and the very different 'new ethnography' and 'ethnomethodology', have not so far aroused any great interest in Britain. Nor do I think they will have much influence, since neither trend is particularly concerned with the study of social life *per se*, but there is certainly a potential for convergence with the work being fostered by some British anthropologists in cultural systems and socio-linguistics. On the other hand, a large number of young American anthropologists have been doing excellent field studies in the British tradition, and so to the extent that the tradition continues to develop, the United States will be one of its centres.

The British anthropologists today look with rather keener interest to developments in the main continental centres of anthropology – France, Holland and, to some extent, Norway. In France Louis Dumont vies with Lévi-Strauss as their favourite structuralist, and Barthes and Althusser are also read with more or less attention. The new Marxist anthropology represented by Meillassoux and others is also beginning to arouse some interest. Holland now harbours 'British social anthropology' in the persons of Beattie and Boissevain, and it has its own distinctive tradition of structuralism and Oriental studies, now, through Needham's efforts, better known and appreciated in Britain. A number of lively Dutch students may be found today in remote corners of the world, pursuing their researches with Malinowskian thoroughness, and they will soon be active in the same enterprises and controversies as their British colleagues. Norway has in Barth the outstanding figure among anthropology's 'action' theorists. Trained in Britain, and writing in English, Barth has been a force in British anthropological circles for over a decade already, and he is training an impressive cadre of students. Although no other European country has yet developed a school of social anthropologists of international importance, there are signs of activity in the other Scandinavian countries, West Germany, and Eastern Europe.

If one were to redraw the theoretical map of British social anthropology, the poles might today be placed outside Britain. Paris is the centre of the new structuralism, and the

ANTHROPOLOGISTS AND ANTHROPOLOGY

most interesting developments of 'transaction theory' are coming from Barth in Bergen. But social anthropologists in Britain can still be placed within the functionalist tradition, with very few exceptions. Radcliffe-Brown's view of social structure as a network of real dyadic relationships has become, ironically, the salvation of Malinowski's manipulative man. These threads have combined in the work of the Manchester anthropologists, with their interest in the strategies of everyday life. The most recent development has been in the field of 'network theory', particularly in the hands of Barnes and Mitchell. Others, notably Bailey, have followed the lead of Barth and tried to interpret social strategies in terms of a series of exchanges, or transactions – so that social life becomes, to quote a recent title of Bailey, a matter of manipulating gifts and poisons. The neo-structuralists (arguably, at least, representatives of another development of the pre-war Oxford orthodoxy) now include Leach, Mary Douglas, Needham, and a number of the younger anthropologists. The other development from Oxford, focusing upon the structure and interrelationship of corporate groups, is perhaps best represented today in the work of Goody, Lloyd and M. G. Smith, though Smith has also introduced more sophisticated notions from the work of Weber and Furnivall. M. G. Smith is today an important figure in political sociology and in general sociological theory. He is the leading authority on racially or ethnically plural societies, and is one of the few social anthropologists in Britain with a commitment to the study of complex societies and social change.

Despite the internationalization of theory – or perhaps following from it – the most creative influences may come from other disciplines. In 1959 David Easton, the American political scientist, published a critique of political anthropology, concentrating upon the mainstream British studies. This provoked wide interest, and a number of people began to study his work and that of other American political scientists, opening a door which will not be shut again. Economics is another area in which a developed theory exists which surely has enormous relevance to social anthropology. So far no British social anthropologist has really come to grips with neo-Keynsian theory, but several American anthropologists have begun to explore the possibilities.

Linguistics, a part of anthropology in the U.S.A., has been brought into British anthropology largely in response to Lévi-Strauss's interest. The reverberations of Chomsky's revolution are now beginning to be felt, but it is impossible to predict the ways in which this might influence social anthropology. Psychology, either in combination with linguistics, or with reference to child-raising and personality formation in different cultures has also been a key influence in American anthropology. Since the loss of interest in Freudian theory, British social anthropologists have neglected psychology, partly, no doubt, because of the poverty of social psychology in Britain. The dearth of sociological theory in British universities has robbed the social anthropologists of another necessary stimulus.

One significant field of cross-fertilization was created by the emergence of 'African studies', in the fifties, embracing not only social anthropologists but also historians, political scientists and lawyers. The African historians, in particular, with their pioneering work on 'oral traditions' have been brought smack up against the classical problems of understanding and explanation with which the British social anthropologists have been grappling. In their turn they are providing a vital historical depth to our understanding of African societies, and incidentally setting some of the classical monographs in a new perspective. There are a number of social anthropologists in Britain who are making a speciality of this borderline area between history and ethnography.

Finally, what about the technological aids now available? American anthropologists have been experimenting with computer simulations and other sophisticated techniques for the manipulation of data. Some of their results have had a considerable impact – notably their demonstrations of the demographic parameters of marriage systems. Once again this is an area of only potential importance for British social anthropology. So far the traditional methods of research and analysis are felt to be adequate.

II

But all this is to assume that British social anthropology – or, at least, social anthropology in Britain – will continue to develop along the lines which have been laid down already. This assumption has been seriously questioned in recent years. Three types of argument have been advanced. First, it has been suggested that social anthropology flourished as a distinct speciality only because it was convenient in a colonial age to concentrate upon the study of 'primitive people', and to separate them conceptually from other men. Now that this no longer has a political value, the social anthropologist is forced to recognize the unity of human societies, and he will soon find that what he is doing is indistinguishable from sociology. The alternative is bleak. As Worsley has warned:

> If social anthropology continues to uphold its traditional concern with the primitive, it must, inexorably, die out with its subject-matter, though this may take a long time still. It will become increasingly dependent on records of now-extinct societies, and therefore a branch of history . . . If this option is taken, the entire realm of contemporary societies will become the province of sociology, as 'primitive' societies become incorporated into 'developing' nation-states and aggregations of nation-states, and of ideological, economic, political, etc. entities often cutting across nation-states, or subsuming them within blocs and groupings.[2]

Needham has indicated another danger. As specialism develops within social anthropology, the discipline will segment. There will be anthropological politics, which will link up with political science; anthropological economics, which will become a branch of economics, etc.[3] This paralleled an argument which Runciman had recently advanced with respect to sociology, in his controversial paper 'Sociology in its Place'. One might suggest that if Worsley, Needham and Runciman are all correct, then social anthropology will not only merge largely with sociology, but will join it in a process of perhaps creative disintegration. Another possibility – though less likely as a fate for the discipline as a whole – is the emergence of regional specialists, who are, say, Africanists first and social anthropologists only a long way after.

The third possibility, represented in the United States, is the reintegration of social anthropology with its traditional stable-mates of archaeology, material culture, linguistics and a modern, non-racialist physical anthropology. Such a discipline would take the evolution of man and of culture as its centre of interest. This is not a likely development, however. Linguistics may be incorporated into social anthropology, but if social anthropology vanishes it will be into some form of sociology, or branches of sociology. The relevant questions, then, are those raised by Worsley and Needham.

Needham seems to me unduly pessimistic – or perhaps, prematurely optimistic about the highly-specialized advances of branches of social anthropology. Although no modern social anthropologist can be an expert on more than two or three ethnographic regions or specialities, we can all quite comfortably keep up with the most important advances in all the branches of the discipline; particularly since these advances tend to be interlinked. The ultimate isolates of social anthropology are not politics, economics, religion or kinship, but social relations, social values, and cultural categories. And the nature of social anthropology is implicit in this break-down: it tries to perceive total social systems. This must remain a valid possibility however much the particular branches of the subject develop. Indeed, their development should contribute to the central enterprise. This may never be realized in a total theory of society – whatever that would be. But it has been progressively realized in the refinement of models which illuminate the structure of particular societies.

Worsley touches a more sensitive nerve. The process of decolonization has had enormous repercussions already for social anthropology. The anthropologist from Britain can no longer assume that if he behaves himself he will be free to study 'natives'. Social anthropology has a bad name through its association with colonialism, and the anthropologist has an even harder time than most of his social science colleagues even getting permission to do fieldwork in the newly-independent states. And once there he is no longer able to rely upon the privileged status of a white man crossing a detested racial barrier; he is now an outsider of a different kind, a foreigner, less secure and perhaps less welcome. Moreover he enters a world in which the politically dominant values are those of 'development' and 'modernization', and he will be challenged to show what his work contributes to nation-building. It is a little galling for the anthropologist to find that he is being slandered while the African historian is fêted for doing more or less what he had done for thirty years, but this is the context in which he must operate.

Yet there is another side to the coin. As an Indonesian scholar recently remarked, anthropologists have traditionally been Euro-Americans studying non-Euro-Americans. Today there are schools of anthropology in India, Japan, the Philippines, South-East Asia, and a few African countries. In these areas citizen-anthropologists are developing a new brand of 'applied anthropology'. Moreover, today virtually any anthropological monograph is bound to be read by some of its subjects. The country in which the study was carried out is in fact becoming a major market for the studies themselves. This by-product of decolonization is one of the most hopeful and neglected factors in the present situation. Anthropology is losing the last traces of its ethnocentricism as it becomes a properly international study of societies all over the world.

The repercussions of decolonization produced some rather unimaginative responses from several members of the older generation of British social anthropologists. Some argued that fieldwork was no longer possible in the traditional sense, and that – as Worsley suggested – all that remained was literary reanalysis and comparison. On the contrary, fieldwork had proceeded with great vigour, not only in the ex-colonial hunting grounds, but with even greater momentum elsewhere, including the hitherto untapped regions of Europe and South America.

There was a more serious concern here, nevertheless. Some actually welcomed the possibility of a pause in the fieldwork effort so that the work of assimilation and theoretical development might be prosecuted more energetically. What was the use of heaping up endless monographs, however meticulous, if they did not lead to theoretical advances? Even if we can still send our students out into the field, is this the wise thing to do? So far these reservations have not seriously altered the pattern of research. The classical solution is still adopted – the young do the fieldwork, and their elders do rather more comparative and theoretical studies. There is a general feeling that serious library studies are more fruitful with the stimulus and critical sense which come from initial field-studies. And, of course, for many recruits to the profession the great attraction is precisely fieldwork in an exotic society. There is the danger nonetheless that the scholar with a mass of unpublished field material in his cupboard will be inhibited about exploring attractive theoretical by-ways, at the expense of neglecting his own data.

But the basic problem which decolonization raised – not perhaps so much in the minds of social anthropologists – was simply whether, with political independence and the drive towards economic development, there were any more peoples suited to the anthropologist's purposes. There were no more tribesmen, only peasants. This assumes that social anthropology is the science of the 'primitive', an assumption which social anthropologists have generally disputed, although one which they have commonly seemed to accept in practice.

One reaction has been to concentrate upon the handful of hunters and gatherers who still manage to maintain some sort of independent existence. This choice is further justified by appeals to humanist values. The poor Bushmen, Hadza, Amazonian Indians, etc., are suffering from abuse, disease, political bullying, exploitation, even, occasionally, virtual genocide. Their plight must be made known. Furthermore their cultures are under such determined attack that they cannot survive for long. Soon the sole survivors of the generations of man the hunter will be gone; they must be studied at once. These are honourable responses, and the fieldwork that has been done recently on hunters and gatherers has been markedly productive of insights. Nevertheless this is an option which can at best employ a minority of anthropologists. It is not an answer for the discipline as a whole.

Another reaction has been to embrace political science; to admit that the living reality is a modern one in the sense that it is determined by centralized state politics and an international economy. The extreme formulation of this position might deny many classical anthropological concerns, but a number of social anthropologists have operated on these assumptions yet within the social anthropological tradition. For to the extent that social anthropology has fulfilled its programme, and abandoned its early racialist and evolutionist assumptions, it is capable of treating all societies within one framework.

These rather disjointed observations are not intended as an answer to Worsley or Needham. I do not know what the future of social anthropology will be. If I did, I would be there already. Still I remain convinced that a certain optimism is in order. Social anthropology is a way of studying all human societies, not a peculiar science of colonized blacks. But within this grand field, shared, of course, with sociology in its broadest sense, anthropologists have staked out a particular field for themselves. They have studied small-scale exotic societies, and tried to understand 'other cultures' from within. They have done this by becoming insider-outsiders, seeing more of the game than the players, but understanding what is demanded of the players. The justification for this method is apparent – to take one example, despite the mass of American social science research, the most valuable studies of American society remain those of the two foreigners, Tocqueville and Myrdal.

The strength of the participant-observer in a foreign situation is that he will necessarily make comparisons, first with his own society and then with other societies which have been analysed by others; and this will yield more powerful abstractions than the hectic movement of the field sociologist between his office and the street outside. Moreover, because he *can* see the wood for the trees he can perceive the society he is studying as a total system which embodies a divergence between stated values and actual relationships. The crucial questions cannot, therefore, be raised by actors, for they must operate in terms of their programme for action.

Nevertheless the anthropologist finds that modern, complex societies pose a problem of method. In many small-scale societies the observed field of social relations is roughly coordinate with the extent of a culture. Even in large African societies the culture in which a community participates is commonly uniform throughout a political realm. This is certainly not the case in an American city, for example. And even if the field area is culturally fairly uniform – say a Norwegian district – the institutions which determine much of the community activity are based outside it. Should the anthropologist then isolate an ethnic unit or a class in a homogenous section of the city or region? Or should he try to transcend the community and establish the cultural norms which are common to all the members of the society, and examine the major organizational structures of the society as a whole? Ideally he should do all these things, but while his familiar routine of participant-observation in closely-knit units must be retained, it will have to be combined with other techniques. And then there is the problem of elaborating a theoretical system which will contain all these elements, and relate them to each other. The most promising candidate for many situations is the new conflict model of the plural society, which originated in the work of Furnivall, and which has been developed particularly by M. G. Smith, Pierre van den Berghe and Leo Kuper. The alternative of a neo-Marxist theoretical framework also exists in sociology, of course, and it has been used by Frankenberg, among British anthropologists, in studies of British society.

Whichever theoretical model is used, the distinctive anthropological perspective remains. This is to begin by assuming that the actors' models are part of the data, not useful analyses of the systems being studied. Therefore the problems of the politicians are not guides to research issues; and in that sense social anthropology denies itself if it seeks to be 'relevant'. This fundamental characteristic of anthropology demands an unusual orientation on the part of its practitioners, but it is the reason why anthropology will remain the eternal outsider of the social sciences, and thus their ultimate touchstone.

This is why I feel that social anthropology will not be assimilated to any other social science, including sociology: sociology as it is rather than as it might have been. The field sociologist, taking his 'problems' from the newspapers and relying on formal questions about attitudes also returns with a hamper of material; and both he and the anthropologist can unpack their hampers only with the aid of sociological theory – in fact their goods only mean anything in terms of that theory. Both have made contributions to the theory too, though the anthropologist, flying the Jolly Roger in uncharted seas has usually brought home the more exciting booty. The anthropological contribution to sociological understanding constitutes a standing reproach to those prissy methodologists and excitable reformists who have made modern sociology so boring and sterile. But it is not only in comparison with their sociological colleagues that the anthropologists can hope that their past achievements do still hold out promise for the future.

Notes

NOTES TO CHAPTER ONE

1. B. Malinowski, *The Sexual Life of Savages*, third edn, London, 1932, p. xxix.
2. E. R. Leach, 'The epistemological background to Malinowski's empiricism', *Man and Culture*, R. Firth (ed.), London, 1957, p. 120.
3. op. cit., p. 124. As a matter of fact, 1915.
4. A. R. Radcliffe-Brown, 'Historical Note on British Social Anthropology', *American Anthropologist*, vol. 54, 1952, p. 276.
5. Report in *Man*, 1906, p. 57.
6. B. Malinowski, *Argonauts of the Western Pacific*, London, 1922, pp. 515-6.
7. A. R. Radcliffe-Brown, 'A Further Note on Ambrym', *Man*, 1929, p. 53.
8. W. H. Rivers, 'Report on Anthropological Research Outside America', *The Present Condition and Future Needs of the Science of Anthropology*, presented by W. H. Rivers, A. E. Jenks, and S. G. Morley, Washington, 1913, p. 6.
9. R. R. Marett, *The Diffusion of Culture*, the Frazer lecture in social anthropology, Cambridge, 1927, p. 4.
10. Henri A. Junod, *The Life of a South African Tribe*, Neuchâtel, Switzerland, 1912, pp. 5-6.
11. E. Sidney Hartland, 'Notes on some South African Tribes', *Man*, 1907, pp. 49-50.
12. A. M. Hocart, review in *Man*, 1915, p. 89.
13. W. H. Rivers, op. cit., p. 7.
14. W. H. Rivers, op. cit., p. 11.
15. R. R. Marett, op. cit., p. 33.
16. Karol Estreicher, 'Zakopane - Leur Amour', *Polish Perspectives*, Warsaw, June 1971.
17. In trying to understand Malinowski's background, and for much else, I am indebted to the three papers on Malinowski by Konstantin Symmons-Symonolewicz in the *Polish Review*, 1958, 1959, and 1960.
18. This and the following quotations are drawn from Wundt's introduction to *Elements of Folk Psychology*, the English translation of which appeared in London in 1916.
19. J. A. Barnes, preface to American paperback edn of Malinowski's *The Family among the Australian Aborigines*, 1963.
20. Review in *Man*, 1914, p. 32.

21. R. R. Marett, *Professor Bronislaw Malinowski: An Account of the memorial meeting held in London on July 13, 1942*, London, 1943, p. 7.
22. B. Malinowski, *A Diary in the Strict Sense of the Term*, London, 1967, pp. 158–9.
23. op. cit., p. 167.
24. B. Malinowski, *Argonauts of the Western Pacific*, p. 13. The references in the following paragraph are to the same introductory chapter, pp. 17, 24, and 25.
25. From a memorandum by R. R. Marett, quoted by Wilson D. Wallis in 'Anthropology in England Early in the Present Century', *American Anthropologist*, 1957, p. 790.
26. Quoted in the leaflet of the department of anthropology at the London School of Economics, p. 5.
27. M. F. Ashley Montagu, 'Bronislaw Malinowski', *Isis*, Harvard, pp. 146–7.
28. Quoted by Raymond Firth, 'Malinowski as Scientist and as Man', *Man and Culture*, R. Firth (ed.), p. 9.
29. E. R. Leach, op. cit., p. 124.
30. M. Fortes, 'Malinowski and the study of Kinship', *Man and Culture*, R. Firth (ed.), p. 157.
31. B. Malinowski, *Argonauts of the Western Pacific*, p. 10.
32. Personal communication from Professor Lucy Mair.
33. *The Autobiography of Bertrand Russell*, vol. 2, London, 1968, pp. 195–6.
34. In an obituary of Malinowski, *Journal of American Folklore*, 1943, p. 208.
35. R. Lowie, *The History of Ethnological Theory*, London, 1937, p. 241.
36. Quoted in R. Firth, op. cit., p. 10.
37. *Crime and Custom in Savage Society*, London, 1926, p. 30.
38. A. Lang, introduction to *Anthropological Essays Presented to Edward Burnett Tylor*, Oxford, 1907, p. 13.
39. B. Malinowski, *Magic, Science and Religion and other essays*, Glencoe, Ill., 1948, p. 15. The following quotation is from p. 70.
40. B. Malinowski, *Myth in Primitive Psychology*, London, 1926, p. 97.
41. B. Malinowski, 'The Impasse on Kinship', *Man*, 1930, pp. 19–29.
42. See Chapter 3.
43. M. Fortes, op. cit.
44. Special preface to the third edn of Malinowski's *The Sexual Life of Savages*, p. xx.
45. A. R. Radcliffe-Brown, review in *Man*, 1914, p. 32.
46. B. Malinowski, *Magic, Science and Religion*, p. 202,
47. Special preface to third edn of Malinowski's *Sexual Life of Savages*, p. xxxv.
48. *Methods of Study of Culture Contact in Africa*, International African Institute, Memorandum XV, London, 1938, p. viii.
49. op. cit., p. xxii.
50. A. R. Radcliffe-Brown, *Structure and Function in Primitive Society*, London, 1952, p. 202.

NOTES

51. B. Malinowski, *Methods of Study of Culture Contact in Africa*, p. xii.
52. B. Malinowski, *Coral Gardens and their Magic*, London, 1935, pp. 479–81.
53. R. Firth (ed.), *Man and Culture*, London, 1957.
54. Review in *Man*, 1930, p. 56.
55. B. Malinowski, *A Diary in the Strict Sense of the Term*, p. 119.

NOTES TO CHAPTER TWO

1. A. R. Radcliffe-Brown, *Structure and Function in Primitive Society*, London, 1952, pp. 188–9.
2. For information on Radcliffe-Brown's early life I have drawn heavily on Firth's obituary in the *Proceedings* of the British Academy, 1956.
3. *The Autobiography of Bertrand Russell*, vol. 1, London, 1967, p. 74.
4. There is a delightful portrait of Rivers in Siegfried Sassoon's *Sherston's Progress*, London, 1936.
5. R. R. Marett, *A Jerseyman at Oxford*, London, 1941, p. 161.
6. See R. Firth, op. cit.; M. Fortes, 'Radcliffe-Brown's Contribution to the study of social organization', *British Journal of Sociology*, 1955.
7. Quoted by R. Firth, op. cit., p. 301.
8. E. L. Grant Watson, *But to What Purpose: The Autobiography of a Contemporary*, London, 1946. This and following quotations from pp. 84–5.
9. A. R. Radcliffe-Brown, *The Andaman Islanders*, Cambridge, 1922, p. 72n.
10. op. cit., p. 22.
11. op. cit., p. 82n.
12. op. cit., p. 230.
13. op. cit., pp. 233–4.
14. op. cit., p. 235.
15. op. cit., p. 243.
16. Grant Watson, op. cit., p. 109.
17. A. P. Elkin, obituary in *Oceania*, 1956, p. 247.
18. J. A. Barnes, *Inquest on the Murngin*, Royal Anthropological Institute Occasional Paper, London, 1967, p. 24.
19. A. R. Radcliffe-Brown, 'Some Problems of Bantu Sociology', *Bantu Studies*, 1922, p. 38.
20. R. Firth, op. cit., p. 302.
21. A. R. Radcliffe-Brown, *A Natural Science of Society*, Glencoe, Ill., 1957, p. 83.
22. C. Lévi-Strauss, 'La Sociologie Française', *La Sociologie au XXe Siècle*, vol. 11, G. Gurvitch and W. Moore (eds.), Paris, 1947, p. 531.
23. A. R. Radcliffe-Brown, *A Natural Science of Society*, p. 45.
24. op. cit., p. 55.
25. Sol Tax and others (eds.), *An Appraisal of Anthropology Today*, Chicago, Ill., 1953, p. 109.

26. A. R. Radcliffe-Brown, *A Natural Science of Society*, p. 58.
27. op. cit., p. 71.
28. op. cit., p. 106.
29. op. cit., p. 102.
30. A. R. Radcliffe-Brown, *Structure and Function in Primitive Society*, pp. 43–4.
31. op. cit., p. 124.
32. op. cit., p. 131.
33. A. R. Radcliffe-Brown, 'The Comparative Method in Social Anthropology', 1952, reprinted posthumously in *Method in Social Anthropology*, Srinivas (ed.), Chicago, 1958, pp. 117–8.
34. C. Lévi-Strauss, *Totemism*, London, 1962. Particularly pp. 83–92.
35. A. R. Radcliffe-Brown, 'The Study of Kinship Systems', *Journal of the Royal Anthropological Institute*, 1941, pp. 63–4. (Reprinted in *Structure and Function*.)
36. Henri A. Junod, *The Life of a South African Tribe*, Neuchâtel, Switzerland, 1912, pp. 227–8.
37. E. E. Evans-Pritchard, 'The Study of Kinship in Primitive Societies', *Man*, 1929.
38. A. R. Radcliffe-Brown, *Structure and Function in Primitive Society*, p. 92.
39. op. cit., p. 95.
40. A. R. Radcliffe-Brown, 'A Note on Functional Anthropology', *Man*, 1946, p. 38.
41. op. cit., pp. 39–40.
42. A. R. Radcliffe-Brown, 'Functionalism: A Protest', *American Anthropologist*, 1949, p. 321.
43. The quotation from Boas and the comment are in Fred Eggan's essay, 'One hundred years of ethnology and social anthropology', *One Hundred Years of Anthropology*, J. O. Brew (ed.), Cambridge Mass., 1968, pp. 136–7.

NOTES TO CHAPTER THREE

1. Hortense Powdermaker, *Stranger and Friend*, London, 1966, pp. 42–3.
2. op. cit., p. 36.
3. M. Fortes's memoir of Nadel, in S. F. Nadel, *The Theory of Social Structure*, London, 1957.
4. Hortense Powdermaker, 'Further Reflections on Lesu and Malinowski's Diary', *Oceania*, 1970, p. 347.
5. R. Firth, 'History of Modern Social Anthropology', preliminary draft, presented at a conference on the history of anthropology held in New York, 1962. Cyclostyled, p. 11. I am grateful to Professor Firth for permission to quote from this paper.
6. G. Bateson, *Naven*, Cambridge, 1936; second edn, Stanford, 1958, p. ix.
7. op. cit., p. 27.
8. op. cit., p. 1.

9. op. cit., second edn, p. 281.
10. op. cit., pp. 262 and 281.
11. op. cit., pp. 278–9.
12. E. E. Evans-Pritchard, *Witchcraft, Oracles and Magic among the Azande*, Oxford, 1937, p. 4.
13. R. F. Fortune, *Sorcerers of Dobu*, London, 1932, p. 150.
14. op. cit., p. 135.
15. E. E. Evans-Pritchard, *Social Anthropology*, London, 1951, pp. 99–100.
16. E. E. Evans-Pritchard, *Witchcraft, Oracles and Magic*, p. 106.
17. op. cit., p. 73.
18. op. cit., p. 114.
19. op. cit., p. 270.
20. op. cit., p. 387.
21. op. cit., p. 405.
22. op. cit., p. 544.
23. op. cit., p. 337.
24. op. cit., pp. 540–41.
25. op. cit., pp. 2–3.
26. op. cit., p. 439.
27. E. E. Evans-Pritchard, *Social Anthropology*, p. 96.
28. E. E. Evans-Pritchard, 'Anthropology and the Social Sciences', *Further Papers on the Social Sciences*, J. E. Dugdale (ed.), London, 1937, pp. 72–3.
29. E. E. Evans-Pritchard, Preface to *Tribes without Rulers*, John Middleton and David Tait (eds.), London, 1958, pp. x–xi.
30. E. E. Evans-Pritchard, *The Nuer*, Oxford, 1940, p. 85.
31. op. cit., p. 110.
32. op. cit., p. 136.
33. op. cit., p. 148.
34. op. cit., p. 159.
35. op. cit., p. 212.
36. op. cit., p. 236.
37. op. cit., p. 248.
38. op. cit., p. 241.
39. *Man*, 1929, pp. 42–3.
40. E. E. Evans-Pritchard, *Nuer Religion*, Oxford, 1956, p. ix.
41. M. Fortes, *The Dynamics of Clanship among the Tallensi*, Oxford, 1945, p. viii.
42. E. E. Evans-Pritchard, *The Nuer*, p. 137.
43. M. Fortes, *Kinship and the Social Order*, London, 1969, p. 28.
44. op. cit., p. 49.
45. op. cit., p. 72.
46. M. Fortes, 'Time and Social Structure: an Ashanti Case-Study', *Social Structure: Studies presented to A. R. Radcliffe-Brown*, M. Fortes (ed.), Oxford, 1949, p. 56.

NOTES TO CHAPTER FOUR

1. Described by Johan Galtung, 'Scientific Colonialism', *Transition*, 30, 1967.
2. C. Lévi-Strauss, *The Scope of Anthropology*, 1967, pp. 51–2. (First published in French, 1960.)
3. Quoted by Conrad Reining, 'A Lost Period of Applied Anthropology', *American Anthropologist*, 1962, p. 593.
4. A. Hingston Quiggin, *Haddon: The Head Hunter*, London, 1942, p. 136.
5. Frazer's inaugural lecture is reprinted in *Psyche's Task*, London, 1913. Quotation p. 161.
6. *Man*, 1909, pp. 85–7.
7. *Man*, 1914, p. 67.
8. *Man*, 1921, p. 93.
9. *Man*, 1921, p. 173.
10. E. E. Evans-Pritchard, 'Applied Anthropology', *Africa*, 1946, p. 97.
11. H. G. Barnett, *Anthropology in Administration*, Evanston, Ill., 1956, p. 7.
12. 'A Five-Year Plan of Research', *Africa*, 1932, p. 1.
13. op. cit., p. 3.
14. W. M. Hailey, *An African Survey*, London, 1938. (Ref. to 1950 edn, p. 51.)
15. op. cit., pp. 59–60.
16. H. J. Braunholtz, 'Anthropology in Theory and Practice', *Journal of the Royal Anthropological Institute*, 1943, p. 8.
17. G. G. Brown and A. B. Hutt, *Anthropology in Action*, London, 1935.
18. Godfrey and Monica Wilson, *The Analysis of Social Change*, Cambridge, 1945.
19. A. I. Richards, 'Practical Anthropology in the Lifetime of the International African Institute', *Africa*, 1944, p. 295.
20. H. G. Barnett, op. cit., p. 49.
21. Joyce Carey, *An American Visitor*, 1952.
22. A. I. Richards, op. cit., pp. 293–4.
23. M. Fortes, 'An Anthropologist's Point of View', *Fabian Colonial Essays*, Rita Hinden (ed.), London, 1945, p. 223.
24. Jacques Maquet, 'Objectivity in Anthropology', *Current Anthropology*, 1964, p. 50.

NOTES TO CHAPTER FIVE

1. R. R. Marett, *A Jerseyman at Oxford*, London, 1941, p. 169.
2. See *Research in Social Anthropology*, Social Science Research Council, London, 1968. For many of these figures I am indebted to Dr K. Garbett, secretary of the A.S.A.
3. E. and S. Ardener, 'A Directory Study of Social Anthropologists', *British Journal of Sociology*, 1965, pp. 300–302.

4. E. E. Evans-Pritchard, letter in *Man*, 1970, p. 704.
5. E. E. Evans-Pritchard, 'Anthropology and the Social Sciences', *Further Papers on the Social Sciences*, J. E. Dugdale (ed.), London, 1937, p. 73.
6. Reprinted in E. E. Evans-Pritchard, *Essays in Social Anthropology*, London, 1962. Reference to p. 26.
7. S. F. Nadel, *The Theory of Social Structure*, London, 1957, p. 158.
8. R. Firth, *Elements of Social Organization*, London, 1951, p. 36.
9. op. cit., p. 211.
10. R. Firth (ed.), *Man and Culture*, London, 1957, p. 1.
11. G. P. Murdock, 'British social anthropology', *American Anthropologist*, 1951, pp. 466–7.

NOTES TO CHAPTER SIX

1. B. Malinowski, *Crime and Custom in Savage Society*, London, 1926, p. 123.
2. E. R. Leach, introductory note to the 1964 reprint, *Political Systems of Highland Burma*, London, p. ix.
3. E. R. Leach, *Lévi-Strauss*, London, 1970, p. 9.
4. M. Gluckman, 'The Kingdom of the Zulu of South Africa', *African Political Systems*, M. Fortes and E. E. Evans-Pritchard (eds.), London, 1940.
5. M. Gluckman, *Analysis of a Social Situation in Modern Zululand*, Rhodes-Livingstone Paper no. 28, 1958 (reprinted from *Bantu Studies*), p. 25.
6. Elizabeth Colson and Max Gluckman (eds.), *Seven Tribes of British Central Africa*, Manchester, 1951.
7. M. Gluckman, *Order and Rebellion in Tribal Africa*, London, 1963, p. 18.
8. E. E. Evans-Pritchard, 'The Divine Kingship of the Shilluk of the Nilotic Sudan' (1948 Frazer Lecture), reprinted in *Essays in Social Anthropology*, London, 1962, quotation p. 83.
9. D. F. Pocock, *Social Anthropology*, London, 1961, pp. 77–82.
10. M. Gluckman, *Order and Rebellion in Tribal Africa*, p. 20.
11. op. cit., p. 28.
12. M. Gluckman, 'Seven-Year Research Plan of the Rhodes-Livingstone Institute . . .', *Human Problems in British Central Africa*, 1945, p. 9.
13. V. W. Turner, *Schism and Continuity in an African Society*, Manchester, 1957, p. xix.
14. op. cit., p. 129.
15. E. R. Leach, *Social and Economic Organisation of the Rowanduz Kurds*, London, 1940, p. 9.
16. op. cit., p. 62.
17. op. cit., p. 9.
18. E. R. Leach, *Political Systems of Highland Burma*, London, 1954, p. 9.

19. op. cit., p. 16.
20. op. cit., p. 203.
21. op. cit., p. 204.
22. op. cit., p. 87.
23. op. cit., p. 263.
24. op. cit., p. 228.
25. op. cit. (1964 reprint), p. xii.
26. op. cit., p. 97.
27. E. R. Leach, *Pul Eliya*, Cambridge, 1961, p. 298.
28. op. cit., pp. 298–9.
29. op. cit., p. 7.
30. op. cit., pp. 300–301.
31. op. cit., p. 130.
32. M. Fortes, *Kinship and the Social Order*, London, 1969, pp. 221–8.
33. E. R. Leach, 'Jinghpaw Kinship Terminology', *Journal of the Royal Anthropological Insti ute*, 1945. Reprinted in *Rethinking Anthropology*, London, 1961, quotation pp. 30–31.
34. E. R. Leach, *Rethinking Anthropology*, London, 1961, p. 2.

NOTES TO CHAPTER SEVEN

1. C. Lévi-Strauss, *Structural Anthropology*, New York and London, 1963, p. 21.
2. E. R. Leach, 'Introduction' to *The Structural Study of Myth and Totemism*, Leach (ed.), London, 1967, p. xv.
3. C. Lévi-Strauss, 'The Future of Kinship Studies', *Proceedings of the Royal Anthropological Institute for 1965*, p. 18.
4. David Schneider, 'Some Muddles in the Models: or, How the System really Works', *The Relevance of Models for Social Anthropology*, Bantom (ed.), London, 1965, p. 69.
5. E. R. Leach, 'Bridewealth and Marriage Stability', *Man*, 1957; reprinted in *Rethinking Anthropology*, 1961, quotation p. 122.
6. M. Fortes, 'Descent, filiation and affinity: a rejoinder to Dr. Leach', *Man*, 1959, p. 209.
7. I am quoting from the translation which appeared in a special 'structuralist' issue of *Yale French Studies*, nos. 36–7, 1966, pp. 41–65.
8. C. Lévi-Strauss, *Totemism*, London, 1962, p. 90.
9. C. Lévi-Strauss, 'The Bear and the Barber', *Journal of the Royal Anthropological Institute*, 1963, p. 9.
10. Introduction to the English edn of *The Elementary Structures of Kinship*, 1969, p. xxix.
11. C. Lévi-Strauss, *Structural Anthropology*, p. 230.
12. Mary Douglas, 'The Healing Rite', *Man*, 1970, p. 303.
13. E. R. Leach, *Lévi-Strauss*, 1970, pp. 7–8.
14. E. Ardener, 'The new anthropology and its critics', *Man*, 1971.

NOTES TO CHAPTER EIGHT

1. E. R. Leach, 'On Certain Unconsidered Aspects of Double Descent', *Man*, 1962, p. 131.
2. P. Worsley, 'The End of Anthropology?', paper for sixth World Congress of Sociology, 1966.
3. R. Needham, 'The Future of Social Anthropology: Disintegration or Metamorphosis?', *Anniversary Contributions to Anthropology*, Leiden, 1970.

Name Index

Abel, C. W., 36
Allan, W., 185
Althusser, L., 229
Ardener, E., 153, 226, 244n, 246n
Ardener, S., 153, 244n
Ardrey, R., 17
Arensberg, C., 147
Asquith, H. H., 125, 126

Bailey, F. G., 157, 176, 203, 230
Banton, M., 246n
Barnes, J. A., 159, 169, 176, 184, 185, 187, 230, 239n, 241n
Barnett, H. G., 139, 244n
Barth, F., 176, 203, 229, 230
Barthes, R., 229
Bates, Daisy, 60
Bateson, G., 121, 165, 242n, 243n
  importance of *Naven*, 95, 96–8, 105, 117
  schisimogenesis, notion of, 98, 181
  structural ideas of, 96–8
Beattie, J., 158, 229
Beemer, Hilda *see* Kuper, Hilda
Beidelman, T. O., 222
Benedict, Ruth, 87
Berghe, P. van den, 237
Beveridge, W., 32
Boas, F., 20, 24, 64, 87, 168, 205, 223, 242n
Bohannan, L., 161
Bohannan, P., 161, 173
Boissevain, J., 229
Braunholtz, H. J., 135, 244n
Brew, J. O., 242n
Brown, A. R. *see* Radcliffe-Brown, A. R.
Brown, E., 90
Brown, G. G., 90, 131, 137, 244n
Bücher, K., 24
Busia, K. A., 148

Cary, Joyce, 140, 244n
Chomsky, N., 212, 231
Clarke, E., 90
Cohen, A., 143
Colson, E., 143, 156, 159, 161, 180, 185, 245n

Conklin, H., 222
Cory, H., 137
Crawley, E., 16
Cunnison, I., 185
Czaplicka, M. A., 26

Doughty, C., 96
Douglas, Mary, 206, 222, 225, 230, 246n
Driberg, J., 90
Dugdale, J. E., 243n, 246n
Dumont, L., 181, 208, 215, 229
Durkheim, É., 21, 24, 25, 35, 72, 86, 110, 180, 207, 224
  Année Sociologique and, 68
  influence of, 17, 21, 119, 197, 205, 208, 214, 216
  Malinowski and, 26, 31, 69, 85
  Radcliffe-Brown and, 17, 51–2, 53–4, 58, 59, 62, 66–9, 71, 84–5, 175, 205
  social solidarity and, 117
  theories of, 66–8
  on totemism, 26, 74

Easton, D., 230
Eggan, F., 64, 87, 223
Elkin, A. P., 64, 241n
Elliot-Smith, G., 15, 16, 17, 20, 35, 39, 63
Epstein, A. L., 159, 184, 185, 186, 188, 189
Epstein, T. S., 159
Estreicher, K., 239n
Evans-Pritchard, E. E., 33, 82, 121, 128, 136, 150, 154, 155, 167, 172, 176, 181–2, 191, 193, 197, 222, 224, 242n, 243n, 244n, 245n
  Azande studies of, 95, 98–105, 108, 122, 164, 205
  on witchcraft, 99–104, 170–71
  history and, 157, 160, 162–3, 166
  on kinship, 107
  lineage theories of, 109–10, 114–16
  Malinowski and, 90, 103, 104
  Marett lecture of, 162–3
  Nuer studies of, 98, 108, 110, 111–19, 120, 122, 164

249

Subject Index

Aborigines, Australian
Malinowski on, 25, 26
Radcliffe-Brown on, 59–61, 78
Africa
anthropological interest in, 107–8, 169–70, 231
colonialism in, 126, 127–9, 130–36, 137, 138, 140–41
Malinowski on change in, 46–7
states in, 169–70
universities in, 143
urbanisation in, 188–90
alliance theory
and descent theory, 214–15
in Leach, 212–13
in Lévi-Strauss, 209–14
in Needham, 212, 213
see also exchange
American critiques
of British anthropology, 167–8
of Lévi-Strauss, 222–3
Andaman Islands, Radcliffe-Brown on, 18, 55, 57–9, 78
Année Sociologique, School of, 68, 77, 84, 122, 157, 160, 205, 216 *see also under name index*, Durkheim; Hertz; Hubert; Mauss
Association of Social Anthropologists, 151, 152, 153, 155, 244n
Australia, influence of anthropologists from, 92
Azande, Evans-Pritchard's studies of, 95, 98–105, 108, 122, 164

British Association for the Advancement of Science, 19, 26, 62, 85, 125, 126
British Government
African colonial policy of, 127–9, 130–36
changes in, 130–31, 143
Colonial Social Science Research Council, 135–6, 143
Royal Anthropological Institute's appeal to, 125–6

Cambridge Expedition to the Torres Straits, 18, 52

Cambridge University, anthropology in, 18, 106, 129, 156, 158–9, 172, 173, 182
Fortes at, 154, 158
Leach at, 155, 158, 190
Radcliffe-Brown at, 52–3
Cape Town University, Radcliffe-Brown at, 52, 62–3, 84, 88, 90
Chicago University, Radcliffe-Brown at, 52, 64, 69, 87, 95
colonial
administration, 135, 136
officers, 125, 129–30, 137, 140
conflict with anthropologists, 139–42
training of, 125
Colonial Social Science Research Council, 135–6, 150, 152, 173
colonialism, 10, 233–4
in Africa, 126, 127–9, 130–36, 137, 138, 140–41, 143, 144
early forms, 124
functionalism and, 132, 145–6
Indian, 127, 135, 136
indirect rule of, 108, 134, 141, 145
Malinowski and, 46–8
in Middle East, 135, 136
in Oceania, 127, 136
Royal Anthropological Institute and, 125–7
conflict
Gluckman and concept of, 98, 160, 171–2, 177
in V. Turner's work, 186–7, 203

descent theory, and alliance theory, 214–15
diffusionism, 14, 15, 16, 17, 18, 21, 106
Egypto-centric, 17
Elliot-Smith and, 15, 17, 39, 63
Malinowski and, 17, 39
Perry and, 15, 17, 34
Rivers and, 17, 20, 53
District Commissioners *see* colonial officers
Durham University, 154

254

East African Institute of Social Research, 143, 152, 173
ecology, interest in, 228
economics
  anthropology and, 173, 230–31
  Firth on, 166, 173
Edinburgh University, anthropology at, 151
ethnography, 14
  'new', 222–3, 228–9
Ethnological Society of London, 124
ethnology, 14, 15, 16, 54, 84, 86
ethology, 228
evolutionism, 16, 17, 18, 208
  Malinowski and, 21–2
  Radcliffe-Brown and, 66
  Victorian, 15
exchange
  in Lévi-Strauss, 49, 207–8, 208–10
  in Malinowski, 49
  in Mauss, 49, 207, 214
expansion of anthropology, 150–54

field methods, 9
  Boas and, 20
  development of, 18–20
  Malinowski and, 20, 23, 26–32, 48, 60, 69, 160
  Rivers and, 19–20
Folklore Society, 125
functionalism, 9, 10, 16, 18, 165
  colonialism and, 132, 145–6
  development of, 17–18, 24–5
  Malinowski and, 13, 22, 23, 31, 35, 39–44, 46, 51, 86, 92, 93, 156
  problems of, 94–5
  Radcliffe-Brown and, 51, 70, 73, 77, 86, 92
future of anthropology, 230–38

government interest in anthropology, 123–4

history
  anthropology and study of, 157, 158, 160, 162–3, 166
  cultural, 17
  evolutionism and, 17
  Malinowski and, 46
  Radcliffe-Brown and, 85
holistic approaches in Malinowski, 39–40

Ibadan University, 152
India
  colonialism in, 127, 135, 136
  School of Oriental and African Studies and study of, 157

International Institute of African Languages and Culture, 91, 107, 155
  Forde and, 157
  history of, 130–33
  Malinowski and, 46

kinship
  alliance theory of, 212–15
  analysis of, 106, 117, 159, 172–3
  descent theory of, 214–15
  Fortes on, 107, 120–21, 172, 198, 200, 214, 215
  Leach on, 172, 194, 198–200, 200–202, 213–15
  Lévi-Strauss on, 172, 206–7, 207–15
  Malinowski on, 42, 43–4, 94, 120
  Morgan on, 77, 78
  Radcliffe-Brown on, 60, 61, 74, 77–83, 86, 110, 120
  Rivers on, 77

law, anthropology and study of, 173, 184
lineage systems, study of, 109–16, 117–18, 175
linguistics, anthropology and, 229, 231
  American, 222–3
  Jakobson and, 205, 217
  Lévi-Strauss and, 204, 205, 217
  and Prague school of, 205, 217
London School of Economics and Political Science (London)
  anthropology at, 106, 129, 156–7
  Firth at, 154, 156, 176, 190
  Leach at, 156–7, 176
  Malinowski and, 13, 22, 23, 25, 26, 32–3, 34, 87, 90, 91, 106, 122, 154
  Nadel at, 154, 156, 165
  Radcliffe-Brown and, 53
  Schapera at, 154
  sociology at, 33
London University, 156, 174
  see also London School of Economics; School of Oriental and African Studies; University College

Makerere University, 152
Manchester University, anthropology at, 151, 154, 156, 159–60, 161, 174, 230
  Gluckman at, 154, 159, 184–5
  'School' of, 185, 190, 199
  urban studies at, 185–6, 188–90

255